BRIDGE

SQUEEZES

COMPLETE

or
WINNING END PLAY STRATEGY

By CLYDE E. LOVE

Dover Publications, Inc., New York

Library of Congress Catalog Card Number: 68-25410

Manufactured in the United States of America
Dover Publications, Inc.
180 Varick Street
New York, N. Y. 10014

CONTENTS

PREFACE

Clyde Love has perhaps produced the finest book on bridge. His first book—*Squeeze Play in Bridge* (1951)—was a more complete exposition of the subject than anything previously written, and now he has gone far beyond his own monumental work.

This book is not to be perused lightly. Instead of racing through, each reader should pace himself to his own capabilities in order to digest thoroughly as he goes. This book is intriguing, fascinating, instructive, comprehensive, and, above all, thoroughly entertaining. Do not put it aside with the thought that it is not for you. It is for *every* bridge player of every gradation of skill. All that is required is interest and a desire to learn.

Bridge Squeezes Complete will polish the expert's technique and will reveal to him hitherto unknown potentialities in other aspects.

Bridge Squeezes Complete will make fine players out of good players by providing them with the means for perfecting and crystallizing their often erratic play of squeeze-type hands.

Bridge Squeezes Complete will intrigue the student beyond description, furnishing him with hundreds of hours of fascinating analyses and squeeze possibilities.

If you are an egotistical bridge player (as most of us are); if, in your opinion, your game is already perfected, leaving little more to learn about the game of bridge—THIS BOOK IS FOR YOU, as well as for the average player. We humbly suggest that your eyes will be opened by *Bridge Squeezes Complete*.

This book is great. It transcends adequate praise from mere bridge players such as we. Full appreciation and ultimate recognition will be forthcoming from you—the bridge players of the world—for whom this masterpiece was written.

We confidently predict this work will become an all-time classic. It is a rare privilege indeed to review this book and to recommend it wholeheartedly and without reservation.

William B. Woodson
John W. Norwood, Jr.

INTRODUCTION

The question is often asked: "Is it possible to win without knowing anything about squeezes?" The answer is: "Yes, certainly." But you won't win as often; more important, you will never experience what is unquestionably the greatest thrill in bridge—the consummation of a squeeze. If you become known as a competent squeezer, a better grade of players will want you as a partner. Second, a squeeze hand requires shaping up according to principles which are in large part unknown to many, and many non-squeeze hands require shaping up *according to those same principles*. This means that this knowledge will make the difference in many hands where no squeeze is present.

This book ultimately gets into the realm of expert play; but it begins at the very beginning, on the assumption that you never saw a squeeze, and the progress is by very easy stages. It follows that anyone who can make a respectable showing in home-town duplicate can read this entire book. However, if you are a squeeze novice, a study of just the first chapter will be of great benefit to your game. (This is merely bait: once you have fully assimilated Chap. I you will never stop there, because squeeze play is habit-forming.)

A word of warning: do not think that you can read this book the way you would read a newspaper—or better, a whodunit. Instead, *lay out each hand as given,* and knuckle down to a bit of serious study.

To acquire a knowledge of squeeze play, the student first encounters two typical forms: the simple squeeze and the double squeeze (each of the "notrump" variety), in which Declarer can win all but one of the remaining tricks without surrendering the lead. Since these are usually the easiest of all squeezes to recognize and execute, it seems proper to call them *elementary squeezes*. Beyond these two types there is a great body of advanced positions.

An earlier work, "Squeeze Play in Bridge" (hereinafter referred to as SP), covered to the best of our ability the elementary field. Readers of this book who are already acquainted with its older brother may want to omit Chaps. I-II following, because those chapters treat the same topics.

Several hands, of types rarely if ever occurring in play, are introduced merely to show the possibility of exceptions to our general statements, or because of their intrinsic interest as curiosities. Those types that are of practical importance in play are discussed to classify the various forms according to their characteristic features, and to reduce the play of each species, so far as possible, to a definite line of procedure. In short, this is a textbook, not an encyclopedia.

A few non-squeeze problems have been included for two reasons: the reader can not assume that every hand must be played with a squeeze; secondly, because the problem is interesting in its own right.

A word about the bidding. Bidding has been included only for the reason that the declarer's plan of play will be influenced by the defenders' bidding, and also that some readers prefer to have this information. This book is primarily concerned with the play of the cards, and it is suggested that the reader concentrate on the play. Except in hands taken from actual play, where your author disclaims all responsibility, there are no artificial bids except those that are familiar to everyone—the "bust" two Notrump, Ace-showing, the Blackwood Convention, etc. Vulnerability is not given: where you think that this would affect the bidding, you may assume the proper conditions to exist, and limitations of space made it impossible to take up a systematic discussion of squeeze defense.

Throughout the writing we have leaned heavily upon that loyal supporter, Dr. Ben Dushnik, of Ann Arbor, Mich. This faithful adherent has gone over the entire manuscript with a microscope, and his help has been invaluable. Messrs. John W. Norwood, Jr., of Greenville, S. C., and William B. Woodson, of Greensboro, N. C., have kept in close touch with the work from the beginning, and have made any number of useful contributions. Our obligation to these three good friends can hardly be overstated, because without their constant encouragement it is doubtful that the book would ever have been completed.

Ann Arbor, Mich.   CLYDE E. LOVE

CHAPTER I

THE SIMPLE SQUEEZE

1. *Definition of squeeze.* As a rule, a bridge hand contains some worthless cards, and some that play a useful role, as prospective winner, stopper, guard, etc. These are called *idle* and *busy* cards respectively.

It may happen that a player is forced to discard a busy card, for the simple reason that his hand no longer contains any idle cards. When this happens, the player is said to be *squeezed*.

In the following end positions the contract is Spades or Notrump, South to lead, one defender's hand worthless.

Example (a):

NORTH
♠ —
♡ 9
♢ A K 10
♣ —

EAST
♠ —
♡ 10
♢ Q J 5
♣ —

SOUTH
♠ —
♡ 5
♢ 8 7
♣ 10

Example (b):

NORTH
♠ —
♡ —
♢ J
♣ A J 3

WEST
♠ —
♡ —
♢ Q
♣ K Q 8

SOUTH
♠ J 10
♡ —
♢ —
♣ 7 6

In (a), on the Club lead North discards his idle Heart, but East is squeezed. If he throws ♡ 10, South's Five is good; if he yields a Diamond, North's Ten makes. So, although South has only three tops, he takes all four tricks.

In (b), on the first Spade West and North throw idle Clubs, but on the second West is squeezed. No matter what he does, North takes the rest.

2. *Vocabulary of squeeze.* Squeeze play has a vocabulary all its own, and our first step is to learn that vocabulary.

A necessary condition for *every* squeeze is that *one adversary must hold busy cards in at least two suits.* In the typical case, Declarer holds in these suits certain cards, one of which will become established by the squeeze. These potential winners are called *threats.* In (a) above the threats are ♡ 5, ◇ 10; in (b), ◇ J, ♣ J.

The suits in which the defender is busy are the *threat-suits;* the others, *free suits.* When a certain stage of play is reached, Declarer begins leading his free winners, and continues without interruption until all are played. The last of these winners, which forces the fatal discard, is the *squeeze-card,* and the trick on which it is played is the *squeeze-trick.* When Declarer is ready to begin playing his string of winners (the "string" might consist of only one card), the squeeze is *established;* when the squeeze-card is about to be played, the squeeze is *reached.* In (a) the squeeze is already reached; in (b) it is established, and is reached after one more trick.

Of Declarer's two hands, the one that lies at the left of the victim is called the *upper hand;* the one at the right, the *lower hand.* In (a), South is the upper hand; in (b), North.

All squeezes fall into one or the other of two general classes. In a *notrump squeeze* (which may occur at a trump contract) the play, after the squeeze is established, is essentially of notrump character: the trumps, if any, are merely run off to force discards. In a *trump squeeze,* on the other hand, Declarer's ability to ruff is an essential ingredient of the squeeze. Since trump squeezes are comparatively rare, their study will be postponed to our last chapter.

3. *The simple squeeze.* Of the many varieties of squeeze that

may arise, the commonest is the *two-suit squeeze,* or *simple squeeze* (simple in the sense of *single,* although by good fortune this commonest squeeze is also the simplest in the more usual meaning of that word). In the typical form of this play, Declarer holds threats in two suits, and the whole burden of defense lies with a single adversary. Further, at the time when the squeeze becomes established Declarer has *only one loser* remaining: that is, he can win all but one trick on tops.

An important property of the simple squeeze is this: *it is impossible that both threats shall lie in the same hand with the squeeze-card.*

To fix ideas, let us suppose in the text of this chapter (though not necessarily in the "Exercises") that South holds the squeeze-card.

4. *The four conditions.* The following statement is the *indispensable foundation stone* for an understanding of squeeze play. In this formulation, it is taken for granted that Declarer has the lead.

A simple squeeze is surely present whenever the following conditions are satisfied:

(B) *One defender is Busy in two suits, his partner being helpless.*

(L) *Declarer has only one Loser remaining.*

(U) *At least one threat lies in the Upper hand.*

(E) *There will be an Entry to the established threat.*

The four conditions must be thoroughly memorized. They may be called to mind by the word BLUE.

There are three possible entry conditions, to be studied in §§ 5, 12, 13 respectively.

(E_1) *North—that is, the hand opposite the squeeze-card—holds a threat accompanied by an entry in its own suit.*

(E_2) *North holds winner-and-small in South's threat-suit, provided further that if East is the victim South also holds a winner in his own threat-suit.*

(E_3) *North holds a winner in South's suit, and South a winner in North's suit.*

The absolute necessity of (B), for all squeezes of whatever type, has already been remarked. The necessity of (E) is obvious. What happens when either (L) or (U) is lacking may be shown by examples: Notrump contract, South to lead.

Example (a):

	NORTH
♠	8
♡	—
◇	A J 8
♣	—

WEST	
♠	—
♡	Q
◇	K Q
♣	9

	SOUTH
♠	J
♡	—
◇	5
♣	7 6

Example (b):

	NORTH
♠	—
♡	—
◇	A J
♣	J

	EAST
♠	—
♡	—
◇	Q 7
♣	Q

	SOUTH
♠	J
♡	—
◇	6 4
♣	—

In (a), Declarer can win only two of the four tricks—that is, he has *two losers*. When he leads the Spade, West has an idle card available, and the squeeze fails. In (b), (U) is lacking—both threats in the lower hand. North has to *discard before East*: no matter which threat he throws, East's guard in that suit is released.

5. *The first entry-condition.* Of the three entry-conditions, the one most frequently appearing in play is

(E_1) *North—that is, the hand opposite the squeeze-card—holds a threat accompanied by an entry in its own suit.*

See, for example, the layouts in § 1.

When (E_1) is present, the threats may be divided between Declarer's two hands, or North may hold both threats, but with this vital proviso: *when North holds both threats, West must hold the stoppers*, because (U) would fail against East.

6. *Exercises*. The squeeze is a machine, and the only way you can learn to operate a machine is by operating it. This means that the "Exercises" are the lifeblood of this book. But to get anything like full value from them, you must scrupulously avoid double-dummy play. So, look at your own hands and the bidding, and form a tentative plan, as you would at the table. Try not to start with a preconceived idea that each hand will produce a squeeze; instead, *just play bridge*. Next, read the data immediately below, and bring your plan up to date. Then and not until then (no peeking!), look at the adverse holdings and read the "Analysis." Do not fail to lay out the full deal and play it trick by trick, watching the wheels go round.

Since (L), (U) and (E) depend mostly on your own holdings, you can determine (tentatively at least) whether these are present. As regards (B), it is usually necessary to *assume* that both threats are stopped by a single adversary. But when a squeeze offers the best—perhaps the only—chance, always try for it.

Exercise 1.

NORTH
- ♠ 6 5
- ♡ A K 4 2
- ◊ A J 8 3
- ♣ J 6 5

SOUTH
- ♠ A 10 3
- ♡ Q 8
- ◊ K Q 7 4 2
- ♣ A K Q

Bidding:

NORTH	EAST	SOUTH	WEST
1 ♡	P	2 ◊	P
3 ◊	P	4 NT	P
5 ♡	P	5 NT	P
6 ◊	P	7 NT	P
P	P		

West leads ♠ 9.

T. 1: East plays ♠ J.

Analysis 1.

WEST
- ♠ 9 8 7
- ♡ J 7
- ◊ 10 6 5
- ♣ 8 7 4 3 2

EAST
- ♠ K Q J 4 2
- ♡ 10 9 6 5 3
- ◊ 9
- ♣ 10 9

You are a trick short, and the only chance is a squeeze. East is marked with ♠ K Q: if he also has four Hearts, he is Busy in two suits, so assume that he does have the Hearts. There is only one loser. One threat, ♠ 10, is in the upper hand. And there will be an entry for the Heart threat. Nothing to do but run the free suits.

Before starting to play, should you try to figure out why or how or when the squeeze will operate? No: when you slip a dime in a parking meter and the needle moves, do you care what went on inside? Or, should you try to visualize what the four hands will look like after eight, or nine, or ten tricks? No— sheer waste of time. During the play, do you watch for Heart discards? No—sublimely uninterested. You *watch for* ♠ K Q *only.* When these have not both appeared, you try the Hearts: either they run or they don't.

One remark, to avert a possible misconception. In a hand offering a choice of contracts—for instance, Spades or Notrump— it may happen that a squeeze is present in one contract but not in the other. But since a squeeze is determined by the placing of the cards, it is totally independent of the *height* of the contract.

Exercise 2.

NORTH
♠ K Q 10 3
♡ 8 6 4
◇ Q 7 5 4
♣ 7 4

SOUTH
♠ A J 5
♡ A K Q 2
◇ A 6
♣ J 9 8 5

Bidding:

NORTH	EAST	SOUTH	WEST
P	P	1 ♡	P
1 ♠	P	2 NT	P
3 NT	P	P	P

West leads ♣ 2.

T. 1: East's King wins.
T. 2: ♣ 6 returned; Ten wins.
T. 3: ♣ Q led. East follows.
T. 4: ♣ A. East discards ♠ 4.
T. 5: ◇ J led. East plays ◇ 8; Ace wins.

Analysis 2.

WEST	EAST
♠ 7 6 2	♠ 9 8 4
♡ J 9	♡ 10 7 5 3
◇ J 10 9 3	◇ K 8 2
♣ A Q 10 2	♣ K 6 3

The Heart division is a frail reed to lean on. Might there be a squeeze? If either defender (undoubtedly East, but who cares?) has ◇ K and four Hearts, (B) is in hand. After four tricks, (L) is right. With the threats—◇ Q, ♡ 2—divided, (U) is OK against either adversary. And (E) for the Heart threat is present. Nothing to do but shell out the Spades. *The only card to watch for is* ◇ K—not interested in Hearts.

We shall insert a remark about defense from time to time, and perhaps it is not too early to begin. One of the most potent anti-squeeze weapons is "the attack on (L)": that is, the defenders try to prevent Declarer from losing enough tricks so that he has only one loser remaining. In Ex. 2, West can see that there is no chance unless East has either an Ace, or ◇ K and a Heart stopper. But in the latter event he can be squeezed if the Clubs are run. West should lead ◇ J, T. 3. Now, just try to make it.

Thus, to the list of reasons why you should study squeeze play, this hand adds another, and one which is of prime importance. Many times no defense is possible (Ex. 1), but sometimes a killing defense can be found (Ex. 2). If you are a non-squeezer you will not take advantage of chances to defend yourself. As for protecting your partner, you will never see his danger until too late—probably not until the bitter incriminations of the post-mortem; and even then, you will offend in exactly the same way next time.

7. *Winners remaining in both threat-suits.* In Exs. 1-2 Declarer, at the point where he gained control, had winners remaining in only one threat-suit. Of course this would not always be the case.

When you hold winners in both suits, you may if you wish keep track of the discards in both suits. But while this would be by no means an onerous task, it can be still further simplified.

Merely decide which suit you will try first, after the squeeze-trick; then keep record of the discards in that suit, *ignoring the other*. After the first suit has been tested, if its threat has not been established the other must be tried, whether or not there have been any discards in that suit.

Exercise 3.

	NORTH		Bidding:			
♠	K 7 2					
♡	9 6		WEST	NORTH	EAST	SOUTH
◇	Q 7 5 4		P	1 ♣	P	1 ♠
♣	A K 7 6		P	2 ♠	P	4 NT
			P	5 ◇	P	6 ♠
	SOUTH		P	P	P	
♠	A Q J 10 9					
♡	Q		West leads ♡ K.			
◇	A K 6 3					
♣	Q 8 3					

T. 1: King wins.
T. 2: ♡ A, ruffed.
T. 3-4: Spades. Both follow.
T. 5: Spade. West discards ♡ 7.

Analysis 3.

	WEST		EAST	
♠	8 3	♠	6 5 4	
♡	A K 7	♡	J 10 8 5 4 3 2	
◇	J 9 8 2	◇	10	
♣	J 10 5 4	♣	9 2	

Even if neither minor runs, there is a chance: the two suits might lie in the same hand. Then, with threats ◇ 6, ♣ 7, BLUE is in hand against either adversary (check it). Naturally you plan to try Diamonds first, after the Spades (although Clubs would do as well): therefore, watch for Diamond discards, disregarding Clubs.

It must be admitted, grudgingly, that no harm would be done by starting the Diamonds, T. 6. (Nevertheless, any habitual squeezer would cash the last Spade, just as a matter of sound policy. Why expose your hand before you have to?) But suppose Diamonds do not break. Then, before running the Clubs, *lead that last trump!**

Exercise 4.

NORTH	Bidding:
♠ —	
♡ K Q 10 8 2	
◊ J 7 6 2	
♣ A J 10 7	

NORTH	EAST	SOUTH	WEST
1 ♡	1 ♠	2 ♣	P
3 ♣	P	4 NT	P
5 ◊	P	5 NT	P
6 ◊	P	7 NT	P
P	P		

SOUTH
♠ A K 5 2
♡ A 4 3
◊ A K Q
♣ K 8 6

West leads ♠ J.

T. 1: Ace wins.
T. 2: ♡ A. Both follow.
T. 3: Heart led. West discards ◊ 3; Queen wins.

Analysis 4.

WEST	EAST
♠ J 7	♠ Q 10 9 8 6 4 3
♡ 5	♡ J 9 7 6
◊ 10 8 5 4 3	◊ 9
♣ Q 9 5 3 2	♣ 4

With East advertising length in Spades, it is a near-certainty that he does not hold four Hearts, and West cannot stop the suit, even with five. So Declarer discards a Club from dummy, expecting to spread the hand after three tricks.

When the bad news is heard, the only chance is that East held seven Spades. If so, BLUE is in hand except that the Club finesse must be risked, and on the first round of the suit, because

---

* Countless multitudes of contracts have failed because Declarer wouldn't lead his last trump, even when (as here) it could not possibly be needed for ruffing.

the King must be preserved for (E). Cash $\diamond$ A K Q; Club finesse; $\diamond$ J; $\clubsuit$ A K; $\spadesuit$ K. Keep strict count of all Spades.*

This hand illustrates a possibility not previously remarked. It is not always necessary that the squeeze-card be *led*—sometimes you merely *lead toward it*.

8. *Both threats in one hand.* When North holds both threats, *West must hold the stoppers*, for lack of (U) against East. In this case, when the squeeze is reached North will have no idle card remaining, and will have to *discard one of the threats* on the squeeze-trick. See Example (b), § 1.

This brings up an important point of play. The saddest outcome of a squeeze hand is to effect the squeeze and then not cash in on it. With North holding both threats, if you have tops remaining in both suits when the squeeze-card is led, you cannot always tell with certainty which suit has been given up by West, and might discard the wrong threat. To avoid all ambiguity —that is, uncertainty as to what has happened—merely follow the

RULE: *When both threats are in one hand and you have winners remaining in both threat-suits, cash all winners in one suit, if possible, before the squeeze-trick.*

Exercise 5.

	NORTH
$\spadesuit$	K Q J 7 4 3
$\heartsuit$	A 5
$\diamond$	A 4 2
$\clubsuit$	K 4

	SOUTH
$\spadesuit$	A 6
$\heartsuit$	K 6
$\diamond$	Q 10 9 8 6
$\clubsuit$	A Q 8 3

Bidding:

WEST	NORTH	EAST	SOUTH
P	1 $\spadesuit$	P	2 $\diamond$
P	3 $\spadesuit$	P	4 NT
P	5 $\heartsuit$	P	5 NT
P	6 $\heartsuit$	P	7 NT
P	P	P	

West leads $\heartsuit$ Q.

* This hand, looking so absurdly artificial, actually occurred in a local (Ann Arbor) game, and was reported to your author by North (Mr. Ben Dushnik), who complained bitterly that his partner discarded a Heart, T 1, made the contract by finessing Clubs twice, and bragged about his performance!

T. 1: King wins.
T. 2-3: Spades. Both follow.
T. 4: Spade. West discards ♡ J.

Analysis 5.

WEST	EAST
♠ 9 5	♠ 10 8 2
♡ Q J 10 9 2	♡ 8 7 4 3
◊ J 5 3	◊ K 7
♣ 6 5 2	♣ J 10 9 7

A squeeze will develop if East—not West—holds ◊ K and four Clubs, the threats being ◊ Q, ♣ 8. If you run off all the free winners, South's squeeze-trick discard cannot be picked with certainty. Instead, somewhere along the line cash ◊ A (Rule), thus removing all ambiguity.

Many hands contain two or even several squeeze possibilities. Here a squeeze will mature, with threats ◊ 4, ♣ 8, if West has four Diamonds and four Clubs. (Play it with ◊ K, ♣ 9 traded for ♡ 9, 2.) However, this is contraindicated by West's discard.

This hand brings out another reason for studying squeeze play. If the prospective Declarer—either yourself or partner—is a skilled squeezer, you can sometimes risk a "try for a top" that you would not otherwise venture, just on the chance that a squeeze can be found if needed.

Exercise 6.

	NORTH		Bidding:			
♠	A K 3 2					
♡	A 9 6 5		NORTH	EAST	SOUTH	WEST
◊	A 9		1 ♣	P	1 ♡	P
♣	A K 9		2 ♠	P	4 NT	P
			5 ♣	P	5 NT	P
	SOUTH		6 ♡	P	7 ♡	P
♠	Q 5 4		P	P		
♡	K Q J 10 2					
◊	K Q		West leads ♣ Q.			
♣	5 3 2					

T. 1: King wins. East plays ♣ 4.

Analysis 6.

	WEST			EAST
♠	10 9 7 6		♠	J 8
♡	7		♡	8 4 3
◊	10 7 6 5		◊	J 8 4 3 2
♣	Q J 10 6		♣	8 7 4

An easier squeeze problem could hardly be constructed. If Spades do not break, the only chance is that West has that suit. Draw trumps; cash ♣ A (Rule); Diamonds followed by Hearts, watching for ♣ J 10 only.

9. *Correcting the count.* In each of our hands so far, the squeeze is already established—all conditions satisfied—at the time when you first get control.

Say now that on checking BLUE, you find that (L) is wrong: there is more than one loser. Then, you must "rectify the count" by losing as many tricks as may be necessary: with two losers in hand, duck (that is, purposely lose) one trick; with three losers duck twice; etc. In effecting this maneuver, Declarer should rigidly follow the

RULE: *Lose the required number of tricks at the first opportunity.*

Of course this Rule must be applied with discretion, for it often happens that certain loose ends must be tied up before the lead can be safely surrendered. Just concentrate on getting rid of those surplus losers *as soon as possible.**

Exercise 7.

NORTH				
♠ A 3				
♡ A 8				
◊ A K Q J 87				
♣ A K 7				

Bidding:

EAST	SOUTH	WEST	NORTH
P	P	P	2 ◊
P	2 NT	P	3 ♣
P	4 ♣	P	6 NT
Dbl.	P	P	P

SOUTH

♠ J 5 4 2
♡ 5 4
◊ 5 4 2
♣ Q 8 4 3

West leads ♡ 6.

Analysis 7.

WEST		EAST	
♠ 10 9 8 6		♠ K Q 7	
♡ Q 9 7 6 3 2		♡ K J 10	
◊ 10		◊ 9 6 3	
♣ 6 5		♣ J 10 9 2	

If Clubs fail, there is a fine chance that East has that suit in addition to ♠ K Q. If so, BLUE is OK except that there are two losers. So, after making sure that no return lead can hurt you, you duck the first trick. East returns ♠ K and you feed him seven reds.

This hand brings out still another way in which a knowledge of squeeze play is rewarding. Our present East, being a non-squeezer, doubles without stopping to think what he will discard on that great mass of Diamonds that Declarer surely holds. True, his double is submoron warfare at its worst; yet such doubles are perpetrated, even in the National Tournament—very seldom, however, by competent squeeze players.

---

* This Rule—lose your sure losers early—finds very broad application in bridge, quite apart from squeeze play, and there are some millions of players whose game would greatly improve if they would assimilate this one fact. Playing three Notrump, the difference between an expert and a dub is roughly this: the expert loses four tricks early, the dub loses five tricks late.

Exercise 8.

NORTH
♠ A K 4 2
♡ 7 5
◇ K 7 4 2
♣ 7 6 3

Bidding:

SOUTH	WEST	NORTH	EAST
1 ♡	1 ♠	Dbl.	2 ♣
4 ♡	P	P	P

West leads ♠ Q.

SOUTH
♠ 8 6 5
♡ A K Q J 6 4
◇ —
♣ A 8 4 2

T. 1: King wins. East plays ♠ 7.
T. 2: Heart. Both follow.
T. 3: Heart. East discards ♣ K.

Analysis 8.

WEST	EAST
♠ Q J 10 9 3	♠ 7
♡ 10 8 3 2	♡ 9
◇ A Q 10 8	◇ J 9 6 5 3
♣ —	♣ K Q J 10 9 5

For his bid, West should hold ◇ A. If so, BLUE is in force, with threats ♠4, ◇ K, except that there are four losers. So, you draw trumps, lay down ♣ A, then lead a Club.

East is helpless. If he takes his three tricks, you ruff the next lead, then show West the last Heart. If East, trying to escape, leads a Diamond instead of finishing the Clubs, you throw a Club, and ◇ K is bound to make.

Exercise 9.

NORTH			
♠ A K Q 2			
♡ Q 4			
◊ 9 8 4 2			
♣ 8 7 5			

Bidding:

EAST	SOUTH	WEST	NORTH
P	1 ♡	P	1 ♠
P	3 ♡	P	4 ♡
P	4 NT	P	5 ◊
P	5 NT	P	6 ◊
P	6 ♡	P	P
P			

SOUTH
♠ 8 5
♡ A K J 10 6
◊ A 7
♣ A K 4 3

West leads ♣ 2.

T. 1: East plays ♣ Q.

Analysis 9.

WEST	EAST
♠ 10 6 4 3	♠ J 9 7
♡ 8 7 2	♡ 9 5 3
◊ K J	◊ Q 10 6 5 3
♣ J 10 6 2	♣ Q 9

If West will be kind enough to have four Spades, BLUE is in hand except that there are two losers. So, stay off the first trick, win the return, run the reds.

This hand is designed to point up the injunction (§ 6) that you should "just play bridge." While the hand does produce a squeeze as the cards lie, this would be a highly odoriferous way to play it, because the odds are against the squeeze—due to the imbalance in Clubs, East is more likely than West to hold four Spades—while the elementary method is heavily odds-on. Win, T. 1; cash the second Club; lead a third Club, intending to ruff the fourth. Even if West is a notorious shyster, you need not fear a 5-1 Club division, because to suppose that West's Deuce was a fifth-best would mean that he led low from J 10 9 xx. And the other danger—trumps 5-1—is only a 15% risk.

Exercise 10.*

NORTH
♠ K 2
♡ K Q 5
◊ A 8 7 3 2
♣ 9 6 3

SOUTH
♠ A Q J 10 9
♡ A 2
◊ J 5 4
♣ A Q 8

Bidding:

SOUTH	WEST	NORTH	EAST
1 ♠	P	2 ◊	P
3 ♠	P	6 ♠	P
P	P		

West leads ♡ J.

T. 1: Ace wins.
T. 2-4: Spades fall 3-3.
T. 5-6: Spades. West discards Clubs, East Hearts.

Analysis 10.

WEST
♠ 8 6 3
♡ J 10 9 8
◊ 9 6
♣ 7 5 4 2

EAST
♠ 7 5 4
♡ 7 6 4 3
◊ K Q 10
♣ K J 10

Success of the Club finesse must be assumed. Even so, without some very lucky break in Diamonds (such as doubleton K Q) the only hope is a squeeze, and the prospects are not good. But we must try. So, lose a Diamond, T. 7. No matter which opponent wins or what he leads in return, the squeeze, if present, remains intact. (Check all variations.)

Practically all rules in bridge are subject to exception. Here, our Rule directs Declarer to correct the count on the fifth trick. But with Dummy still holding two idle cards, no harm can be done by finishing the Spades at once, and just possibly (although it does not happen here) some helpful discards might be obtained from the enemy. Hence in this instance the best technique is as shown above. (Look ahead to § 35.)

10. *Ruffing out a stopper.* In a notrump squeeze played at a

* This hand was played by Dr. Walter E. Reichart, of Ann Arbor, Mich.

trump contract, the trumps may serve in various ways in getting the squeeze set up. The most important of these ways is in *ruffing out a stopper* held by the victim's partner.

Do not confuse this play with the genuine trump squeeze, in which Declarer's ability to ruff plays an essential role *after the squeeze is established.*

Exercise 11.

	NORTH			
	♠ 7 4 3 2			
	♡ A 6			
	◊ Q J 7			
	♣ K 7 6 2			

Bidding:

WEST	NORTH	EAST	SOUTH
P	P	P	2 ♡
P	3 NT	P	4 NT
P	5 ◊	P	6 ♡
P	P	P	

SOUTH
♠ Q
♡ K Q J 10 5 3
◊ A K 4
♣ A J 8

West leads ♡ 9.

T. 1: East follows.

Analysis 11.

WEST	EAST
♠ K 9 8	♠ A J 10 6 5
♡ 9 8 7 4	♡ 2
◊ 10 8 6 3	◊ 9 5 2
♣ Q 5	♣ 10 9 4 3

Beside the Club finesse, there is one other chance. If one opponent holds five Spades and ♣ Q, he can be squeezed.

So you win the first trick in the closed hand and lead the Spade (Rule, § 9). West's King wins, and East, who knows nothing about squeeze play, drops his Jack. But West, who sees what Declarer is up to, leads another Heart (as good as anything). You ruff a Spade; return in Clubs and ruff a Spade; finish the trumps; cash ◊ A K Q. When East has played to the Club return it is certain that his last card is ♠ A, so you drop West's Queen.

The hand raises an interesting point of logic. Since East holds a stopper in only one suit, is he "Busy in two suits"? In other words, is this a genuine squeeze? The answer is definitely yes. Though worthless in themselves, East's Clubs (while they last) are busily engaged in concealing the fact that West's Queen will drop.

11. *The Vienna Coup.* Suppose that East is to be pulverized. The threats, of necessity, are divided. When the squeeze is reached North must have an idle card remaining, for if not, the squeeze would pinch North rather than East.

As a rule, the mere presence of a threat in South's hand makes room for an idle card opposite. But there is one situation where trouble arises, viz. when *North holds a winner in each threat-suit and South has no winner in either suit.* Then, unless you take precaution the trouble will be fatal.

Example (a):

NORTH	
♠	5
♡	—
◇	10 4
♣	A 5

EAST	
♠	—
♡	—
◇	9 8
♣	K 8 7

SOUTH	
♠	J 7
♡	—
◇	5
♣	Q 6

Example (b):

NORTH	
♠	5
♡	—
◇	10 4
♣	A 5

WEST	
♠	—
♡	—
◇	9 8
♣	K 8 7

SOUTH	
♠	J 7
♡	—
◇	5
♣	Q 6

In Example (a), if you lead the Spades now, on the last one North will have to discard ◇ 4, releasing East's Diamond guard, or ♣ 5, which releases East's Club guard because *South's threat is now blocked.* The remedy is easily found: cash ♣ A, return in Spades and turn on the heat. North's ♣ 5 is now idle, and East is helpless.

This play is called the *Vienna Coup*. A formal definition:

The Vienna Coup is a play in which Declarer cashes all winners in one threat-suit before the squeeze-trick in order to prevent that threat from becoming blocked.

Or in other words, the Coup *saves Declarer from squeezing himself.*

Look now at Example (b)—the same position except that West is on the spot. Here, with North discarding *after* West, the squeeze will surely occur if the Spades are run now (check it); but tricky discarding by West might make it impossible to tell which threat has been set up. The difficulty is exactly the same as in § 8, and the remedy is the same: merely cash North's winners in South's suit before the squeeze trick. This play, together with the one of § 8, might be called a *pseudo Vienna Coup.*

Let us summarize all this in the form of a

RULE: *When South, holding the squeeze-card and one threat, has no winner in either threat-suit, and North holds winners in both threat-suits, cash North's winners in South's suit before the squeeze-trick: that is, execute the Vienna Coup.*

To recapitulate: against East the (genuine) Coup, if indicated, *must* be made. If for any reason this is impossible (as happens occasionally) the squeeze will fail, even though at first check all conditions appear to be present.* Against West the (pseudo) Coup is not absolutely required; but to avoid the danger of ambiguity, the Coup should be made against West unless to do so would involve some other, and greater, risk.

---

* Actually, BLUE is not satisfied: there will not be "an Entry to the established threat," because that threat will become blocked.

Exercise 12.

	NORTH
♠	A K 3
♡	A 10 6 3
◇	J 5
♣	Q 8 6 4

Bidding:

NORTH	EAST	SOUTH	WEST
1 ♡	P	2 ♣	2 ◇
3 ♣	P	4 ♣	P
5 ♣	P	P	P

	SOUTH
♠	J 9 7
♡	K 4
◇	10 6 4
♣	A K J 9 2

West leads ◇ K.

T. 1: East plays ◇ 2.
T. 2: ◇ Q led. East plays ◇ 8.
T. 3: ♡ 9 led. East plays ♡ 5; King wins.
T. 4: ♣ A. Both follow.
T. 5: Club. West discards a Diamond.

Analysis 12.

	WEST		EAST
♠	8 6 5 2	♠	Q 10 4
♡	9 8 7	♡	Q J 5 2
◇	A K Q 7 3	◇	9 8 2
♣	5	♣	10 7 3

If either opponent holds the major pictures, he is squeezeable (check it). Watch your step! North has winners in both threat-suits, South in neither: you must cash the Spades while you still have a means of return. So, Diamond ruff; ♠ A K (Vienna Coup); Clubs. Keep an eye out for ♠ Q only. Do not fail to observe that if you had carelessly won in Dummy, T. 5, you would have missed the boat.

x x x x

Many glowing adjectives—"spectacular," "abstruse," "stupen-dous"—have been showered on the Vienna Coup, none of which it deserves. Various functions other than the one covered by our Rule have been ascribed to it, none of which it performs. It has even been called a "species of squeeze"! The obvious truth is that as regards "difficulty" of recognition and execution, this play is on an exact par with the one of § 8. Any squeeze novice who will memorize the above Rule and *keep it in mind,* for use when required, will handle the Coup as adeptly as any expert.

In short, the aura of glamor which has always seemed to surround this play is wholly fictitious.

Exercise 13.

	NORTH			
	♠ A K 3 2			
	♡ A 9 6 5			
	◇ A 9			
	♣ A K 5			

Bidding:

NORTH	EAST	SOUTH	WEST
1 ♣	P	1 ♡	P
2 ♠	P	4 NT	P
5 ♣	P	5 NT	P
6 ♡	P	7 ♡	P
P	P		

SOUTH
♠ Q 5 4
♡ K Q J 10 2
◇ K 5
♣ 9 3 2

West leads ♣ 8.

T. 1: King wins. East plays ♣ Q.

Analysis 13.

WEST	EAST
♠ J 8	♠ 10 9 7 6
♡ 8 4 3	♡ 7
◇ J 8 4 3 2	◇ Q 10 7 6
♣ 8 7 4	♣ Q J 10 6

An easier squeeze problem could hardly be constructed. If Spades do not break, the only chance is that East has that suit. Draw trumps; cash ♣ A (Vienna Coup); Diamonds followed by Hearts, watching for ♣ J 10 only. (Compare Ex. 6.)

Exercise 14.

	NORTH	Bidding:			
♠	A J 4				
♡	10 7 4	EAST	SOUTH	WEST	NORTH
◇	A K J	1 ♡	P	P	Dbl.
♣	A Q J 9	P	2 ♠	P	4 ♠
		P	P	P	
	SOUTH				
♠	K Q 9 8 5 2	West leads ♡ Q.			
♡	J 5 3				
◇	5 3				
♣	8 4				

T. 1: East plays ♡ 8.
T. 2: ♡ 9 led. King wins.
T. 3: ♡ A. West discards ◇ 2.
T. 4: ♠ 3 led. West follows.

Analysis 14.

	WEST		EAST
♠	10 7 6	♠	3
♡	Q 9	♡	A K 8 6 2
◇	9 8 6 4 2	◇	Q 10 7
♣	7 6 3	♣	K 10 5 2

The Club finesse is no good, on the bidding. Beside the Diamond finesse, there is one other chance: if East has ◇ Q and ♣ K 10, he can be squeezed. So you cash ♣ A (Vienna Coup) and ◇ A, then run the trumps.

After 11½ tricks we are in a dilemma, of a sort that fairly often arises: has the squeeze operated, or is a mere finesse required? (Imagine ◇ Q traded for ◇ 9.) East's ◇ 10 means nothing, because it could just as easily be a false card. Drop-failure means one down, finesse-failure two down; also, without ◇ Q East's bid would be a minimum. So you would probably play for the drop, but it could be wrong. (All the experts with whom we are personally acquainted would go up, on this "reasoning." If a finesse works, so what? If a squeeze works, oh boy!)

Note that the Vienna Coup does not "transfer a threat" from North to South. North, holding the Diamond threat, is incapable of holding a second threat against East, and you cannot transfer from North to South something that North never possessed.

Of course East should have played ♡ 2, T. 1. But West can see that the bidding probably marks his partner with ♣ K: thus West might well disobey his partner and lead the Club.

12. *The second entry-condition.* Although not as common as the first (§ 5), our second entry-condition is by no means rare.

(E_2) *North holds winner-and-small opposite South's threat, provided further that if East is the victim South also holds a winner in his own threat-suit.*

It is of course understood that North has no entry in his own suit, for in that case (E_1) would be present.

Example (a):	*Example* (b):
NORTH	NORTH
♠ —	♠ —
♡ —	♡ —
◊ 8	◊ 8 5
♣ A 6	♣ A 6

	EAST		EAST
	♠ —		♠ —
	♡ —		♡ —
	◊ 9		◊ 9
	♣ J 10		♣ J 10 6

SOUTH		SOUTH	
♠ J		♠ J	
♡ —		♡ —	
◊ —		◊ —	
♣ 9 7		♣ K 9 7	

In (a) the proviso is lacking, and North, having to *discard before East*, is squeezed. But if West holds the stoppers (transfer East's cards to West), he is helpless: if West discards ◊ 9, North gives ♣ 6, or if West yields ♣ 10, North throws ◊ 8. In (b) the proviso is satisfied: South's Club winner makes room for an idle card in North's hand without relaxing the pressure on East.

Exercise 15.

NORTH
♠ 10 7 2
♡ J 8 6 3
◇ A K Q
♣ A 5 3

SOUTH
♠ A
♡ A K Q 7 5 4 2
◇ 8 6 5
♣ Q 6

Bidding:

SOUTH	WEST	NORTH	EAST
1 ♡	1 ♠	2 ◇	P
2 ♠	P	4 ♡	P
4 NT	P	5 ♡	P
5 NT	P	6 ◇	P
6 ♡	P	P	P

West leads ♠ K.

Analysis 15.

WEST
♠ K Q J 8 4
♡ 9
♣ K J 10 9 2
◇ 9 7

EAST
♠ 9 6 5 3
♡ 10
◇ J 10 4 3 2
♣ 8 7 4

There is a fine chance that West holds ♠ Q J and ♣ K. If so, we pick up that handsome overtrick, because BLUE is airtight, thanks to (E₂) in Clubs. Draw trumps, clear the Diamonds, ruff a Spade, finish the trumps.

Exercise 16.

NORTH
♠ A 10 7
♡ K 8 4
◇ K 6 5 4
♣ 10 8 3

SOUTH
♠ 4 3
♡ A Q J 5 3
◇ A J 2
♣ J 5 2

Bidding:

EAST	SOUTH	WEST	NORTH
P	1 ♡	2 ♣	2 ♡
2 ♠	3 ♡	P	P
P			

West leads ♣ K.

T. 1: East plays ♣ 9.
T. 2-3: ♣ Q A. East discards ♠ 9, 5.
T. 4: ♠ K led.

Analysis 16.

WEST	EAST
♠ K 2	♠ Q J 9 8 6 5
♡ 10 7 2	♡ 9 6
◊ Q 9	◊ 10 8 7 3
♣ A K Q 7 6 4	♣ 9

Finesses are nasty things: might there be a squeeze? East certainly holds ♠ Q J: if he also has four Diamonds, BLUE is present except that there are two losers. Thus the duck, T. 4, is clearly indicated. West's Spade continuation removes (E₁) but leaves (E₂) still in hand, including the vital proviso. Just run the trumps, watching for ♠ Q J. After East plays to the twelfth trick it is certain that he does not have ◊ Q, so you play the Ace.

If you have not thought far enough ahead to have the hand sized up, still you should duck the Spade, just on general principles. (Footnote, Ex. 6.) Any time you get a chance to lose a trick at no cost, lose it!*

13. *The third entry-condition: criss-cross squeeze.* The last of our three entry-conditions is comparatively rare in play, yet not so very rare that you can afford to overlook it.

(E₃): *North holds a winner in South's threat-suit, and South a winner in North's threat-suit.*

These examples show how the squeeze works. North will always have an idle card available for discard on the squeeze-trick. If the defender (either one) parts with a Diamond, Declarer cashes ◊ A, then crosses to ♣ A. If he yields a Club, cash ♣ A, then return via ◊ A.

---

* If the contract is *four* diamonds, however, your best play is to take the first spade, finesse the ♦ J and run the trumps, discarding spades from dummy. You win ten tricks if the diamond finesse works, provided that East has only three diamonds or that West cannot cope with the threat of ♠ 4. (Trade ♦ Q and ♦ 10, and the squeeze succeeds.)

Example (a):

Example (b):

	NORTH	
♠	—	
♡	—	
◇	J 8 7	
♣	A	

	NORTH	
♠	—	
♡	—	
◇	J 8 7	
♣	A	

WEST
♠ —
♡ —
◇ K Q
♣ J 9

EAST
♠ —
♡ —
◇ K Q
♣ J 9

SOUTH
♠ J
♡ —
◇ A
♣ 7 4

SOUTH
♠ J
♡ —
◇ A
♣ 7 4

For an obvious reason, this play is called the *criss-cross squeeze*.

Exercise 17.

NORTH
♠ K 7 3
♡ J 8 4 3
◇ 7 4 3 2
♣ A 2

SOUTH
♠ A Q J
♡ A K Q 9 2
◇ A K Q
♣ Q 6

Bidding:

WEST	NORTH	EAST	SOUTH
P	P	P	2 ♡
P	3 ♡	P	4 NT
P	5 ◇	P	5 NT
P	6 ◇	P	7 ♡
P	P	P	

West leads ♠ 10.

T. 1: Queen wins.
T. 2-3: Hearts. Both follow.
T. 4: Heart. West discards ♣ 3; East, ♣ J.

Analysis 17.

	WEST		EAST
♠	10 9 8 5	♠	6 4 2
♡	6 5	♡	10 7
◇	9 5	◇	J 10 8 6
♣	9 7 5 4 3	♣	K J 10 8

Assume that one adversary (apparently East, from his stupid signal) holds ♣ K and four Diamonds, for this gives a chance via criss-cross squeeze, in addition to the possible Diamond break. (Check BLUE$_3$.) Cash all the majors followed by ◇ K A, then make your choice.

The criss-cross squeeze suffers from a built-in defect. By the very terms of (E$_3$) you have remaining, after the squeeze, one or more winners in each threat-suit. This introduces exactly the same kind of difficulty that was discussed in § 8. There, we found a remedy—the "Rule": here, no remedy is available. Thus in some hands, against a skillful and shifty defender, the choice —whether to cash South's winner or North's—might be little better than a guess.

14. *The failing case.* Looking over our three entry conditions— §§ 5, 12, 13—we find that one case is not covered: East is the defender, North's only entry in South's threat-suit, South with no winner in either threat-suit.

Example:

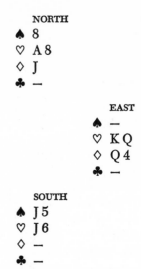

NORTH
♠ 8
♡ A 8
◊ J
♣ —

EAST
♠ —
♡ K Q
◊ Q 4
♣ —

SOUTH
♠ J 5
♡ J 6
◊ —
♣ —

In this Example, on the first Spade no one is hurt; but the second squeezes North. If he throws the Diamond East's guard is released; if he parts with the Heart East can discard a Heart, for South's threat is blocked. And there is no "out." The only alternative would be to start by cashing North's Ace (à la Vienna Coup), and this leaves North with no entry at all. That is:

When East is the defender, North's only entry is in South's threat-suit, and South has no entry in either threat-suit, the squeeze fails.

Note that BLUE, appearing at first glance to be present, is actually not so. (Footnote, Ex. 11.)

Let us return to Ex. 17. One's first thought might be to cash all the Diamonds before the last Spade-Heart. But this puts us in the failing case. (Play it.)

Exercise 18.*

NORTH
♠ A K 6 5 3
♡ K Q 2
◇ 2
♣ K J 8 4

SOUTH
♠ 8 7 2
♡ J 10 9 6 5 4
◇ 9 7
♣ 5 3

Bidding:

WEST	NORTH	EAST	SOUTH
1 ◇	Dbl.	Rdbl.	1 ♡
2 ◇	2 ♡	3 ◇	P
P	3 ♡	4 ◇	P
P	Dbl.	P	4 ♡
Dbl.	P	P	P

West leads ◇ K.

T. 1: King wins.
T. 2: ♣ 2 led. Jack to East's Ace.
T. 3: ♣ 7 returned. West plays Nine; King wins.
T. 4: ♡ K led. East follows; West's Ace wins.
T. 5: ♣ Q led. East plays ♣ 6.

Analysis 18.

WEST
♠ 10 9 4
♡ A
◇ A K 10 5 3
♣ Q 10 9 2

EAST
♠ Q J
♡ 8 7 3
◇ Q J 8 6 4
♣ A 7 6

After five tricks, (B) is in hand if the holder of ♣ 10 also has three Spades. (L) is right. (U) is—wait up! With North's Six as the Spade threat, (U) fails against East; with ♠ 8 as the threat, we are in the failing case if East is the busy defender—North's only entry in South's suit, South with no entry in either suit. So, since there is no squeeze against East, assume perforce that West has the stoppers. Evidently (E₁) is present in Spades. Ruff your Diamond with the Queen, then finish the Hearts, watching for ♣ 10 only.

15. *Choice of threat-suits.* Suppose you know that only a simple squeeze is present, but you have promising threats *in three*

* This hand was played by Mr. Frank Owens, of Kinston, N. C.

suits, and cannot determine (at an early stage) just which two are the threat-suits. This question may in some cases be very baffling; but usually, by close analysis you can find the answer.

Exercise 19.°

	NORTH
♠	A Q 9
♡	7
◇	K 7 6 2
♣	A K 8 5 2

	SOUTH
♠	6 3
♡	A K Q J 10 3
◇	A 8 5 4
♣	9

Bidding:

SOUTH	WEST	NORTH	EAST
1 ♡	1 ♠	2 ♣	P
3 ♡	P	3 ♠	P
4 NT	P	5 ♡	P
5 NT	P	6 ♡	P
7 ♡	Dbl.	P	P
P			

West leads ♠ J.

T. 1: Queen wins. East plays ♠ 2.
T. 2: Heart. Both follow.
T. 3-5: Hearts. West discards ♠ 4, 8, ♣ 3; North, ◇ 2, 6, ♣ 2.
T. 6: Heart. West discards ◇ 10.

Analysis 19.

	WEST
♠	K J 10 8 4
♡	2
◇	Q 10
♣	Q J 7 6 3

	EAST
♠	7 5 2
♡	9 8 6 5 4
◇	J 9 3
♣	10 4

A Spade-Diamond or Spade-Club squeeze, but which? In this instance, we don't care. If West has Diamonds, the Clubs must be cashed (free winners), and the Diamonds may be cashed without doing any harm. If West has Clubs, the Diamonds are free winners; the Clubs should be cashed and a Club ruffed, to remove East's stopper if the suit is 4-3 (§ 10). Thus the same

---

° This hand was played by Mr. John W. Norwood, Jr.

sequence will inflict either squeeze. Discard ◊ 7, T. 6; ◊ K; ♣ A K; Club ruff; ◊ A.

Let us play it with ♣ 6 3 traded for ◊ 9 3. Now the squeeze occurs on the ruffing trick.

While the above certainly suffices for the bridge table, there is one other possibility: West might have both minors. But this case will play itself, for if West is responsible for three suits, the one-loser triple squeeze will grind him to mincemeat. (Play it with ◊ 3, ♣ 3 switched.)

16. *Transferring a stopper.* It frequently happens that all conditions for a squeeze are favorable except that (B) is lacking: one threat stopped by West, the other by East. In such a spot, it is possible sometimes to *transfer a stopper.**

Example:

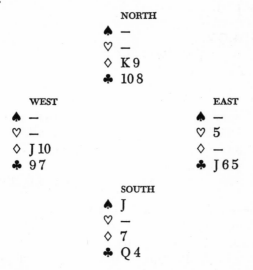

NORTH
♠ —
♡ —
◊ K 9
♣ 10 8

WEST
♠ —
♡ —
◊ J 10
♣ 9 7

EAST
♠ —
♡ 5
◊ —
♣ J 6 5

SOUTH
♠ J
♡ —
◊ 7
♣ Q 4

With North on lead, suppose you know the location of the outstanding honors. A squeeze is in force except that West stops Diamonds, East Clubs. You lead ♣ 10, smothering East's Jack and setting the squeeze if West happens to hold ♣ 9.

* Discovery of this stratagem is due to Mr. Oswald Jacoby.

It seems likely that opportunities for use of the stopper transfer occur with appreciable (though certainly not great) frequency, but that they are apt to be overlooked.

Exercise 20.

NORTH	Bidding:
♠ Q 10 7	
♡ Q J 7	
◊ A K 8 6	
♣ 7 6 5	

EAST	SOUTH	WEST	NORTH
1 ♣	1 ♡	P	2 ◊
P	3 ♡	P	4 ♡
P	P	P	

SOUTH
♠ A 4
♡ A K 10 9 3 2
◊ J 4
♣ J 8 3

West leads ♣ 9.

T. 1-2: ♣ Q K.
T. 3: ♣ A. West discards ◊ 7.
T. 4: East leads ◊ 5.

Analysis 20.

WEST	EAST
♠ J 9 3 2	♠ K 8 6 5
♡ 6 4	♡ 8 5
◊ Q 10 9 7 2	◊ 5 3
♣ 9 2	♣ A K Q 10 4

His bid marks East with ♠ K, but West may hold the Jack. Declarer draws trumps, ending in Dummy; he leads ♠ Q, covered by King and captured by Ace; he runs the trumps.

17. Fraternal care. Perhaps by this time you will agree that, as regards difficulty, Declarer's play of squeezes is greatly overrated. Squeeze defense, on the other hand, is probably the most difficult department of bridge; and in this difficult subject, the toughest assignment is *protection of your partner*. To succeed in this, you must try to look at the hand from Declarer's viewpoint, and figure out what your plans or hopes would be if you were in his place.

Exercise 21.

NORTH	Bidding:

NORTH
- ♠ A 10 7 4
- ♡ A J 10
- ◇ A Q 5
- ♣ 7 6 2

SOUTH	WEST	NORTH	EAST
P	1 ◇	Dbl.	P
2 ♡	3 ♣	3 ♡	P
4 ♡	P	P	P

EAST
- ♠ 9 8 5 2
- ♡ 9 8 7 3
- ◇ 6 4 2
- ♣ 9 3

West leads ♣ K.

T. 1-2: ♣ K Q. South follows.
T. 3: ♣ A led. Plan East's defense.

Analysis 21.

WEST
- ♠ K Q J
- ♡ —
- ◇ K J 10 8 3
- ♣ A K Q 10 5

SOUTH
- ♠ 6 3
- ♡ K Q 6 5 4 2
- ◇ 9 7
- ♣ J 8 4

No chance unless West has something pretty good in Spades. Then, if Declarer has nine tricks, as seems likely, West will be Spade-Diamond squeezable. But look! On the bidding South probably has no more than two Diamonds; thus the threat will be Dummy's Five. You hang tight to that Diamond stopper through thick and thin.

East's ♣ 9 exposes the whole situation to West. What does West expect Declarer to do with all those losers—eat them? He should lead ♠ K as a mere matter of routine. But a nice comfy nap is so refreshing, especially when one has a big brother to watch over him.

Exercise 22.

```
              NORTH
            ♠ 9 6 5
            ♡ 6 5
            ◇ A Q J 7 6
            ♣ 9 5 2
     WEST
   ♠ A K Q 10 3
   ♡ 8 2
   ◇ 9 8 3
   ♣ 10 4 3
```

Bidding:

NORTH	EAST	SOUTH	WEST
P	P	2 ♣	2 ♠
3 ◇	P	3 ♡	P
4 ♣	P	4 NT	P
5 ◇	P	6 ♣	P
P	P		

West leads ♠ K.

T. 1: East plays ♠ 2, South ♠ 7.

Analysis 22.

```
                              EAST
                            ♠ J 8 4 2
                            ♡ J 10 7 4 3
                            ◇ K 10 5 4
                            ♣ —
              SOUTH
            ♠ 7
            ♡ A K Q 9
            ◇ 2
            ♣ A K Q J 8 7 6
```

Unless Declarer is an imbecile, he has no more Spades. Thus the only chance is that East has ◇ K and a Heart stopper. If so, he is squeezable—but not if you lead a Diamond, because (E) will be lacking.

In case Declarer runs the trumps, get your Diamonds on the table so that East can count the suit. But of course he will try to ruff the third round of Hearts, which is your dish.

18. *The pseudo squeeze.* Even with no hope of a genuine squeeze, do not abandon the hand if there is any chance that one defender may think that he is being squeezed, for in a surprising percentage of cases he will make a fatal blunder in discarding. This type of play is called a *pseudo squeeze.*

One point should be emphasized. A pseudo (of the "simple" variety, which is all that we are considering at present) will seldom succeed when (L) is missing. Thus with more than one loser in hand you should prepare for a pseudo just as for a real squeeze by ducking the required number of tricks as early as possible.

That word "blunder" is hardly fair to the defense. There are pseudos which are absolutely indefensible: that is, hands where a dunderhead might stumble into the winning defense, but a capable player, never.

Another important possibility is that the victim's partner may make a discard that converts the pseudo into a genuine squeeze. For example, in Ex. 21 many Easts would throw one of those "worthless" Diamonds. West's bid shows that he can stop Diamonds!

Exercise 23.

NORTH
- ♠ J 8 4 3
- ♡ 8 2
- ◇ A Q 8 5
- ♣ 8 4 3

SOUTH
- ♠ A K Q 10 9 5
- ♡ 9 4
- ◇ 4
- ♣ A K 6 5

Bidding:

SOUTH	WEST	NORTH	EAST
1 ♠	Dbl.	2 ♠	3 ♡
4 ♠	P	P	P

West leads ♡ A.

T. 1: East plays ♡ Q.
T. 2: ♡ K led. East plays ♡ 3.
T. 3: Spade. Both follow.
T. 4: Spade. East discards ♡ 5.

Analysis 23.

WEST
- ♠ 7 2
- ♡ A K
- ◇ K J 9 6 2
- ♣ Q 10 7 2

EAST
- ♠ 6
- ♡ Q J 10 7 6 5 3
- ◇ 10 7 3
- ♣ J 9

In rubber bridge Declarer would concede a Club and claim the rest, but in match play a bolder course is advisable. If the

Diamond finesse is good, as is all but certain, it can cost no money to run those Spades. With nine Diamonds and seven Clubs in sight, West can see that East is much more likely to hold a Club than a Diamond stopper. A thoughtful West would be very apt to abandon Clubs.

East can see that his Clubs are worthless, while his Diamonds might possibly help. He should discard ♡ J, T. 4, to tell his partner that he (East) has a little something in the higher suit.

PROBLEMS*

Problem 1.

<pre>
          NORTH   Bidding:
       ♠ K 4
       ♡ 8753   NORTH   EAST   SOUTH   WEST
       ◊ A K Q 7 5 4   1 ◊   P   7 NT   P
       ♣ 8   P   P

          SOUTH   West leads ♡ J.
       ♠ A Q 6
       ♡ A K Q
       ◊ —
       ♣ A K Q 9 6 3 2
</pre>

Plan Declarer's play.

Solution 1.

<pre>
          WEST   EAST
       ♠ J 8 7 5 3   ♠ 10 9 2
       ♡ J 10 9 6   ♡ 4 2
       ◊ 10 6 2   ◊ J 9 8 3
       ♣ 10   ♣ J 7 5 4
</pre>

Of course you cash the Hearts followed by the Spades. Even if Clubs are stopped, this succeeds in case both minor suits are in one hand.

Any question? What would you discard from East's hand? Declarer's failure to cash the Diamonds when in Dummy proves

---

* These review "Problems" are of the same general character as our "Exercises." The different term is used merely to distinguish the two groups.

(if proof were needed) that he has at least one Diamond; thus a Diamond discard closes out the hand.

A fine player would therefore surely discard a Club from the East hand. It would take an imbecile or a genius to discard a Diamond!

*Problem 2.**

NORTH	Bidding:
♠ A K 8 4	
♡ A 5 2	
◇ A 10 7	
♣ A K Q	

EAST	SOUTH	WEST	NORTH
P	P	P	2 NT
P	3 ♣	P	3 NT
P	4 ♣	P	6 ♣
P	P	P	

SOUTH
♠ 3 2
♡ Q 9 6 4
◇ 8
♣ J 10 7 4 3 2

West leads ♡ J.

T. 1: East's King wins.
T. 2: ♡ 3, 6, 7, A.

Solution 2.

WEST	EAST
♠ 10 9 7 6	♠ Q J 5
♡ J 10 8 7	♡ K 3
◇ K J 3 2	◇ Q 9 6 5 4
♣ 5	♣ 9 8 6

Since West probably stops Hearts, he can be squeezed if he has four Spades. Draw trumps; ♠ A K; Spade ruff; Clubs; ◇ A.

As no doubt you saw, this would be a very bad method. The sequence, beginning with the third trick, should be ◇ A; Diamond ruff; Spade cross; Diamond, ruffed with the Seven; Spade cross; Spade, ruffed with the Ten; Club cross; Spade, ruffed with the Jack; Club cross; Club; Heart. This wins except against a very bad division in Spades, Diamonds or Clubs, whereas the squeeze is rather less than an even bet.

This would seem to be as pretty a dummy reversal as one often sees, simply because of the exquisite timing required. Any slightest deviation from course, and no dividends.

* This hand was played by Mr. Michel Dufrenne, of Ann Arbor, Mich.

Problem 3.*

	NORTH
♠	K Q 6 4
♡	9 7 4 3
◇	A J
♣	A 10 3

	SOUTH
♠	9 5 3 2
♡	A K Q
◇	K Q 10 8
♣	K Q

Bidding:

NORTH	EAST	SOUTH	WEST
1 ♣	P	2 ◇	P
2 ♠	P	3 ♠	P
4 ◇	P	4 NT	P
5 ♡	P	6 NT	P
P	P		

West leads ♣ 5.

T. 1: East plays ♣ 8; King wins.
T. 2: ♠ Q to East's Ace.
T. 3: Club led.

Solution 3.

	WEST
♠	J 7
♡	10
◇	9 7 6 4 2
♣	J 9 7 5 2

	EAST
♠	A 10 8
♡	J 8 6 5 2
◇	5 3
♣	8 6 4

As usual, forget the Heart break—it either is or is not there. Thanks to East's complaisance in winning the first Spade, the contract is sure by criss-cross squeeze if either defender stops both majors. Cash Dummy's Aces; finish the Diamonds. No ambiguity arises, because of West's singleton Heart.

Problem 4.

	NORTH
♠	5 4 2
♡	Q J 9 2
◇	A 5 4
♣	A Q J

	SOUTH
♠	A K Q J 9 8 6
♡	—
◇	K 8 3
♣	K 6 5

Bidding:

WEST	NORTH	EAST	SOUTH
P	1 ♣	1 ♡	2 ♡
3 ◇	3 NT	P	4 ♣
P	4 ◇	P	7 ♠
P	P	P	

West leads ◇ Q.

* This hand was played by Dr. Ben Dushnik.

T. 1:   East plays ◊ 7.
T. 2-4: Spades. West discards ◊ 2, 9, 10.

Solution 4.

	WEST		EAST
♠	—	♠	10 7 3
♡	10 7 4 3	♡	A K 8 6 5
◊	Q J 10 9 6 2	◊	7
♣	9 8 2	♣	10 7 4 3

We got over the first hurdle anyway—East had a Diamond. Now, cross in Clubs and ruff ♡ 2; cross again and crash ♡ Q; cross and jam ♡ J through, hoping to smother the Ten from West. When this does not happen, there is still a chance. (Footnote, Ex. 3.)

Problem 5.

NORTH
♠ K 9 7 4 2
♡ A K J 7 2
◊ 4
♣ K J

SOUTH
♠ A 10 5
♡ 10 4
◊ A K 10
♣ A Q 9 3 2

Bidding:

NORTH	EAST	SOUTH	WEST
1 ♠	P	3 ♣	P
3 ♡	P	4 NT	P
5 ◊	P	5 NT	P
6 ♠	P	7 NT	P
P	P		

West leads ◊ 5.

T. 1:   Queen to Ace.
T. 2:   ♡ 10, Q, K, 3.
T. 3-4: ♣ K, J. Both follow.

Solution 5.

	WEST		EAST
♠	Q 6	♠	J 8 3
♡	Q 5	♡	9 8 6 3
◊	J 9 8 5 2	◊	Q 7 6 3
♣	10 8 6 5	♣	7 4

This hand, based on one that occurred in local (Ann Arbor) play, is a fine example of the problem discussed in § 15. The crucial question, location of the Spade stopper, is a 50-50 guess. There are two possible sequences. (a) Cash Hearts, ♠ A, minors, for success if West has Spades, failure (§ 14) if East has that suit. (b) Cash ♠ K A and the minors, succeeding when East has Spades, *also* when West has Spades provided West also has Hearts. Since in a large number of trials (a) would succeed half the time and (b) decidedly more than half, (b) must be chosen.

As the cards lie, the cashing of ♠ K is a Vienna Coup, executed at a time when South holds a winner in his own threat-suit. This brings out the fact that for scrupulous accuracy the Rule of § 11 should be slightly amended: "When South . . . has or will have no winner," etc.

CHAPTER II

THE DOUBLE SQUEEZE

19. *Terminology.* The *double squeeze* is a play in which both opponents are squeezed. The two squeezes, resulting all told in the gain of one trick, may occur simultaneously or sequentially— that is, on the same trick or on different tricks. In the typical case, one adversary defends one suit, his partner defends another, while each (before the squeeze culminates) can stop a third suit.

Declarer thus holds three threats. For a reason to appear in a moment, it is impossible that all three threats shall lie in one hand: invariably we have a single threat in one hand, two threats opposite. In the text of this chapter (not necessarily in the exercises), South will denote the hand *containing the single threat.*

The suit stopped at the *right* of the single threat will be called Suit R; the one stopped at the *left,* Suit L; the one stopped by *both,* Suit B. The fourth, or *free,* suit is F. Since Suits R and L are each free against one opponent, they may be called *semi-free* suits.

It will be necessary to fix in mind the meaning of the four letters, since all will be used constantly. Without some such device, we would lose our way in a maze of words.

20. *The necessary condition.* We may take it as self-evident that:

If a double squeeze is to occur, each defender must be subject to a simple squeeze when his partner's support in Suit B is withdrawn.

This shows why it is impossible that all three threats shall lie in one hand: (U) would fail against the adversary at the left of the threats.

Thus, to determine whether a double squeeze is or may be present, Declarer's first step (of course after identifying the threats) is to check BLUE against each opponent in turn. Second, he plans the play, making sure that all conditions will remain in effect until each squeeze has matured. Third, he runs the winners: in the typical case, he keeps record of all cards *higher than the two singly-guarded threats*, disregarding discards in Suit B.

This may look at first glance like a somewhat formidable task. But we shall presently proceed to classify all double squeezes in three easily distinguishable types, and to lay down explicit rules for the execution of each type. Armed with these rules, you will find that in most cases the double squeeze is only slightly more complicated than the simple squeeze.

We shall not undertake to play any hands until the above-mentioned classification has been made, but let us look at two end positions.

Example (a):

	NORTH	
♠	—	
♡	5	
◇	K 8	
♣	A 5	

WEST		EAST
♠ —		♠ —
♡ 6		♡ 9 8
◇ Q J		◇ 9
♣ Q J		♣ K 9

	SOUTH
♠	J
♡	J 7
◇	7
♣	8

Example (b):

	NORTH
♠	—
♡	6
◇	8 7
♣	Q 5

WEST		EAST
♠ —		♠ —
♡ J 8 7		♡ Q 9 5
◇ Q 9		◇ —
♣ —		♣ J 9

	SOUTH
♠	J
♡	A K 3
◇	—
♣	4

Example (a): The threats are R, ♡ 7; L, ◊ 8; B, ♣ 5. Cash the Diamond; return in Hearts; lead the Spade. Both adversaries are squeezed on the same trick. West must give up a Club to guard the Diamond; North discards the Diamond; East surrenders.

Example (b): A sequential squeeze, with threats R, ♣ 5; L, ◊ 8; B, ♡ 3. On the Spade West and North throw idle Diamonds, but East is squeezed out of Hearts. And now the Club extorts a Heart from West.

Note that in these examples, unless the F, L and R winners are run *in proper order* the squeeze will fail, and this is true of double squeezes in general. In retrospect at the end of this chapter one fact will stand out: in the vast majority of double squeezes, *it is safe to run the L winners at an early stage,* and in many cases it is advisable or even necessary to do so.

You are warned not to adopt this statement as a universal guiding principle, since it is not universally applicable. The remark is inserted for this reason. Theoretically, with a double squeeze in hand you should be able to plan the sequence to the end. Actually, with the whole table waiting impatiently for you to play, it is easy to "get mixed up." In such a case, cash the L winners. The chances are that this will have done no harm, and it may simplify the problem to a point where you can get back on the beam.

21. *Two fundamental propositions.* In simple squeeze, you may have winners remaining in each threat-suit after the squeeze is completed. See, for example, Ex. 3.

In double squeeze the fact is radically different. A double squeeze culminates when the last of the F, L and R tops is played: that is, when a double squeeze is complete, Declarer has winners remaining only in the B suit.

From this fact, two important results are easily established.

I. *In every double squeeze, the B threat must be accompanied by an entry in its own suit.*

II. *In every double squeeze, if all the B winners are in the same hand with the B threat, the final squeeze-card must lie in the opposite hand.*

22. *Classification of double squeezes.* All double squeezes belong to one or the other of two general types, called Type R and Type B.

Type R: *The R threat is alone, opposite the L and B threats.*

Type B: *The B threat is alone, opposite the L and R threats.*

The third possibility, that South (say) holds the L threat, North R and B, results in failure, for lack of (U) against East.

We shall find that Type B squeezes divide into two widely different subclasses, to be called Type B_2 and Type B_1. Thus we should say that there are really three basic forms of double squeeze. Specific directions for the execution of Types R, B_2 and B_1 will be laid down in §§ 23, 27, 28 respectively. Of the three forms, Type R is undoubtedly the commonest in play.

Situations occasionally arise where, due to a multiplicity of threats, the hand may be viewed and played as either Type R or Type B, at Declarer's choice. (An example later.)

23. *Type R double squeeze.* Suppose that South holds the R threat, North L and B. The play of this form is covered by the following general

RULE: *In every Type R double squeeze, the L winners should be cashed early. The last of the F-R group must lie in and be led from the one-threat hand.*

Theoretically, that word "every" is a shade too strong: hands can be constructed where all the F-R's must precede the last L, and yet the squeeze matures. But since you are unlikely ever to hold such a hand, the wording as it stands is satisfactory for practical purposes.

In § 20 you were told to cash the L winners when in doubt. We have now learned that for Type R—commonest of the three forms—this is standard procedure. Thus in planning the execution of a double squeeze, the first step (after identifying the threats) is to note whether the squeeze is Type R or Type B. If Type R, get rid of those L winners! In most cases, the rest of the hand will play itself.

Let us point out explicitly the failing case. If South holds neither a B winner nor the last L, then all L's *must* be cashed while South has remaining an F or R *entry*, in addition to the

last F-R winner (squeeze-card). That is, Declarer must be able
to re-enter the South hand and *then* lead the final squeeze-card.
In the rare case when this is not possible, the squeeze fails. (An
example presently.)

Exercise 24.

NORTH	Bidding:			
♠ Q J 7 3				
♡ Q 10 9 6 5	EAST	SOUTH	WEST	NORTH
◊ A 7 6 2	3 ♣	3 ♠	4 ♣	5 ♣
♣ —	P	5 ♡	P	6 ◊
	P	7 ♠	P	P
SOUTH	P			
♠ A K 10 9 8 5 2				
♡ A	West leads ♠ 4.			
◊ 10				
♣ 7 6 5 3				

T. 1: East follows.

Analysis 24.

WEST	EAST
♠ 4	♠ 6
♡ K J 8 7 2	♡ 4 3
◊ K J 9 3	◊ Q 8 5 4
♣ J 9 4	♣ A K Q 10 8 2

But for that naughty lead the hand would be a laydown, but
it is practically that anyway. Cash ♡ A, then ruff Clubs and
Hearts, hoping to drop ♡ K. When this does not happen, you
have a Type R double squeeze with threats R, ♣ 7; L, ♡ Q;
B, ◊ 7.

Do not fail to realize that this double squeeze literally does
play itself. You wish to ruff three Hearts; therefore, automatically,
the L winner gets cashed "early." When the King roosts too high,
what can you possibly do but finish the trumps?

Exercise 25.

NORTH
- ♠ K 2
- ♡ A 10 7 4
- ◇ 9 8 3
- ♣ 7 6 5 3

SOUTH
- ♠ A Q 6 4
- ♡ 8
- ◇ A K Q 7 4 2
- ♣ 9 4

Bidding:

EAST	SOUTH	WEST	NORTH
P	1 ◇	2 ♣	P
P	2 ♠	3 ♣	3 ◇
P	5 ◇	P	P
P			

West leads ♣ K.

T. 1: East plays ♣ 10.
T. 2: ♣ Q led. East plays ♣ 2.
T. 3: ♣ 8 led. East plays ◇ 6; ◇ 7 wins.
T. 4: ◇ A. East discards ♡ 2.

Analysis 25.

WEST
- ♠ 9 5
- ♡ K 9 6
- ◇ J 10 5
- ♣ A K Q J 8

EAST
- ♠ J 10 8 7 3
- ♡ Q J 5 3 2
- ◇ 6
- ♣ 10 2

The first thought might be to try to ruff a Spade. But with West holding eight minors, to give him three Spades would mean that Hearts are 6-2, which is less likely than that Spades are 5-2. On the other hand, West is highly unlikely to hold four Spades, and if not, the Type R double squeeze is on, with threats R, ♠ 6; L, ♣ 7; B, ♡ 10. Run the Diamonds, erasing East; then the Spades, polishing off West. Count Spades and Clubs.

Exercise 26.

	NORTH
♠	A 6 5 4 2
♡	10 6 5 2
◊	A 2
♣	10 7

	SOUTH
♠	K Q
♡	A K Q 4
◊	Q J
♣	A K Q J 8

Bidding:

WEST	NORTH	EAST	SOUTH
P	P	P	2 ♣
P	2 ♠	P	3 ♡
P	4 ♡	P	4 NT
P	5 ♡	P	7 NT
P	P	P	

West leads ♠ J.

T. 1: East plays ♠ 8. Queen wins.
T. 2: ♠ K. East discards ◊ 3.
Spread the hand for contract.

Analysis 26.

	WEST		EAST
♠	J 10 9 7 3	♠	8
♡	9	♡	J 8 7 3
◊	10 7 5 4	◊	K 9 8 6 3
♣	5 3 2	♣	9 6 4

Two rounds of Hearts will expose the situation. If East has a stopper, Type R double squeeze with threats R, ♡ 4; L, ♠ 6; B, ◊ 2. Cross in Clubs; cash ♠ A (last L winner); run the Clubs. If West stops Hearts, Spade-Heart simple (left to you).

Note that with ♣ 10, 9 switched, the simple squeeze would still make but the double would fail. (§ 23, fifth paragraph.)

24. *Simple squeeze played as a double squeeze.* In the typical double squeeze, both defenders presumably stop the B suit. If it turns out that only one can do so, there is actually a simple squeeze against that one, with the other out of the picture. (For example, in Ex. 25 trade ♡ K for ♡ 2.) However, this is a mere technicality, in no way affecting the play and certainly doing no harm, since a load that would be too heavy for both defenders cannot possibly be carried by one alone.

Suppose now that West stops Hearts, East Diamonds, while Declarer's Clubs are such that only one opponent can stop that suit (for example, A K Q x opposite x x); also that there is no way to locate the Club stopper. Technically there is no double squeeze—merely a simple squeeze against the Club holder. However, if the necessary conditions are present, Declarer can *obviate the guess by playing the hand as a double squeeze.* Again, the fact that only one defender stops the B suit has no weight.

This device must be kept always in mind, because it finds frequent application.

Exercise 27.

NORTH
♠ A Q J 6 4
♡ 9 8 4
♢ A 10 5
♣ J 6

SOUTH
♠ K 5
♡ A K Q 5 2
♢ K Q J 7
♣ A 5

Bidding:

NORTH	EAST	SOUTH	WEST
1 ♠	P	3 ♡	P
3 ♠	P	4 NT	P
5 ♡	P	7 NT	P
P	P		

West leads ♣ K.

Show that the contract is guaranteed on the one assumption that West holds ♣ Q.

Analysis 27.

WEST
♠ 10 9 8 7 3
♡ 3
♢ 8 3 2
♣ K Q 8 3

EAST
♠ 2
♡ J 10 7 6
♢ 9 6 4
♣ 10 9 7 4 2

At the bridge table this hand would be very easy to miss— or at least, your author cheerfully admits that he himself would be very apt to miss it—simply because it is so easy to take for granted that Spades will run. Before starting to run a suit that looks solid but may not be, we *should* always consider what will happen if that suit fails.

Instead, of course, you cash two Hearts. If East refuses, run

Diamonds and Spades to execute the child's-size Heart-Club simple squeeze. If West refuses Hearts, you have (provided Spades are stopped) a Spade-Club simple against West or Spade-Heart simple against East. Which? You don't care. Merely play Type R double with threats R, ♡ 5; L, ♣ J; B, ♠ 6. Just run the reds.

x x x x

When faced with a choice between two simple squeezes, do not think that you can always "obviate the guess" by resort to double-squeeze technique, because there was a proviso—"if the necessary conditions are present".

For a prime example, play Ex. 27 with ♡ 4, ♣ 5 traded. Now your best bet is to run the Diamonds in hope of adducing a little information, but all you get is two meaningless Clubs. So you cash ♠ K and ♡ A, then flip a coin. If on their toes the opponents can help (?): West drops ♠ 9 under your King, East ♡ 10 under Your Ace.

25. *Choice between simple squeeze and double squeeze.* Do not confuse the problem above—choice between two simple squeezes—with the totally different problem of choice between a simple and a double squeeze. In a hand which may contain one or the other of these squeezes, quite obviously you should play as many tops as you can that will leave both roads open. While this is going on, new information may come to light which will point out infallibly the right path. We are concerned here only with those hands in which uncertainty remains. It might be thought that in this case also the double squeeze would be the right play, but not so. In § 24, "if the necessary conditions are present, Declarer can obviate the guess"; but not here, because the techniques of the two squeezes will inevitably diverge.*

Hands can be constructed which leave the choice a mere toss-up; but in most cases one can pick the route with at least some probability of success. The point to be emphasized is that there is no *a priori* reason to incline toward the double squeeze, because (other things being equal) the simple is just as likely to be present. And you can't have it both ways!

* With rare exceptions. An example in due course.

Exercise 28.

NORTH
♠ 8 7 4 3
♡ A K 7 2
◇ 9 7 4
♣ 10 4

Bidding:

WEST	NORTH	EAST	SOUTH
P	P	P	2 ◇
P	2 ♡	P	3 ♣
P	3 ◇	P	3 ♠
P	4 ♡	P	6 NT
P	P	P	

SOUTH
♠ A K 6
♡ 8 4
◇ A K Q 8
♣ A K Q J

West leads ♠ 2.

T. 1: East's Queen wins.
T. 2: ♠ 9 returned. West plays ♠ 5.
T. 3: Spade. East discards ♣ 2.
T. 4: Heart. West plays ♡ 5, East ♡ 3.
T. 5-6: Clubs. Both follow.
T. 7-8: Clubs. West discards ♡ 6, J.
T. 9: Diamond. Both follow.

Analysis 28.

WEST	EAST
♠ J 10 5 2	♠ Q 9
♡ J 6 5	♡ Q 10 9 3
◇ J 10 5 3	◇ 6 2
♣ 9 7	♣ 8 6 5 3 2

If West stops Diamonds, Spade-Diamond simple squeeze. If East has the Diamonds, Type R double with threats R, ◇ 8; L, ♠ 8; B, ♡ 7. After nine tricks the evidence is strong that West is protecting Diamonds. So you lead the Heart.

Exercise 29.*

	NORTH
♠	A K
♡	10 9 5 4
◇	A 8 6 4
♣	A 10 3

	SOUTH
♠	Q J 10 8 7 6 3 2
♡	A
◇	Q
♣	K 7 4

Bidding:

WEST	NORTH	EAST	SOUTH
P	1 ◇	P	2 ♠
P	3 ♠	P	4 ♠
P	5 ♠	P	6 ♠
P	P	P	

West leads ♣ 9.

Plan Declarer's play.

Analysis 29.

	WEST		EAST
♠	9 4	♠	5
♡	J 8 6 3 2	♡	K Q 7
◇	J 9 7 5	◇	K 10 3 2
♣	9 5	♣	Q J 8 6 2

The key play of this brilliant hand comes on the first trick. The only hope of the overtrick is to set up ♡ 10 as a threat for a squeeze. With Dummy's Ten as the Club threat, no double squeeze because all three threats would be in one hand, and no Heart-Club simple because if West has Hearts, (B) is lacking, and if East has Hearts, (U) will fail. Thus the Club threat must be the Seven: to preserve (E), the first trick must be won with the Ace. Although we have no information on the point, it seems likely that East would play ♣ 8, T. 1, thus boosting Declarer's hopes.

The preparatory sequence, obviously, is ♡ A, Spade, Heart ruff, Spade, Heart ruff. Now, if East has the Hearts, Heart-Club simple: Spades followed by Diamond. If West has the Hearts, Type R double with threats R, ♣ 7; L, ♡ 10; B, ◇ 8: Spades followed by Club. When the decision-point is reached, the indications are that West has the Heart stopper.

* This hand was played by Mrs. Mildred Erskine, of Mt. Clemens, Mich., and reported by Mr. Frank S. Eaton in the Detroit Free Press.

With Hearts 4-4 and the pictures divided, there would be no genuine squeeze in the hand. There would, however, be a pseudo compound squeeze which only a very knowledgeable East would be able to defend. (Ex. 116.)

26. *The Type B squeezes.* With rare exceptions, noted in § 23, all Type R squeezes are essentially alike.

For the Type B squeezes—B threat opposite L and R—the fact is quite otherwise. These squeezes divide into two subgroups, differing widely in their rules of play.

Type B_2: *The B threat is accompanied by two (or more) B winners.*

Type B_1: *The B threat is accompanied by one B winner.*

Of course the subscripts "1" and "2" do not mean "first" and "second"; they merely denote the number of winners accompanying the B threat.

When a genuine double squeeze exists—both adversaries stopping the B suit—the B threat can be accompanied by more than two B winners only if the holding is exactly A K Q x opposite x. But of course our theory must cover the case of a simple squeeze played as double: thus Declarer may hold a maximum of five B winners—A K Q J 10 x opposite x—or as many as four divided between the two hands (as in Ex. 27).

27. *Type B_2 double squeeze.* Suppose that the B threat is alone, opposite the L and R threats, and that the B threat is *accompanied by two B winners.* The play of this type of squeeze goes as follows:

RULE: *In every Type B_2 double squeeze,*
(a) *if the two-threat hand has no B winner, the final squeeze-card must lie opposite the B threat;*
(b) *if the two-threat hand has a B winner, the free and semi-free winners may be cashed in any order whatever.*

Do not forget that the B winners must still be in hand when the squeeze is reached. If it becomes necessary earlier to cash one of the B pair, the hand goes at once into Type B_1, for which (as we shall find presently) the rules of play are very much more strict.

Of course the phrase "in any order" does not—nothing can—supersede the fundamental requirement, dominating every situation whether squeeze play or not, that entries must be conserved. In this example, with threats R, ◇ 9; L, ♡ 9; B, ♣ 9, unless ♠ J is led now South's hand will have to be re-entered in Clubs, which ruins everything. But with ♡ 4 replaced by a Spade, "any order" is right.

Example:

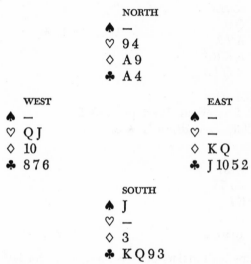

NORTH
♠ —
♡ 9 4
◇ A 9
♣ A 4

WEST
♠ —
♡ Q J
◇ 10
♣ 8 7 6

EAST
♠ —
♡ —
◇ K Q
♣ J 10 5 2

SOUTH
♠ J
♡ —
◇ 3
♣ K Q 9 3

In the Rule, the letters R and L do not appear. As a logical consequence it follows that Declarer does not care which suit is R and which is L. The only requirement is that the stops be divided, either way.

In Case (b), Declarer's minimum holding in the B suit is A K x x opposite Q x, or the equivalent—see the Example. Since it is now impossible that both defenders stop the suit, it follows that Case (b) can arise only when a simple squeeze is being played as double.

We know that for Type R it is usually advisable, and frequently necessary, to cash the L winners early. The Rule above shows that for Type B₂ the same procedure, though not in most cases especially advisable, is *allowable* unless entry difficulty would be created thereby. Thus the suggestion of § 20 (last two paragraphs) is valid for Type B₂ as well as for Type R.

Exercise 30.

	NORTH
♠	A K 6 4
♡	K Q 9 5
◊	7 4
♣	7 6 4

	SOUTH
♠	Q 9
♡	A 7 2
◊	A K 6 5
♣	K Q J 3

Bidding:

NORTH	EAST	SOUTH	WEST
1 ♠	P	2 ◊	P
2 ♡	P	4 NT	P
5 ◊	P	6 NT	P
P	P		

West leads ♣ 10.

T. 1: Ace wins.
T. 2: ♣ 5 returned. West plays ♣ 2.
T. 3: Club. East discards ♠ 3.

Analysis 30.

	WEST		EAST
♠	J 8 5 2	♠	10 7 3
♡	6 4	♡	J 10 8 3
◊	Q 8 2	◊	J 10 9 3
♣	10 9 8 2	♣	A 5

If East stops both majors there is no squeeze, for lack of (U). If West has both, then East has six Diamonds, which does not jibe with his Spade discard. If the stops are divided, either way, there is an easy Type B_2 double with B threat ◊ 6. The only requirement is that the final squeeze-card lie opposite the B threat. So you cash the last Club followed by the majors, counting Spades and Hearts.

Exercise 31.*

	NORTH
♠	Q 9 5 2
♡	K 8
◇	10 6
♣	A K Q 5 3

	SOUTH
♠	10 6
♡	A Q 6 2
◇	A J 3 2
♣	9 7 6

Bidding:

NORTH	EAST	SOUTH	WEST
1 ♣	P	1 ♡	P
2 ♣	P	2 ◇	P
2 ♠	P	2 NT	P
3 NT	P	P	P

West leads ♠ 7.

T. 1: East's King wins.
T. 2: ♠ 4 returned. West's Ace wins.
T. 3: ◇ 9 led. East plays Queen; Ace wins.
T. 4-5: Clubs. Both follow.
T. 6: ♠ Q led. East discards ◇ 5.

Analysis 31.

	WEST		EAST
♠	A J 8 7 3	♠	K 4
♡	9 7 5	♡	J 10 4 3
◇	9 8 4	◇	K Q 7 5
♣	4 2	♣	J 10 8

With West holding ◇ K there would be no Spade-Diamond simple squeeze, for lack of (E). But it is unthinkable that West would lead away from the King into South's bid: undoubtedly East has that card. If so, Type B₂ simple-played-as-double with threats R, ◇ 10; L, ♠ 9; B, ♡ 6. Just finish the Clubs.

This hand illustrates the possibility mentioned in § 22 (last paragraph). Due to the presence of a competent Diamond threat *in each hand,** the squeeze may equally well be considered as Type R with threats R, ♠ 9; L, ◇ J; B, ♡ 6.

---

* This hand was played by Mr. John W. Norwood, Jr.
* While the dual-threat, dual-type possibility seems obvious enough, it had escaped your author's notice until it was pointed out to him by Mr. Norwood in this very hand.

Exercise 32.

	NORTH
♠	J 10 5 3
♡	10 5 4
◇	K Q 5 4
♣	5 2

	SOUTH
♠	7 4
♡	A K Q 9 6
◇	A 8
♣	A K J 4

Bidding:

SOUTH	WEST	NORTH	EAST
1 ♡	1 ♠	P	P
3 ♣	P	3 ♡	P
4 ♡	P	P	P

West leads ♠ K.

T. 1: East plays ♠ 9.
T. 2: ♠ Q. East plays ♠ 6.
T. 3: ♠ 2 led. East plays ♡ 8; ♡ 9 wins.
T. 4: Heart. West plays ♡ 2, East ♡ 3.
T. 5: Heart. West plays ♡ 7, East ♣ 3.

Analysis 32.

	WEST		EAST
♠	A K Q 8 2	♠	9 6
♡	J 7 2	♡	8 3
◇	9 7 2	◇	J 10 6 3
♣	9 7	♣	Q 10 8 6 3

Since most tables will play the hand in 3 NT, making four, it behooves us to pick up the overtrick.

After recoiling in terror from the Club finesse, one's first thought might be to ruff a Club; but in view of West's holding of eight cards in the majors, this involves a serious risk.

What are the squeeze possibilities? If West stops Diamonds, Spade-Diamond simple squeeze. But this would mean that Clubs are 6-1. Very much more likely, East has the Diamonds, which means Type B_2 double with threats R, ◇ 5; L, ♠ J; B, ♣ J. Finish the Hearts, then the Diamonds.

28. *Type B_1 Double squeeze.* When the B threat is alone, opposite the L and R threats, and the B threat is *accompanied by one B winner,* the squeezes fall into two clearly separable classes.

RULE: *In every Type B_1 double squeeze,*

(a) *if the two-threat hand has a B winner, the last R must precede the last F;*

(b) *if the two-threat hand has no B winner, that hand must contain an L winner with a small card opposite, and the last winners must be cashed in the precise order RFL.**

To help us keep in mind the rigidly prescribed sequence of winners in Case (b), that case will be called *the RFL squeeze.*

A vital point: any Type B_1 squeeze—either case—will fail unless the last F winner is *in the same hand with the B threat.* Also (see the Rule) the RFL squeeze will fail unless the L threat is *accompanied by an entry in its own suit,* to serve as final squeeze-card.

Since in every Type B_1 squeeze the last R must precede the last F, it is almost always desirable, and frequently necessary, to *cash the R winners early.* In Case (a) it is also allowable, as a rule, to cash the L winners early, just as we have been doing in Type R and Type B_2.

Evidently the two cases above compare in this way. In each, the last R *must* precede the last F. In (a) the last L usually *may,* in (b) the last L always *must,* be kept in hand for use as final squeeze-card.

Example (a):

```
              NORTH
            ♠ 8
            ♡ A J
            ◇ K 4
            ♣ A 8
  WEST                    EAST
♠ —                     ♠ —
♡ 9 8                   ♡ K Q
◇ Q 9 3                 ◇ J 8 2
♣ J 9                   ♣ 7 6
              SOUTH
            ♠ J 9
            ♡ 7
            ◇ A 7 5
            ♣ 5
```

Example (b):

```
              NORTH
            ♠ 8
            ♡ A J
            ◇ 4
            ♣ A 8
  WEST                    EAST
♠ —                     ♠ —
♡ 9 8                   ♡ K Q
◇ Q 9                   ◇ J 8
♣ J 9                   ♣ 7 6
              SOUTH
            ♠ J 9
            ♡ 7
            ◇ A 7
            ♣ 5
```

* Rural Free 'Livery!

In (a), the threats are R, ♡ J; L, ♣ 8; B, ◇ 7. Since the two-threat hand has a B winner, the L winners may be cashed early and the last R must precede the last F. So, ♣ A, ♡ A, Spades. It is true that the squeeze would surely operate if the order were ♡ A, Spades, ♣ A, but in some cases there might be danger of ambiguity.

In (b), the threats are R, ♡ J; L, ♣ 8; B, ◇ 7. Since the two-threat hand has no B winner, this is an RFL squeeze. The formula says Hearts-Spades-Clubs. Be sure to verify the fact that with any other sequence the squeeze would fail.

The RFL squeeze, though by no means rare, is undoubtedly the least common of the various forms, for an obvious reason: even when the necessary threats are present and properly placed, very often the squeeze cannot be executed due to inability to cash the winners in proper order.

Exercise 33.

```
        NORTH
     ♠ A K Q J
     ♡ A 4 2
     ◇ 6 2
     ♣ 9 6 5 3

        SOUTH
     ♠ 10 4
     ♡ K J 10
     ◇ Q 9 4 3
     ♣ A K Q 4
```

Bidding:

SOUTH	WEST	NORTH	EAST
1 ♣	P	1 ♠	P
1 NT	P	3 NT	P
P	P		

West leads ◇ 5.

T. 1: King wins.
T. 2: ◇ A led. West plays ◇ 7.
T. 3: ◇ 10 led. Queen wins; West plays ◇ 8.
T. 4: Club. Both follow.
T. 5: Club. West discards ♠ 2.

Analysis 33.

```
        WEST                    EAST
     ♠ 7 6 3 2              ♠ 9 8 5
     ♡ Q 7 6 3              ♡ 9 8 5
     ◇ J 8 7 5              ◇ A K 10
     ♣ 8                    ♣ J 10 7 2
```

The Type B_1 squeeze, with threats R, ◊ 9; L, ♣ 4; B, ♡ 4, is as good as proved. "The last R must precede the last F": this has already been attended to. So you cash the last Club followed by the Spades (or vice versa). Do not fail to find out what will happen if a Heart is discarded, T. 3.

Exercise 34.

	NORTH	Bidding:
♠	A K Q 10 2	
♡	Q	
◊	K Q 4	
♣	K J 10 7	

SOUTH	WEST	NORTH	EAST
1 ♡	P	2 ♠	P
2 NT	P	3 ♣	P
3 ◊	P	4 NT	P
5 ♡	P	6 NT	P
P	P		

	SOUTH
♠	J 5
♡	K 9 8 2
◊	A 10 8 5 3
♣	A 6

West leads ♠ 9.

T. 1: East plays ♠ 3. Jack wins.
T. 2: ◊ K. Both follow.
T. 3: ◊ Q. East discards ♡ 5.
T. 4: ♡ Q led. East wins; West follows.
T. 5: ♡ J led.

Analysis 34.

	WEST		EAST
♠	9 8 6	♠	7 4 3
♡	7 6 3	♡	A J 10 5 4
◊	J 9 7 6	◊	2
♣	Q 5 2	♣	9 8 4 3

The Type B_1 squeeze, with threats R, ◊ 10; L, ♡ 9; B, ♣ J, may be taken as proved. Cash the R winner, then run the Spades.

Exercise 35.

	NORTH
♠	A 10
♡	A 10 2
◇	A 6 5 3
♣	A 9 8 6

	SOUTH
♠	K 8 7 6
♡	K Q 8 7 4 3
◇	—
♣	K Q 5

Bidding:

NORTH	EAST	SOUTH	WEST
1 NT	3 ◇	3 ♡	P
4 ♡	P	4 NT	P
5 ♣	P	7 ♡	P
P	P		

West leads ◇ 9.

T. 1: East plays ◇ K; Declarer ruffs.
T. 2: ♡ K led. East discards ◇ Q.

Analysis 35.

WEST			EAST
♠ 9 5 4		♠	Q J 3 2
♡ J 9 6 5		♡	—
◇ 9 8		◇	K Q J 10 7 4 2
♣ J 10 7 4		♣	3 2

It is likely on the bidding, and must be assumed anyway, that West cannot stop Diamonds. If East stops Clubs the Diamond-Club squeeze will fail for lack of (U), and the hand along with it, so give West the Clubs. Then, Type B₁ double with threats R, ◇ 6; L, ♣ 9; B, ♠ 8. Entries must be carefully watched. The sequence is ♡ 10, ♡ A, ♣ K, ♡ Q, ♣ A, ◇ A, ♣ Q, Heart.

Declarer's original intention is to ruff two Diamonds, on the chance that West had three. But when the 4-0 division shows up, he doesn't have enough trumps for two ruffs. (Play it with ◇ 2, ♠ 4 traded.)

Exercise 36.

NORTH	Bidding:
♠ Q 10 5	
♡ A K 8 5	
◊ 6 4	
♣ A 6 5 4	

EAST	SOUTH	WEST	NORTH
P	1 ◊	P	1 ♡
P	2 NT	P	6 NT
P	P	P	

SOUTH
♠ A 4
♡ Q 7 6
◊ A K Q J 7
♣ K 8 2

West leads ♣ 3.

T. 1: East plays ♣ Q; Declarer ducks.
T. 2: ♣ 10 led. King wins; West plays ♣ 7.
T. 3-4: Diamonds. Both follow.

Analysis 36.

WEST	EAST
♠ K 7 6	♠ J 9 8 3 2
♡ J 9	♡ 10 4 3 2
◊ 9 8 3 2	◊ 10 5
♣ J 9 7 3	♣ Q 10

The contract is assured. If West has Hearts, Heart-Club simple squeeze. If East has Hearts, RFL double with threats R, ♡ 8; L, ♣ 6; B, ♠ 4. RFL reads Hearts-Diamonds-Clubs: therefore, to keep both squeezes in force, cash the Hearts followed by the Diamonds. (Play it as above, and again with ♡ 3 2 traded for ◊ 3 2.)

Exercise 37.*

	NORTH
♠	K Q 8
♡	6
◇	A K Q 6 2
♣	A K Q 4

	SOUTH
♠	A J 7 5 2
♡	A J 10 4
◇	7 4
♣	5 2

Bidding:

NORTH	EAST	SOUTH	WEST
2 ◇	P	2 ♠	P
3 ♣	P	3 ♡	P
4 ♠	P	4 NT	P
5 ♡	P	5 NT	P
6 ♠	P	7 NT	P
P	P		

West leads ◇ J.

T. 1: Queen wins. East plays ◇ 3.

Analysis 37.

WEST		EAST	
♠	10 6 4	♠	9 3
♡	K 9 7 5	♡	Q 8 3 2
◇	J 10 9 8	◇	5 3
♣	J 7	♣	10 9 8 6 3

West is very likely to have Diamonds stopped. If he also has Clubs, Diamond-Club simple squeeze. If East has the Clubs, an RFL squeeze with threats R, ♣ 4; L, ◇ 6; B, ♡ J. RFL translates into Clubs-Spades-Diamonds, which means that all the blacks can be run, in order Clubs-Spades, without disturbing either squeeze.

Due to the 5-2 Club division, the position is clear (granted the Diamond assumption) after four tricks. But with Clubs 4-3 —play it with ♣ 3, ♡ 5 traded—Dummy's choice of discard on the last Spade would be little better than a guess. (§ 25.)

---

* This hand was played by Mr. Harold S. Hemrick, of Kinston, N. C.

Exercise 38.*

NORTH
♠ K 5
♡ 10 5 2
◊ A 9 3 2
♣ A 6 5 2

SOUTH
♠ A J 7 6
♡ A K Q 3
◊ K Q 8
♣ K 8

Bidding:

SOUTH	WEST	NORTH	EAST
2 NT	P	6 NT	P
P	P		

West leads ♣ 3.

T. 1:   East plays ♣ J. King wins.
T. 2-3: Hearts. Both follow.
T. 4-5: ◊ K Q. Both follow.
T. 6-7: ♠ K J. Both follow.
T. 8:   ♠ A. East plays ♠ Q.

Analysis 38.

WEST	EAST
♠ 10 8 4 2	♠ Q 9 3
♡ 8 4	♡ J 9 7 6
◊ 10 5 4	◊ J 7 6
♣ Q 10 4 3	♣ J 9 7

On the assumption that no false cards have been played, it is known after eight tricks that West has only one red card remaining, but whether a Heart or a Diamond is an exact 50-50 guess. At any rate, since one red suit will break, the contract is assured (granted the assumption above).

Does this mean that there is nothing to choose between the two leads—Heart or Diamond? By no means. If the Heart is led and the suit breaks (trade ◊ 10 for ♡ 9), there is no squeeze because each of the singly-guarded threats, ♠ 7 and ◊ 9, lies below the stopper. But if the Diamond is led and that suit falls, we have an RFL squeeze with threats R, ♠ 7; L, ♡ 3; B, ♣ 6. Thus the Heart lead will produce the contract; the Diamond lead produces the contract with a 50% chance of the overtrick. Declarer made seven for a clean top.

* This hand was played by Mr. Marion L. Powell, of Aiken, S. C.

29. *A point of defense.* Although the subject is large and important, space is lacking for an extensive study of double-squeeze defense. But let us pause long enough to make just one point which might otherwise escape your notice. When threatened with a Type B_2 double squeeze, if you are able to *change the squeeze to Type B_1* there is a good chance that Declarer will have to work for his supper.

In the next two hands, say that East is known to be a master player. (We'll try not to let such a thing happen often, because it merely makes trouble.)

Exercise 39.

NORTH
♠ A K 6 4
♡ K Q 9 5
◇ 7 4
♣ 7 6 4

SOUTH
♠ Q 9
♡ A 7 2
◇ A K 6 5
♣ K Q J 3

Bidding:

NORTH	EAST	SOUTH	WEST
1 ♠	P	2 ◇	P
2 ♡	P	4 NT	P
5 ◇	P	6 NT	P
P	P		

West leads ♣ 10.

T. 1: East plays ♣ 5. Jack wins.
T. 2: ♡ Q. West plays ♡ 4, East ♡ 3.
T. 3: ♣ 7 led. East plays Ace.
T. 4: ◇ J led. King wins; West plays ◇ 8.
T. 5: ♡ A led. West plays ♡ 6, East ♡ 10.
T. 6: ♠ Q led. West plays ♠ 2, East ♠ 3.

Analysis 39.

WEST	EAST
♠ J 8 5 2	♠ 10 7 3
♡ 6 4	♡ J 10 8 3
◇ Q 8 2	◇ J 10 9 3
♣ 10 9 8 2	♣ A 5

Forget as usual the Heart run. (a) If East stops Hearts, West Spades, RFL says Hearts-Clubs-Spades. (b) If East stops Spades, West Hearts, the sequence is Spades-Clubs-Hearts. All signs point to (b); but East is a known crook. Anyway, it's your play.

Be sure to see that East's shift to Diamonds is not an aimless shot in the dark. If South has the three top Diamonds, nothing can be done; but if only two, he will have to "work for his supper." (Compare Ex. 30.)

Exercise 40.

	NORTH	Bidding:			
♠	A K 5 4 3				
♡	K Q 7	SOUTH	WEST	NORTH	EAST
◊	Q 8 2	1 ♣	P	1 ♠	P
♣	7 6	2 NT	P	6 NT	P
		P	P		

	SOUTH	
♠	J 7	West leads ◊ J.
♡	A 4	
◊	K 7 6 5	
♣	A K Q J 2	

T. 1: East's Ace wins.
T. 2: ♠ 10, J, Q, K.
T. 3: ◊ Q. East discards ♡ 3.
T. 4: Club. East plays ♣ 5, West ♣ 3.

Analysis 40.

	WEST		EAST
♠	Q 8 6	♠	10 9 2
♡	8 6 5 2	♡	J 10 9 3
◊	J 10 9 4 3	◊	A
♣	3	♣	10 9 8 5 4

Declarer pauses to see what will happen if Clubs do not run. If West has that suit, failure. With East stopping Clubs, RFL double squeeze with threats R, ◊ 7; L, ♣ 2; B, ♠ 5: cash the Diamond followed by the Hearts. Now Diamonds were 5-1, greatly increasing the chance that Clubs were 5-1 the other way; also, East is known to be the kind of player who, if holding five Clubs in a spot like this, might be smart enough to play just as he has played, T. 2-4. Nevertheless—! Anyway, it's your play.

One's first thought might be that East must have taken a peek, but not so. He has merely taken a really careful look before leaping—a thing which most players, certainly including your author, frequently fail to do at the bridge table. (It must be admitted that the study table and the bridge table are two quite different articles of furniture. This book might be viewed as an attempt to bring the two closer together.) East can see that if Spades run, the hand is undoubtedly solid, so as the only hope he gives West the Queen. Then, South surely must hold all the invisible points. Even so, he is somewhat out of bounds for his jump rebid: a step which could only be justified by a massive Club suit. On these hypotheses, the Type B_2 double squeeze is in plain sight. (Play it with a Heart or a Club lead, T. 2.)

PROBLEMS

Problem 6.

	NORTH
♠	K Q J 6 3
♡	J 9 8 2
◊	8 2
♣	5 4

	SOUTH
♠	A 2
♡	Q 10 4
◊	A K Q J 6
♣	Q 8 2

Bidding:

EAST	SOUTH	WEST	NORTH
P	1 ◊	P	1 ♠
P	2 NT	P	3 NT
P	P	P	

West leads ♣ J.

T. 1: East's King wins.
T. 2: ♣ 3 led. Nine wins.
T. 3-4: ♣ A 10. East follows.
T. 5: ♠ 10 led. East plays ♠ 4; Ace wins.

Solution 6.

	WEST		EAST
♠	10 9 8 7 5	♠	4
♡	K 5 3	♡	A 7 6
◊	5	◊	10 9 7 4 3
♣	A J 10 9	♣	K 7 6 3

Assume that neither long suit will run. Give West the Spades as indicated, and East the Diamonds. Now, no double squeeze because the B threat (Heart) is not accompanied by a winner.

East has ♡ A, for if holding that card West would have led it, T. 5. West has ♡ K, for if holding both tops East would have laid down the King, T. 2. If we run the Diamonds West will discard ♡ K, because a Spade discard would be sudden death. But if we cash the Spades East will suffer torment, and it is long odds that he will yield a Diamond.

Problem 7.

NORTH
♠ A Q 5 3
♡ 7 6 3
◇ K Q J 6 4
♣ 5

SOUTH
♠ K 7 6
♡ A K 5
◇ A 5 3
♣ A K Q 4

Bidding:

SOUTH	WEST	NORTH	EAST
2 NT	P	3 ◇	P
3 NT	P	4 NT	P
5 ♠	P	5 NT	P
6 ♠	P	7 NT	P
P	P		

West leads ◇ 10.

T. 1: East discards ♠ 2.
Spread the hand for contract.

Solution 7.

WEST
♠ 10
♡ Q 9 8
◇ 10 9 8 7 2
♣ 10 8 6 2

EAST
♠ J 9 8 4 2
♡ J 10 4 2
◇ —
♣ J 9 7 3

Cash the Spades. If West has that suit, the easiest kind of Spade-Diamond simple squeeze. If East stops Spades, Type B₂ double with threats R, ♠ 5; L, ◇ 6; B, ♣ 4 (or ♡ 5). Run the Hearts (or Clubs) followed by the Diamonds.

This is the first hand we have had where either of two suits will serve equally well as the B suit.

Problem 8.*

NORTH				
♠ J				

Bidding:

SOUTH	WEST	NORTH	EAST
P	1 ♣	2 ◊	2 ♡
2 ♠	P	4 ◊	Dbl.
4 NT	P	5 ♠	P
6 ♠	P	P	Dbl.
P	P	P	

NORTH
♠ J
♡ A Q
◊ A J 10 9 8 7 2
♣ A 6 2

SOUTH
♠ A Q 9 8 7 5 4 3 2
♡ J 4
◊ 4
♣ 9

West leads ♣ K.

T. 1: Ace wins. East plays ♣ 4.
T. 2: ♠ J, 6, A, K.

Solution 8.

WEST	EAST
♠ K	♠ 10 6
♡ 9 8 5 3	♡ K 10 7 6 2
◊ 6	◊ K Q 5 3
♣ K Q J 10 8 5 3	♣ 7 4

Declarer goes for the drop, T. 2, on the theory that East, if holding ♠ K, would not have doubled. Now, the play is for the overtrick.

Give ♡ K to East. (a) If East had ◊ K Q as indicated by his bidding, he is Heart-Diamond squeezable: run all the trumps, merely taking care to cash ♡ A (Vienna Coup) and return by Club ruff. (b) If West has the Diamonds, as seemingly required for his original bid, it is necessary to assume that East had only two Clubs: then, West is Diamond-Club squeezable. (Trade ◊ K Q for two Hearts.) (c) If the Diamonds are divided and East had only two Clubs, Type R double with threats R, ♡ J; L, ♣ 6; B, ◊ J. (Trade ◊ Q for a Heart.) The striking feature is that all three squeezes require exactly the same technique. (Footnote, §25.)

* This hand was played by Mr. Grant Marsee, of Detroit, and reported by Mr. William S. Mouser in the Detroit News.

Problem 9.

NORTH
♠ A K 7 4
♡ A K J 2
◇ Q 9 6
♣ 5 2

SOUTH
♠ Q 2
♡ 6 5
◇ A K 8 4 2
♣ J 8 7 3

Bidding:

EAST	SOUTH	WEST	NORTH
P	P	P	1 ♠
P	2 ◇	P	2 ♡
P	2 NT	P	3 NT
P	P	P	

West leads ♣ K.

T. 1: East plays ♣ 9.
T. 2: ♣ 4 led. Ace wins.
T. 3: ♣ 6 led. Ten wins.
T. 4: ♣ Q. East discards ♠ 3.
T. 5: ♠ J led. East plays ♠ 6; Queen wins.

Solution 9.

WEST	EAST
♠ J 10 8 5	♠ 9 6 3
♡ 10 9 7 4	♡ Q 8 3
◇ 3	◇ J 10 7 5
♣ K Q 10 4	♣ A 9 6

West very probably stops Spades. Then, (a) West also has a Diamond stopper: Spade-Diamond simple squeeze. Or, (b) East stops Diamonds: Type R double squeeze with threats R, ◇ 8; L, ♠ 7; B, ♡ J. So, cash the Spades, because this will not interfere with either squeeze. Now, if (a) is present, East held six Hearts: this, unlikely anyway, is negated by his Spade discard. Thus (b) is clearly indicated.

CHAPTER III

THE ELIMINATION PLAY

30. *An explanatory remark.* It may be taken for granted that every prospective reader of this book is thoroughly familiar with the elimination play, or strip, in each of its forms—"trump strip" and "notrump strip." However, many hands embody the salient features of both squeeze and strip to such an extent, and so closely interwoven, that it would be impossible to separate them. Thus it seems worth while, if only for purposes of review, to preface our study of advanced squeezes with a brief discussion of the strip.

31. *The trump strip.* In the typical case, to effect a *trump strip* Declarer must have *at least one trump remaining in each hand* after the throw-in has occurred. Then, it may happen that any return lead that the opponent can make will enable Declarer to make his trumps separately by "ruff-and-discard": that is, he ruffs in one hand while throwing a loser from the other. More often, the defender has a choice of this lead or some other equally ruinous—usually a lead into a tenace.

In playing a trump contract, one should always keep in mind the following

RULE: *When you have or will have trumps remaining in both hands with no obvious way of making them separately, always look for a strip.*

Of course this Rule is inoperative when you have only one loser remaining, because no throw-in can gain; but that is precisely the case in which a squeeze is most likely to be present.

Exercise 41.

	NORTH
♠	9 5 2
♡	Q 10 7 3 2
◊	7 6 4
♣	10 8

	SOUTH
♠	A K Q 8
♡	A K J 6
◊	A Q 9
♣	Q J

Bidding:

EAST	SOUTH	WEST	NORTH
P	2 ♠	P	2 NT
P	3 ♡	P	4 ♡
P	P	P	

West leads ♣ K.

T. 1-2: ♣ K A.
T. 3: Heart led. East follows.

Analysis 41.

WEST		EAST	
♠	10 4	♠	J 7 6 3
♡	9 5 4	♡	8
◊	K J 8 3	◊	10 5 2
♣	A K 4 3	♣	9 7 6 5 2

After three tricks the contract is in your pocket. Draw trumps, then cash the Spade tops. If the suit fails to break, ruff the fourth and lead a Diamond. In case East plays Ten or Jack, put up the Queen: if West wins, he will have to return into the A 9 tenace or permit ruff and discard. But if East plays low, don't touch that Queen—the Nine instead. Again West is caught.

You should make mental note of this particular combination A Q 9, since the fact that this holding is just as good as A Q 10, for throw-in purposes, is not instantly apparent. Evidently another sure-fire combination is A Q 8 with either Ten or Nine opposite.

Exercise 42.

	NORTH			
	♠ 7 6 3			
	♡ 9 4			
	◇ —			
	♣ J 9 8 6 5 4 3 2			

Bidding:

SOUTH	WEST	NORTH	EAST
2 ♣	3 ◇	P	4 ◇
4 ♡	P	6 ♣	P
P	P		

SOUTH
♠ A K J
♡ A Q 6 5
◇ K
♣ A K Q 10 7

West leads ◇ A.

Analysis 42.

WEST	EAST
♠ Q 9 4	♠ 10 8 5 2
♡ K 7 3 2	♡ J 10 8
◇ A Q J 10 7 5	◇ 9 8 6 4 3 2
♣ —	♣ —

Our Rule says, "always look for a strip." Doing so, you quickly find that (at least in rubber bridge) only one play is permissible: discard a Spade or a Heart from Dummy, then claim the rest.

When you go looking for an "endplay," better get an early start!

32. *A remark on terminology.* Exercise 42 suggests an interpolated remark. Sharp distinction should be drawn between the terms "end play" and "endplay." *The* end play of a hand—every hand—is a vague term meaning the play of the last few tricks. *An* endplay is a play belonging to the group known as squeezes, strips, and trump coups, or combinations thereof: this name is used because such plays usually occur toward the end of the hand. But this example shows that a strip may be completed on the first trick; later we shall exhibit a squeeze culminating on the first trick. Although a strip or a squeeze that occurs very early is not a part of the end play in the usual sense, there is no impropriety in calling it an endplay. A wildcat may conceivably be tamed: in that event, though no longer a wild cat, he is still a wildcat. The dictionary bulges with this sort of thing.

Some writers have applied the term "endplay" to the strip exclusively. But this is clearly a misnomer: such usage would be correct only if the strip occurred, on the average, at a later stage of the hand than the other plays in question, and this is not the case. Instead, "endplay" should be the generic name covering the three species listed. And some writers have done even worse, by labelling the play now in hand a "strip and endplay." Executing a strip and endplay is like eating some beef and meat, or planting a pine and tree.

33. *Repeated throw-in.* Under exceptionally favorable circumstances it may be possible to throw a defender in for gain of one trick, and then to repeat the maneuver for gain of another trick.

Exercise 43.

NORTH
♠ 6 4 2
♡ A Q 8 4 3
◇ 8 5
♣ J 10 4

SOUTH
♠ A Q 3
♡ K 10 6 5 2
◇ A Q
♣ A 6 5

Bidding:

NORTH	EAST	SOUTH	WEST
P	P	1 ♡	Dbl.
2 ♡	P	3 NT	P
4 ♡	P	P	P

West leads ♡ 9.

T. 1: East follows.
T. 2: ♡ Q. West discards ♠ 9.

Analysis 43.

WEST
♠ K J 9 8
♡ 9
◇ K 10 7 4 3
♣ K Q 3

EAST
♠ 10 7 5
♡ J 7
◇ J 9 6 2
♣ 9 8 7 2

West's double, light in any case, seems to call for the missing high cards. If so, the contract, looking so hopeless at first sight, is surely in hand. Lead ♣ J to West. If he returns a Spade, cash the other winner and exit with ♠ 3. In case West holds the exit-trick, you are home. If East wins the Spade and returns a minor, go up with the Ace and exit in that suit. If West returns a minor, T. 4, the procedure is equally obvious.

34. *The notrump strip.* We know that in a typical trump strip the victim must hand Declarer a plain-suit trick or else give ruff-and-discard. To insure this, Declarer must strip his own hands of two plain suits—possibly only one (Ex. 42). It may happen that nothing more than this is needed. At the worst, it is merely necessary to direct the throw-in, which involves the adverse holdings in one suit only; and as a rule, those holdings must be favorable to begin with or nothing can be done. That is, Declarer must get *his own two hands* into proper shape.

A *notrump strip* (which, like the notrump squeeze, may occur at a trump contract) is one in which the ruff-and-discard possibility is not present: the victim's return must usually be such as to give Declarer a trick in the suit led. And now, Declarer's problem is not to ready up his own hands, but *to remove from the defender's hand all cards of exit,* leaving him ripe for the throw-in. (Technically, in the trump strip also all cards of exit are removed; but this is done indirectly, by stripping Declarer's hands of certain suits, rather than that of the opponent.) It follows that here, just as in squeeze play and to a much greater extent than in trump-strip play, Declarer is passionately interested in all features of the adverse distributions.

Exercise 44.

NORTH
♠ A Q 5 4 2
♡ K Q 9
◇ A J 6
♣ 6 2

SOUTH
♠ 10
♡ A 5 4 3
◇ K Q 7
♣ A 8 7 4 3

Bidding:

EAST	SOUTH	WEST	NORTH
P	1 ♣	P	1 ♠
P	1 NT	P	3 NT
P	P	P	

West leads ♣ K.

T. 1:   East discards ♠ 9; Ace wins.
T. 2-3: Hearts. Both follow.
T. 4.   Heart. East discards ♠ 3.
T. 5-6: Diamonds. Both follow.

Analysis 44.

WEST	EAST
♠ J	♠ K 9 8 7 6 3
♡ J 10 7 6	♡ 8 2
◇ 5 2	◇ 10 9 8 4 3
♣ K Q J 10 9 5	♣ —

After six tricks Declarer can claim his contract, because it is known that West has no more than one Spade. Cash ◇ K to close the exit; then lead the Spade. If West plays low, let the Ten ride to East, for an ultimate return into the tenace. When West comes up with the Jack, play the Ace and return a low Spade. The Queen is bound to take the last trick.

Quite possibly you don't care for South's bidding, but it worked out all right in this hand, didn't it?

Exercise 45.

NORTH				
♠ A Q 5 4	**Bidding:**			
♡ 9 6 3	NORTH	EAST	SOUTH	WEST
◇ K 7	1 ♣	P	1 ◇	P
♣ A K J 7	1 ♠	P	2 NT	P
	3 NT	P	P	P

SOUTH	
♠ 10 8 7	West leads ♡ Q.
♡ A K 4	
◇ A Q 8 5 4	
♣ 6 4	

T. 1: Queen wins.
T. 2: ♡ J led. King wins.
T. 3-4: ◇ K A. Both follow.
T. 5: ◇ Q. West discards a Club.

Analysis 45.

WEST	EAST
♠ K 6 3	♠ J 9 2
♡ Q J 10 8 2	♡ 7 5
◇ 10 6	◇ J 9 3 2
♣ 9 3 2	♣ Q 10 8 5

In a spot like this—all other suits well protected—the first thought of any experienced player would be to stay off: if not for a clean-cut reason, then just on general principles.

Here a reason for ducking is not far to seek. Granted normal Diamond division, the hand is a parade. So, assume that suit to be 5-1. No matter where the Diamonds may lie, you plan to put East in, but his Hearts must first be eliminated. Since he may have three Hearts, the smooth and sure road to that elimination is by passing the first trick.

When the 4-2 Diamond break appears, you put East in at once, since to cash the third Heart would leave no entry to make the thirteener Diamond. But maybe East had only two Hearts, in which case you pick up an overtrick! As the cards lie, East would probably return ♠ 2. Your Eight drives the King. Whereupon you cash ♠ Q (Vienna Coup) on the chance of a Spade-Club squeeze—may as well try—and come out with five odd.

Exercise 46.

	NORTH
♠	6 2
♡	10 8
◇	A K 9 8 4
♣	A J 5 2

	SOUTH
♠	A K 10
♡	A Q 7 4
◇	Q J
♣	K Q 6 3

Bidding:

WEST	NORTH	EAST	SOUTH
P	1 ◇	P	6 NT
P	P	P	

West leads ♠ Q.

T. 1: King wins.
T. 2: ◇ Q. Both follow.
T. 3: ◇ J. East discards a Spade.
T. 4: ♣ Q. Both follow.
T. 5: ♣ K. West discards a Heart.

Analysis 46.

	WEST		EAST
♠	Q J 9 8	♠	7 5 4 3
♡	J 9 3	♡	K 6 5 2
◇	10 7 5 3 2	◇	6
♣	10	♣	9 8 7 4

The first thought might be to cross in Clubs and put West in with the last Diamond. But this requires three discards from the closed hand, and only two are available.

Yet, everything is under control. Cross to Dummy and lead a Heart (either one). If East covers, play the Queen; otherwise duck. No matter how the Hearts are placed, West's return will give you a trick.

In a top-level tournament the above would not earn you many points. Instead of letting the Heart go through, finesse the Queen. If West wins, his Heart return will drive the Ace, but you have a laid-down Spade-Diamond squeeze, for contract. And if the finesse holds, ♡ A followed by the Club will crucify West, for an overtrick.

Exercise 47.

NORTH	Bidding:			
♠ K 8 6				
♡ A 3	SOUTH	WEST	NORTH	EAST
◇ K 7 4 2	1 ♡	2 ♣	Dbl.	P
♣ Q 10 6 3	3 ♣	P	3 NT	P
	4 ◇	P	5 ◇	P
SOUTH	6 ♡	P	P	P
♠ A J 2				
♡ K Q J 10 7 4	West leads ♣ K.			
◇ A Q 6 3				
♣ —				

T. 1: East plays ♣ 7. Declarer ruffs.
T. 2-3: ♡ A K. Both follow.
T. 4: ♡ Q. West discards a Club.
T. 5: Diamond. Both follow.
T. 6: Diamond. West discards a Club.

Analysis 47.

WEST	EAST
♠ Q 10 7 4	♠ 9 5 3
♡ 9 5	♡ 8 6 2
◇ 10	◇ J 9 8 5
♣ A K 9 5 4 2	♣ J 8 7

Outside of his Clubs, West can hold only a few rags. Thus he must have had at least six Clubs. If so, he is sure to get caught in a throw-in or squeeze.

Lead a third Diamond to Dummy's King and return ♣ Q, discarding ◊ 6. West must win and must return a Club, since a Spade would yield a free finesse.

You play ♣ 10 from Dummy, hoping that West has led from ♣ J. East covers, and you ruff. You now lead the last trump, squeezing West in the black suits and East in Diamonds-Spades.

Exercise 48.*

NORTH
♠ A Q 2
♡ 8 7 6
◊ A 7 5 4
♣ A 8 6

SOUTH
♠ 10 4
♡ A 5 4 3 2
◊ K 8
♣ K Q 7 5

Bidding:

NORTH	EAST	SOUTH	WEST
1 ♣	P	1 ♡	P
2 ♡	P	4 ♡	P
P	P		

West leads ◊ Q.

T. 1: East plays ◊ 2. King wins.
T. 2: ♡ 2 led. West plays ♡ 9, East ♡ 10.
T. 3: ♡ K led. Ace wins; West discards ♠ 3.

Analysis 48.

WEST
♠ 8 6 5 3
♡ 9
◊ Q J 10 3
♣ J 10 9 4

EAST
♠ K J 9 7
♡ K Q J 10
◊ 9 6 2
♣ 3 2

The only chance of avoiding the Spade finesse is to strip East's minors. Therefore, ◊ A; Diamond ruff; ♣ K; ♣ A; Club. If East ruffs, he is caught; if he discards a Spade (as he did), ♣ Q wins and a Club is ruffed by Dummy. If East discards a Spade (as again he did), the Diamond is returned and East is through.

* This hand was played by Mr. William B. Woodson.

Exercise 49.

	NORTH
♠	K 8 6
♡	A 3
◇	K 7 4 2
♣	Q 10 6 3

	SOUTH
♠	A J 2
♡	K Q J 10 7 4
◇	A Q 6 3
♣	—

Bidding:

SOUTH	WEST	NORTH	EAST
1 ♡	2 ♣	Dbl.	P
3 ♣	P	3 NT	P
4 ◇	P	5 ◇	P
6 ◇	P	P	P

West leads ♣ K.

T. 1: Ruff.
T. 2: Diamond. Both follow.
T. 3: Diamond. West discards a Club.

Analysis 49.

	WEST
♠	Q 10 7 4
♡	9 5
◇	10
♣	A K 9 5 4 2

	EAST
♠	9 5 3
♡	8 6 2
◇	J 9 8 5
♣	J 8 7

This hand is about as exciting as a saunter in the park. Of course you merely bombard East with Hearts until he decides to ruff. Just one point: unless you win with ◇ A Q, T. 2-3, preserving the Six, a Club return by East would set the contract. With the Six still in hand you ride home on solid tops, no matter what East does.

x   x   x   x

From time to time there will be a hand which may seem to be out of place. For instance, Ex. 47 leads to a squeeze instead of the expected strip, while Ex. 49 involves no endplay of any kind. The reason, of course, is to insure that the reader will keep ready to hand all the weapons in his arsenal, not merely the one whose use is being exemplified at the moment.

35. *An elementary principle of play.* It is a truism that beginners tend, in a general way, to cash their quick, sure winners early and then look around for something else to do, while good

players reverse the process. It may be worth while to point out that occasionally there appears a hand that *must* be played à la novice.

RULE: *When no harm can possibly be done thereby, run your solid suit at the earliest opportunity.*

In the hands of a weak player this Rule would be poison, because he would read it as encouragement to continue his bad habits; but readers of this book can be trusted to apply the Rule with intelligence and discretion. Usually the solid suit cannot be run at once, for one or more of a dozen reasons—no need to elaborate; but always keep on the watch for that occasional hand where "no harm can possibly be done thereby." Then, make those defenders paw for discards at the earliest possible moment: very often they will hand you a bouquet of roses.

Exercise 50.

	NORTH			
	♠ 7 4 3			
	♡ K Q J 6 3			
	◇ 9 6			
	♣ 7 5 2			

Bidding:

SOUTH	WEST	NORTH	EAST
1 ◇	P	1 ♡	P
3 NT	P	P	P

	SOUTH
	♠ A J 6
	♡ 9 7
	◇ A K Q J
	♣ A K 9 3

West leads ♠ 2.

T. 1: East plays Queen; Ace wins.

Analysis 50.

WEST	EAST
♠ K 10 8 2	♠ Q 9 5
♡ A 10 8	♡ 5 4 2
◇ 7 5 3	◇ 10 8 4 2
♣ 8 6 4	♣ Q J 10

Declarer has to assume that West holds ♡ A, for if not, there is hardly a chance.

The "average player" might lead a Heart, T. 2, then return

in Diamonds and lead another Heart, hoping that West will stay off again. But if West has only one small Heart, he will win the second round willy-nilly; if he has two or three small, East will have used the doubleton convention (lowest of three, higher of two) to give his partner the count, so that West will surely win the second Heart. That is, against competent defense any thought of two Heart tricks is a pipe-dream.

A better player would lead a Club from Dummy, T. 3, hoping for some sort of lucky break in that suit. This plan has a good prospect of success, but it fails as the cards lie.

The point of interest is this: if either opponent can be induced to discard a Club, the contract is sure (granted that West has ♡ A). Thus the only conceivable play is to run the Diamonds, T. 2-5. Now, suppose that a Club has been discarded—any Club, by either adversary. Declarer takes the Heart, cashes the Club tops, then puts West in with the Heart. His only chance of exit would be that he has a Club and East a higher Club still in hand, which is not possible following a Club discard. And if no Club has been discarded, every chance that was available to begin with *is still intact*.

Exercise 51.

NORTH			
♠ K Q J 10 3 2			
♡ A J			
◇ A 7 3			
♣ A K			

Bidding:

NORTH	EAST	SOUTH	WEST
2 ♠	P	3 ♠	P
4 ♣	P	4 NT	P
5 ♠	P	5 NT	P
6 ♡	P	7 NT	P
P	P		

SOUTH
♠ A 9 8 6
♡ 4
◇ K Q 5 4
♣ 10 6 4 3

West leads ♡ K.

Analysis 51.

WEST	EAST
♠ 5 4	♠ 7
♡ K Q 9 7 6 5 2	♡ 10 8 3
◇ 10	◇ J 9 8 6 2
♣ Q 9 2	♣ J 8 7 5

Believing that the hand will be played at other tables in seven Spades, South goes all out for a top board.

Apart from the 3-3 Diamond chance, there are squeeze possibilities. If West has Diamond length, an easy simple squeeze. If East has ♣ Q J, Type R simple-played-as-double with threats R, ♡ J; L, ♣ 10; B, ◇ 5, succeeding no matter how the Diamonds are distributed. If East has the Diamonds with the Club honors divided, no squeeze because the B threat, ♣ 10, is not accompanied by an entry.

One Declarer cashed two Diamonds; another laid down the Clubs, eliciting a high-low from West. After either of these forays in folly, the hand cannot be made.

Instead, let us run some Spades. On the fifth Spade East must choose, with exactly nothing to go on except that his hand and Dummy held eight Diamonds as against six Clubs, which means that the closed hand is more likely to be long in Clubs than in Diamonds. If East is any part of a bridge player, he will yield another Diamond.

The point is this: neither of the squeeze possibilities mentioned above is damaged by the running of five Spades. If Diamonds and/or Clubs are favorably placed, *they will stay that way*, so why give information about them?

x x x x

Exercise 50 is a pseudo strip; the one above, a pseudo squeeze. The two together show how magically our Rule sometimes works in either form of counterfeit endplay.

It would seem that this Rule is very elementary, to be learned at an early stage of bridge education; yet surprisingly often good players and writers overlook it. Don't! It will win games for you.

PROBLEMS

Problem 10.

	NORTH
♠	Q 10 6
♡	10 6 4 3
◇	A 10 7
♣	J 9 2

	SOUTH
♠	A K J 9 8 7 4
♡	A Q
◇	K J 2
♣	A

Bidding:

SOUTH	WEST	NORTH	EAST
2 ♠	P	3 ◇	P
3 ♠	P	4 ♠	P
4 NT	P	5 ◇	P
5 NT	P	6 ♣	P
6 ♠	P	P	P

West leads ♣ K.

T. 1: East plays ♣ 6.
T. 2: Spade. West discards a Club.

Solution 10.

	WEST		EAST
♠	—	♠	5 3 2
♡	K 9 8 7	♡	J 5 2
◇	9 6 5	◇	Q 8 4 3
♣	K Q 10 5 4 3	♣	8 7 6

You win in Dummy, T. 2, and ruff ♣ 9; return in trumps and lead ♣ J, discarding ◇ 2.

This stratagem, where one defender is thrown in at a time when his partner still holds one or more trumps, might be called a *semi-strip*. Many times the risk of an untimely ruff by the partner would be slight; in other cases, so great as to preclude the method. Here, this danger is negligible compared to the risk of depending on the finesses.

Problem 11.

	NORTH		Bidding:			
♠	J642					
♡	A84		SOUTH	WEST	NORTH	EAST
◊	2		1 ♠	Dbl.	2 ♠	P
♣	Q10963		4 ♠	Dbl.	Rdbl.	P
			P	P		
	SOUTH					
♠	A98753		West leads ♣ K.			
♡	K105					
◊	AQJ4					
♣	—					

T. 1: Ruff.

T. 2: ◊ A.

T. 3: ◊ Q led; West plays King; Dummy ruffs.

Solution 11.

	WEST			EAST	
♠	KQ10		♠	—	
♡	QJ3		♡	9762	
◊	K87		◊	109653	
♣	AKJ7		♣	8542	

Since there is no suit that West can lead without costing him a trick, the hand fairly shouts throw-in; but a trifle of preliminary stripping might be good clean fun.

T. 4: Club ruff. T. 5: ◊ J, Heart discarded. T. 6: ♡ A. T. 7: Club ruff. T. 8: ♡ K. T. 9: Heart ruff. T. 10: Club ruff. And now in the fullness of time the Diamond return puts West on lead, for two fat, juicy overtricks.

Moral: Before doubling, make sure your hand is not too strong! And this is not entirely kidding. When you hold a bulldozer with the adversaries bidding their heads off, your partner will be unable to help at all, and your strength must be greatly discounted.

Problem 12.*

```
        NORTH
      ♠ A 9 8 3
      ♡ J 9 8 3
      ◇ K 2
      ♣ K 5 3

        SOUTH
      ♠ K J 6 4
      ♡ —
      ◇ A Q J 10 9
      ♣ A J 7 4
```

Bidding:

SOUTH	WEST	NORTH	EAST
1 ◇	P	1 ♡	P
1 ♠	P	3 ♠	P
4 ♣	P	4 ♠	P
4 NT	P	5 ◇	P
5 NT	P	6 ♡	P
6 ♠	Dbl.	P	P
P			

West leads ♡ K.

T. 1: Ruff.
T. 2: ◇ K.
T. 3: Heart ruff.
T. 4: ♣ K.
T. 5: Heart ruff. West plays ♡ A.
T. 6: ♠ K. Both follow.

Solution 12.

```
        WEST                      EAST
      ♠ Q 10 7 2                ♠ 5
      ♡ A K 5                   ♡ Q 10 7 6 4 2
      ◇ 7 6 5                   ◇ 8 4 3
      ♣ Q 10 8                  ♣ 9 6 2
```

Declarer decides that if holding only Q x x in trumps West would not have doubled for fear of exposing his Queen to a finesse; therefore he probably holds four. On that basis, with East now blank in trumps, the Diamonds can be safely run. When West ruffs the fourth Diamond with ♠ 10—his best play—Declarer underruffs, and the rest is obvious. An equally good method would be to capture West's Ten with the Ace and return ♠ 9.

* This hand was played by Mrs. Godfrey Stone, of Detroit, and reported by Mr. William S. Mouser in the Detroit News.

Problem 13.*

	NORTH
♠	A Q 8
♡	Q 10 9 5 2
◇	A 5
♣	10 6 3

	SOUTH
♠	10 6 5
♡	A K J 8 7
◇	J 4
♣	A 9 5

Bidding:

SOUTH	WEST	NORTH	EAST
1 ♡	P	3 ♡	P
4 ♡	P	P	P

West leads ♣ K.

T. 1: East plays ♣ 7; King wins.
T. 2: ♣ Q led. East plays ♣ 2; Ace wins.
T. 3: Heart. Both follow.
T. 4: Heart. East discards ◇ 9.

Solution 13.

	WEST		EAST
♠	K J 3 2	♠	9 7 4
♡	4 3	♡	6
◇	10 8	◇	K Q 9 7 6 3 2
♣	K Q J 8 4	♣	7 2

The second round of Diamonds puts East on lead. A low Spade is returned, West's King going to the Ace. Now the Club puts West in, and his Spade return rides around to the Ten, for contract.

In Ex. 43 West was thrown in twice. Problem 14 exhibits the less common case, where first one defender, then the other is mistreated.

---

* This hand was played by Dr. Eugene Davidson, of Ann Arbor, Mich., and reported by Mr. William S. Mouser in the Detroit News.

Problem 14.*

NORTH		
♠ 10 7		
♡ K J 9 6 2		
◇ A 8 6		
♣ J 9 2		

Bidding:

EAST	SOUTH	WEST	NORTH
1 ◇	1 ♡	P	3 ♡
P	4 ♡	P	P
P			

SOUTH
♠ A Q 6
♡ Q 10 8 7 3
◇ 7 4 2
♣ A 7

West leads ◇ J.

T. 1: East's Queen wins.
T. 2: ◇ K returned. West plays ◇ 3; Ace wins.

Solution 14.

WEST	EAST
♠ 9 5 4 3 2	♠ K J 8
♡ A	♡ 5 4
◇ J 3	◇ K Q 10 9 5
♣ Q 10 8 5 3	♣ K 6 4

The point of the hand appears on the first trick. At first glance Declarer sees no reason for ducking, but also no argument against it, because even if the lead was a singleton, no harm will have been done by the duck. So he passes the first trick as a matter of sound procedure—"lose your sure losers early." On further study one faint ray of hope appears. If West held a Diamond doubleton, if East holds ♠ K, if West holds either ♣ K 10 or ♣ Q 10, and if West holds ♡ A blank, this leaky ship may make port. T. 3: ♠ Q. T. 4: ♠ A. T. 5: ♠ 6, ruffed. T. 6: Heart. T. 7: low Club returned, Nine finessed. Etcetera. Note that without that general-principles duck, the hand could not be made.

A mountainous array of ifs, yet that is the way things were. If you wish to become a master of end play, the first rule to be learned is "never say die!"

* This hand was played by Mr. John W. Norwood, Jr.

CHAPTER IV

THE TWO-SUIT STRIP-SQUEEZE

36. *Boundaries of squeeze.* Many books on bridge play are devoted wholly or in part to the squeeze. Unfortunately, very few of the authors concerned have given an explicit definition of the word, apparently taking for granted that everyone will understand what is meant, and that everyone's understanding will be the same. But until a technical term such as this is sharply defined, its meaning remains vague. Especially, its *boundaries* cannot be unmistakably located: just what plays are to be called squeezes and what ones are not?

Webster's Dictionary defines the squeeze as "a play in which an opponent is forced by his discard to give up command of one suit or to unguard his possible taking card in another." Everyone will agree that this definition is inaccurate, in that a defender may squeeze his partner, or Declarer may squeeze himself.

If "an opponent" were changed to "a player," it may be that many authors and players would accept the resulting form. But according to the conception of squeeze that motivates this book,* the dictionary definition must still be rejected as being much too narrow. For instance, it would exclude all those types that form the subject-matter of this chapter; also those hands in which the forced discard blocks a suit, a good example being hands where Declarer should have played a Vienna Coup and neglected to do so.

* See § 1. Though differently worded, the definition there adopted is exactly equivalent to the one laid down by Mr. Ely Culbertson (Red Book, p. 399).

In Chaps. I-II we have considered the standard and best-known forms of one-loser squeeze, but such a study leaves a broad hinterland of squeeze play unexplored. It is time to begin a foray into the hinterland.

37. *The two-suit strip-squeeze.* As our first objective, let us discuss that large and highly important group of hands which "embody the salient features of both squeeze and strip to such an extent, and so closely interwoven, that it would be impossible to separate them." All such hands may be collected under the family name of *strip-squeeze*. In this chapter we are concerned only with the two-suit strip-squeeze.

This group divides into three major classifications. Other forms* can be found; but these three are the ones most likely to appear and be recognizable in play. The three species will be studied in §§ 38, 39, 43. As a preliminary, two definitions will be needed.

Say that a notrump strip (§ 34) is in prospect. At the moment when you get control, the victim has in hand potential cards of exit in one or more suits. You must hold in the exit suits enough winners to remove all possible exit cards; when this has been done, you put the enemy on lead, in circumstances where sooner or later he must give you a trick. Very often, when the throw-in is reached he will have still in hand one or more of what may be called *surplus winners*: that is, winners over and above the one on which the throw-in is to occur. He may also have idle cards remaining. Thus in Ex. 44, East's last five cards are ♠ 8, throw-in winner; ♠ K and ◊ 10 9, surplus winners; ♠ 7, idle card.

When a player stops a suit, but the position is such that if he leads away from that stopper he will lose it, let us say that the stopper in question is *vulnerable:* for example, East holds K x, North A Q, or West holds Q x x, North J x x, South A K x. In the majority of cases the success of a notrump strip is due to the fact that the defender holds, and is ultimately compelled to lead from, a vulnerable stopper.

38. *Squeeze to remove surplus winners.* Let us look at an

* See George S. Coffin, Endplays, Chap. 15.

example. Declarer cashes the Heart to complete the strip; the first Spade forces out the last idle card, ♣ 6. Now the second Spade squeezes West: he must choose between discarding the vital guard, ♣ 10, or one of his surplus winners. Of course he parts with a Diamond, so that the throw-in permits him to take two tricks only.

Example:

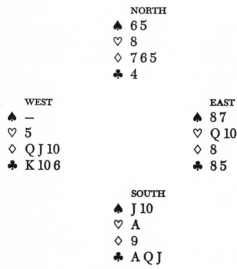

NORTH
♠ 6 5
♡ 8
◊ 7 6 5
♣ 4

WEST
♠ —
♡ 5
◊ Q J 10
♣ K 10 6

EAST
♠ 8 7
♡ Q 10
◊ 8
♣ 8 5

SOUTH
♠ J 10
♡ A
◊ 9
♣ A Q J

This layout illustrates an important possibility. The defender holds a *vulnerable stopper*. Declarer is able (just as in Chap. III) to play winners in the exit suit or suits (above, Hearts) until all exits are closed. He has remaining enough free winners (above, ♠ J) to force out all idle cards. If only just enough for this purpose, the hand belongs in Chap. III—pure strip. But if he has still in hand one or more free winners (above, ♠ 10), the lead of these *squeezes* the opponent: he must discard surplus winners, which reduces the number of tricks he can take after the throw-in.

The question might be asked, what happens if the defender has no surplus winners? This question is easily answered. If, after excision of all idle cards and exit cards, Declarer has so much as one free winner remaining and the defender has no surplus winner, the hand is a pure squeeze—not a strip at all.

Exercise 52.

NORTH	Bidding:
♠ Q 10 6 5	
♡ A K J	
◊ 5 3 2	
♣ A Q 4	

SOUTH	WEST	NORTH	EAST
P	1 ◊	Dbl.	P
2 NT	P	3 NT	P
P	P		

SOUTH
♠ A 9 8
♡ Q 9 5
◊ Q J 10
♣ K 9 7 3

West leads ◊ 7.

T. 1: East plays ◊ 8.

Analysis 52.

WEST	EAST
♠ K J 7	♠ 4 3 2
♡ 7 4	♡ 10 8 6 3 2
◊ A K 9 7 6 4	◊ 8
♣ 8 2	♣ J 10 6 5

The saving feature is West's bid, placing ♠ K in his hand. So, after three Hearts and three Clubs, he will have remaining four winners plus ♠ K x, and the throw-in will compel him to lead away from his King on the twelfth trick. Of course the Hearts must be cashed before the Clubs, on the chance of getting a Club discard from someone. The third Club exacts a Diamond (surplus winner) from West, whereupon the throw-in functions according to schedule.

With one of West's Diamonds traded for a card of any other suit, the hand would have been a pure strip, yet every feature of the plan and play would have been the same. That is: so far as the original plan is concerned, it makes (in some cases at least) little or no difference whether a pure strip or the combined form is to develop. In making his blueprint, Declarer neither knows nor cares about such matters.

Exercise 53.

	NORTH		Bidding:			
♠	A K 6 4					
♡	9 5 2		SOUTH	WEST	NORTH	EAST
◇	9 4		1 NT	P	3 NT	P
♣	A 8 7 3		P	P		

	SOUTH		West leads ♡ K.
♠	Q 5 2		
♡	A 10		
◇	A Q 7 6		
♣	K Q 6 4		

T. 1: King wins. East plays ♡ 4.
T. 2: ♡ Q led. East plays ♡ 6.
T. 3: ♣ K. Both follow.
T. 4: ♣ Q. West discards ◇ 8.
T. 5-6: ♠ Q K. Both follow.
T. 7: ♠ A. West discards ◇ 2.

Analysis 53.

	WEST		EAST
♠	J 8	♠	10 9 7 3
♡	K Q J 8 7 3	♡	6 4
◇	K J 8 2	◇	10 5 3
♣	2	♣	J 10 9 5

After seven tricks there can be no question about the next play—lead ♣ A to extract more testimony from West. As soon as that party sloughs a Heart, he is a ripe cherry.

Endplays are tough, aren't they?

x x x x

Notice that under the dictionary definition of squeeze the "surplus-winner squeeze" does not qualify, because the card squeezed out is neither a stopper nor a guard. (But the victim will testify that it feels like a squeeze, anway!) The same remark applies in §§ 39, 43.

39. *The two-loser squeeze: vulnerable stopper.* Let us look at Example (a). On the Spade, West discards an idle card. Whether

you put him in now or after cashing the Heart, he will be able to avoid leading a Club.

Example (a):

	NORTH	
♠	—	
♡	8 7	
◊	7 6	
♣	A 7	

WEST		EAST
♠ —		♠ —
♡ 9 6		♡ K Q
◊ Q 5		◊ 9 8
♣ K 8		♣ J 9

	SOUTH
♠	J
♡	A 5
◊	J
♣	Q 6

Example (b):

	NORTH	
♠	—	
♡	8 7	
◊	7 6	
♣	A 7	

WEST		EAST
♠ —		♠ —
♡ 9 6		♡ K Q
◊ Q 5		◊ 9 8
♣ K 8		♣ J 9

	SOUTH
♠	J 8
♡	A
◊	J
♣	Q 6

Next, Example (b). On the first Spade West discards ◊ 5, but on the second he is hooked. If he discards a Diamond or a Club, disaster is instant (provided Declarer reads the situation correctly); instead, he will yield a Heart. Whereupon you lay down ♡ A, closing the exit, then lead the Diamond. And what is the difference between these two layouts? Just this: in (a) you have three losers, in (b) *only two losers*.

The general problem is easily formulated. Throughout Chap. III and in § 38, you have enough tops in the exit suits to exhaust the victim in those suits. Suppose now that one adversary defends two suits and holds a potential card of exit in a third suit; also that you are not able to remove that card by follow-suit because the defender holds more small cards in the exit suit than you have winners in that suit. Don't give up! If *one stopper is vulnerable* and if you have *only two losers*, you can squeeze out the exit card every time.

The reason why this squeeze functions with two losers still in hand, instead of one as in simple squeeze, is easily found:

the necessity of keeping a card of exit puts an extra busy card in the opponent's hand. This squeeze fails with three losers for exactly the same reason that simple squeeze fails with two losers.

Strictly speaking, the play now in hand is a three-suit squeeze: the defender holds stoppers in two suits with an equally vital exit card in a third suit. Thus it might seem that this material properly belongs in a later chapter. But this play is much more closely related to the notrump strip than to the triple squeeze: hence, this is certainly the logical place to study it. We call it a two-suit squeeze in order to distinguish it from the case where the victim holds stoppers in all three suits.

Similar remarks will apply in § 43.

Exercise 54.

NORTH	Bidding:			
♠ 9 7 6 3				
♡ K 5 3	SOUTH	WEST	NORTH	EAST
◊ A 6	P	1 ♠	Dbl.	P
♣ A K 4 2	3 ♡	P	4 ♡	P
	P	P		

SOUTH	
♠ 10 2	
♡ A Q J 10 6	West leads ♠ K.
◊ 5 2	
♣ Q 10 5 3	

T. 1-2: ♠ K Q. East follows.

T. 3: ♠ J. East follows; Declarer ruffs.

T. 4: Heart. Both follow.

Analysis 54.

WEST	EAST
♠ A K Q J	♠ 8 5 4
♡ 7 2	♡ 9 8 4
◊ K J 10	◊ Q 9 8 7 4 3
♣ J 8 7 6	♣ 9

You are assured of the contract after four tricks. (a) Clubs run. Or (b) East has four: a proved finesse. Or (c) West has four. If so, he is measured for an elementary Spade-Club squeeze except that there are two losers. The only possible duck is in Diamonds, whereupon West will erase the Spade threat. Nevertheless the two-loser strip-squeeze is bound to produce, because the Club stopper is vulnerable; and there is no possible ambiguity, because all the cards are placed.

However, there is a concealed trap. Suppose that you draw trumps, then lay down ♣ K A, T. 7-8. Now the squeeze fails. (Footnote, Ex. 3.)

Exercise 55.

	NORTH	Bidding:
	♠ A Q J	
	♡ 9 6 3 2	

	EAST	SOUTH	WEST	NORTH
♢ A J 5 2	1 ♡	1 ♠	P	3 ♠
♣ Q 6	P	4 ♠	P	P
	P			

	SOUTH	
	♠ K 10 8 7 6 5	West leads ♡ 8.
	♡ Q 5	
	♢ K 10 6	
	♣ A 3	

T. 1: ♡ K wins.
T. 2: ♡ A. West plays ♡ 7.
T. 3: ♡ J led. ♠ 10 wins; West discards ♣ 4.
T. 4: ♠ A. East discards ♣ 2.

Analysis 55.

WEST	EAST
♠ 9 4 3 2	♠ —
♡ 8 7	♡ A K J 10 4
♢ Q 8 4	♢ 9 7 3
♣ J 10 9 4	♣ K 8 7 5 2

If Spades are 2-2 the hand is a routine trump strip: draw trumps, ruff the fourth Heart, cash ♣ A, exit in Clubs.

After four tricks this plan is out. But East's bid presumably places ♣ K in his hand. If so, the King is vulnerable, and there are only two losers. T. 5-6: Spades. T. 7: ◇ K. T. 8-9: Spades. T. 10: ◇ A. T. 11: Heart.

x   x   x   x

Very often, in executing a "vulnerable-stopper squeeze," you will bring down a number—possibly a bagful—of surplus winners (Heart in Ex. 55). This is a mere side-issue, of no interest or importance. The big game, the only game you are hunting, is that wary old exit card.

40. *Orientation.* In studying a series of closely related plays, there is danger that the reader may reach a point where he "can't see the town for the houses": that is, he may lose sight of the characteristic features that distinguish the various plays. At the risk of being merely repetitious, let us pause long enough to take a bird's-eye view of our recent activities.

In the pure strip (Chap. III) no element of squeeze is involved. You are able to remove all possible cards of exit by follow-suit; having done this, you put your adversary on lead at once. He may or may not have a vulnerable stopper. He may have still in hand surplus winners, or idle cards, or both. Within the limitations of a deck of cards, you may have any number of losers, from two up: for instance, five in Ex. 44.

In the "surplus-winner squeeze" (§ 38), again you are able to remove all possible cards of exit by follow-suit. The defender holds a *vulnerable stopper.* After closing the exits, you have enough free winners to force the discard of all idle cards, and one or more free winners still remaining. The play of this last group squeezes out surplus winners. Again, you may have any number of losers.

In the "vulnerable-stopper squeeze" (§ 39), you are *not* able to remove all possible cards of exit by follow-suit. The defender holds a *vulnerable stopper.* If you have *only two losers,* you can squeeze out the last exit card.

41. *Correcting the count.* We know that to establish a simple squeeze, if you have two or more losers in hand you must rectify the count by ducking down to one loser.

Precisely the same problem may arise in strip-squeeze play. If you can surely extract the card of exit by follow-suit, no need to worry about the number of losers; but if that card will have to be squeezed out, you must *duck down to two losers*.

Exercise 56.

NORTH	Bidding:

NORTH
♠ J 9 7 3
♡ A 7 3 2
◊ A 6 5
♣ 9 6

SOUTH	WEST	NORTH	EAST
5 ♣	P	P	P

West leads ◊ K.

SOUTH
♠ —
♡ Q 8
◊ 10 8 2
♣ A K Q J 8 5 3 2

Analysis 56.

WEST	EAST
♠ 10 8 6 5 2	♠ A K Q 4
♡ K 9 5	♡ J 10 6 4
◊ K Q J 4 3	◊ 9 7
♣ —	♣ 10 7 4

The only chance is that West has the Diamond pictures plus ♡ K. Stay off the first trick; win the second lead; run all the trumps. The risk of a 6-1 Diamond division is serious in a hand of this shape, but that risk must be run.

42. *Simple squeeze or strip-squeeze.* Say that a simple squeeze is established, except that there are two losers. Then, one usually tries to correct the count as soon as possible. But perhaps there is danger that the defender, if left on lead, will be able to kill the squeeze, or to do damage in some other way. In such a spot, always look to see if one stopper is vulnerable; for if so, the strip-squeeze will serve equally well, thus obviating the need of a duck.

Another point, important in match play. Suppose that a single duck will establish a simple squeeze, for contract; or, if a certain as yet untested suit is on its good behavior, this also will produce the needed trick. If the strip-squeeze will serve as well as the one-loser squeeze, postpone the duck; for if said suit runs, the new winner thus created will set the elementary squeeze, for an overtrick.

Exercise 57.

	NORTH
♠	A 6
♡	A 8 7
◇	A 10 9 5
♣	A K 9 8

	SOUTH
♠	K Q 10
♡	K Q 6 2
◇	K Q 7 2
♣	7 5

Bidding:

SOUTH	WEST	NORTH	EAST
1 ♡	P	3 ♣	P
3 NT	P	6 NT	P
P	P		

West leads ♣ Q.

Analysis 57.

	WEST		EAST
♠	5 3 2	♠	J 9 8 7 4
♡	J 9 5 3	♡	10 4
◇	J 6	◇	8 4 3
♣	Q J 10 3	♣	6 4 2

The contract arrives automatically if Diamonds are 3-2. In case West has four, the laydown of ◇ K Q will develop a proved finesse; if East has four, K A will produce the same result. Which to play for?

It doesn't matter how Diamonds are divided. Merely duck the first trick; then on getting in, cash ◇ K A. If West has a stopper he is measured for a squeeze, already established, with threats ◇ 7, ♣ 9.

The above might suffice in rubber bridge, but in match play a closer look is advisable. Following the play of ◇ K A, the contract is in hand automatically unless West has shown up with ◇ J x x x. But in that case he is subject to a vulnerable-stopper Diamond-Club strip-squeeze. It follows that the safety-duck is not required. (Play it with two of East's Diamonds replaced by two of West's majors.)

When the Diamonds fall, an overtrick arrives if Hearts are 3-3. But it is better than that: in case West stops Hearts he is in the grip of a typical simple squeeze with threats ♡ 6, ♣ 9. Thus as the cards lie you make seven.

Exercise 58.

	NORTH
♠	Q 8 7 2
♡	J 10 5
◊	A K J
♣	Q 8 3

	SOUTH
♠	A K 10 9 4 3
♡	7 4
◊	10 9 7
♣	A 4

Bidding:

SOUTH	WEST	NORTH	EAST
1 ♠	P	2 ◊	2 ♡
2 ♠	P	4 ♠	P
P	P		

West leads ♡ 3.

T. 1: East's King wins.
T. 2: ♡ A led. West plays ♡ 6.
T. 3: ♡ 2 led.

Analysis 58.

	WEST
♠	J 6 5
♡	Q 6 3
◊	8 6 5
♣	7 6 5 2

	EAST
♠	—
♡	A K 9 8 2
◊	Q 4 3 2
♣	K J 10 9

East has bid two on five to A K, opposite a passing partner with both opponents bidding: he surely holds ♣ K, and quite likely ◊ Q as well. Thus the first thought might be to discard a Diamond, to establish the Diamond-Club squeeze with threats ◊ J, ♣ Q. But this play will fail—both threats in the lower hand. Instead, discard ♣ 4 to set a criss-cross with threats ◊ 10, ♣ Q. But West will respond to his partner's ♡ 2 by returning a Club, leaving the failing case (§ 14). That is, there is no simple squeeze in the hand.

Instead, go for the two-loser squeeze. Ruff the third trick; draw trumps; cash ◊ A; finish the trumps. And now, while it is no certainty, the throw-in looks like a better bet than the finesse.

Evidently, the hand has defensive possibilities. If East keeps ◊ Q, ♣ K 10 9 and drops his Ten under the Ace, Declarer will have to be a good guesser.

This hand exhibits the rather surprising fact that sometimes, when you have two losers, you cannot afford to part with either of them; or to put it more succinctly, in some cases *two losers are better than one.*

43. *The two-loser squeeze: delayed duck.* The last of the three species mentioned in § 37 might be called the *delayed-duck squeeze.* This play is intimately related to the elementary simple squeeze, and *all conditions for that squeeze must be present,* except that there are *two losers* with no way to drop just one trick. Then, it fairly often happens that by means of a strip-squeeze the defender can be trimmed down to a size where the one-trick duck can be effected.

Example:

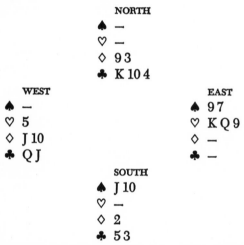

The first Spade forces West to part with a Diamond, the second squeezes out the card of exit; Dummy discards Clubs. And now the lead of ◇ 2 establishes the Nine. The reason why the play succeeds, with two losers still in hand, is the same as in "vulnerable stopper": the victim must retain a card of exit, which puts an extra busy card in his hand. With rare exceptions, the delayed-duck squeeze fails with three losers, in the same way as in § 39.

The requirements for this play are now clearly visible. One threat must have a *companion*—a small card of the same suit

(above, ◇ 3 accompanying ◇ 9). After the squeeze has occurred, it must be possible to *lead* either the companion or a
small card of the same suit from across the table (above, ◇ 2).
And there must be an *entry* to the established threat (above,
♣ K). To assist in remembering these three essentials, let us
coin the word CLE—*companion, lead, entry.*

One further requirement is almost too obvious to need pointing out—yet sometimes the obvious is overlooked! You may or
may not hold the top card of the throw-in suit—in the Example,
not—but *you must hold the master card in the other threat-suit,*
for if the defender holds that card, following the throw-in he
will be able to take his second trick at once. In the Example,
Declarer could discard Diamonds on the Spades, then duck a
Club to establish the Club threat; but West would simply lay
down his Diamond winner.

At first reading this may look like a formidable amount of
machinery, but it is actually not so. With a little practice you
can learn to recognize the presence of this squeeze, and to execute it, as easily as a mere simple squeeze.

Exercise 59.

NORTH

♠ A K 3
♡ 9 6 3
◇ 10 6
♣ A J 8 5 2

SOUTH

♠ Q J 10 8
♡ A 10
◇ A K Q J 4
♣ 7 4

Bidding:

NORTH	EAST	SOUTH	WEST
1 ♣	P	2 ◇	2 ♡
P	P	2 ♠	P
3 ♠	P	4 NT	P
5 ♡	P	6 NT	Dbl.
P	P	P	

West leads ♡ K.

T. 1: East plays ♡ 8.

Analysis 59.

WEST

♠ 9 6
♡ K Q J 5 4 2
◇ 8 2
♣ K Q 9

EAST

♠ 7 5 4 2
♡ 8 7
◇ 9 7 5 3
♣ 10 6 3

For his brash double of this brash bid, West should have the Heart-Club pictures. Granted this, the contract is in the bank.

One's first impulse would be to lose the first trick, to rectify the count. But if West is a bridge player he will lead ♣ K, destroying (E) for the simple squeeze. Fortunately the duck is not necessary, because the delayed-duck squeeze is already established: companion ♡ 6, lead ♡ 10, entry ♣ A. Merely run off all the Spade-Diamond tops.

Do not proceed until you see clearly that this is nothing but a simple squeeze, except for a slight change in the order of ceremonies: instead of rectifying the count on the first trick, you do so on the eleventh.

Exercise 60.

NORTH
- ♠ A Q 3 2
- ♡ A 8 3
- ♢ A K Q 6 2
- ♣ 6

SOUTH
- ♠ K J
- ♡ K Q 6 5 4
- ♢ 8 5 4 3
- ♣ A 7

Bidding:

NORTH	EAST	SOUTH	WEST
1 ♢	P	1 ♡	2 ♣
2 ♠	P	3 ♣	P
3 ♢	P	3 NT	P
6 NT	P	P	P

West leads ♣ K.

T. 1: East plays ♣ 3; Ace wins.
T. 2: Diamond. West discards a Club.
T. 3: ♡ A. Both follow.
T. 4: ♡ K. West discards a Club.

Declarer concedes one and claims the rest.

Analysis 60.

WEST
- ♠ 10 9 8 6 4
- ♡ 9
- ♢ —
- ♣ K Q J 10 9 5 2

EAST
- ♠ 7 5
- ♡ J 10 7 2
- ♢ J 10 9 7
- ♣ 8 4 3

After four tricks the delayed-duck squeeze is proved. But unlike Ex. 59, the hand will not "play itself"; instead, careful planning is required. The three elements are: companion ◊ 2, lead ◊ 2, entry ◊ Q. The sequence must be ♠ K J, ◊ K, ♠ A Q. For discard on the Spades the closed hand will have available ♣ 7, ♡ 5 (don't touch those Diamonds—they're busy). The last Spade squeezes out the exit card, whereupon the Rule of § 9 comes into play: "at the first opportunity," which is now, Declarer ducks a Diamond.

Be sure to see that failure will result if a Heart is led, T. 10; also if one of South's Diamonds has been discarded. Also note that if North-South could have seen each other's hands they would have bid seven. Ouch!

In Ex. 59 the squeeze pinches out a surplus winner (Heart); here, an exit card (Club). No matter—all is grist that comes to this mill.

Exercise 61.

	NORTH
♠	A K 8 4
♡	A
◊	Q 4
♣	A K 8 5 3 2

	SOUTH
♠	Q 3
♡	Q 6 2
◊	A K J 10 3
♣	9 7 6

Bidding:

WEST	NORTH	EAST	SOUTH
P	1 ♣	P	1 ◊
P	1 ♠	P	2 NT
P	6 NT	P	P
P			

West leads ♡ 3.

T. 1:   East plays ♡ 10.
T. 2:   ♣ K. Both follow.
T. 3:   ♣ A. East discards ♡ 4.
T. 4-5: ◊ Q K. Both follow.
T. 6:   ◊ A. West discards ♡ 7.

Analysis 61.

	WEST		EAST
♠	10 7 6 2	♠	J 9 5
♡	J 8 7 3	♡	K 10 9 5 4
◊	8 2	◊	9 7 6 5
♣	Q 10 4	♣	J

Granted that the lead was an honest fourth-best, West's hand can be counted after six tricks, and he is under the thumb of a delayed-duck Spade-Club squeeze: companion ♣ 5, lead ♣ 7, entry ♠ K. Lead ◊ J, discarding ♣ 3; ◊ 10 squeezes out the exit card, with a Spade thrown from Dummy; lead of ♣ 7 establishes the Eight.

x   x   x   x

You must be sure to see clearly the difference between the vulnerable-stopper squeeze (§ 39) and the delayed duck. In each, there are two losers. In each, the last free winner reduces the enemy to a holding where one trick may be safely ducked. In § 39, the duck in one suit compels him to *lead away from his vulnerable stopper*, usually in the other suit. In § 43, the duck *establishes a new winner* in the throw-in suit.

Also, it should hardly be necessary to point out that the remarks made in § 42 (both paragraphs) apply here as well.

When you have a simple squeeze, except that there are two losers with no way to correct the count, look to see if one stopper is vulnerable. Lacking that, look to see if one threat suit is of extra length: if so, there is a good chance that the other conditions for delayed duck will be satisfied.

Exercise 62.

```
        NORTH
     ♠ A 10 7
     ♡ K 10 4
     ◊ K 6 5 4
     ♣ 10 8 3

        SOUTH
     ♠ 4 3
     ♡ A Q J 5 3
     ◊ A J 2
     ♣ J 5 2
```

Bidding:

EAST	SOUTH	WEST	NORTH
P	1 ♡	2 ♣	2 ♡
2 ♠	3 ♡	P	P
P			

West leads ♣ K.

T. 1: East plays ♣ 9.
T. 2-3: ♣ Q A. East discards ♠ 9 2.
T. 4: West leads ♠ 8.

Analysis 62.

WEST	EAST
♠ 8	♠ K Q J 9 6 5 2
♡ 8 7 6 2	♡ 9
◇ Q 9	◇ 10 8 7 3
♣ A K Q 7 6 4	♣ 9

In Ex. 16 the duck, being perfectly safe, was "clearly indicated." Here, if you stay off, East will return a Spade, for instant disaster in case the Eight was a singleton. So, win the trick and run the Hearts, for the same result as in Ex. 16.

Of course, Ex. 16 also could just as well have been played this way.

44. *Losing squeeze-card.* Let us play a hand of bridge.

Exercise 63.

NORTH
♠ A K Q 10
♡ 3
◇ A Q J 7 2
♣ J 9 5

SOUTH
♠ J 7 5
♡ A Q 7 5 2
◇ K 4
♣ A 6 4

Bidding:

NORTH	EAST	SOUTH	WEST
1 ◇	1 ♡	Dbl.	P
2 ♠	P	3 NT	P
6 NT	P	P	P

West leads ♡ 10.

T. 1: East plays ♡ 4. Queen wins.
T. 2: ◇ K. Both follow.
T. 3: Diamond. East discards ♡ 6.
T. 4-5: Spades. Both follow.

Analysis 63.

WEST	EAST
♠ 8 4 3 2	♠ 9 6
♡ 10	♡ K J 9 8 6 4
◇ 10 9 6 5 3	◇ 8
♣ 8 7 3	♣ K Q 10 2

It seems likely on the bidding, and from his discouragers in Hearts, that East has ♣ K Q. So, finish the Spade and Diamond tops, then throw West in with the last Diamond, squeezing East at the same time.

x x x x

The play employed in Ex. 63 is evidently this. A simple squeeze is in hand except that there are two losers. Then, your thoughts turn to "delayed duck," but you find that CLE is not present. (In Ex. 63, "lead" is lacking. With ♡ 2 traded for ♣ 5, the hand would be a standard delayed duck.) In such a spot, it may be possible to *lose a trick to the victim's partner, executing the squeeze at the same time.* Be sure to see that in its timing, and in every other respect, this play is identical with the simple squeeze, except that the squeeze-card is a loser.

Of course you must make sure that the thrown-in partner cannot make a damaging return. With ♠ 6, ♣ 3 traded, Ex. 63 would fail.

Exercise 64.

NORTH
♠ A 6 4 2
♡ 8 6 5 4
♢ J 7
♣ K Q 9

SOUTH
♠ K Q J 9
♡ 9 2
♢ A 9 5
♣ A 5 4 3

Bidding:

WEST	NORTH	EAST	SOUTH
P	P	P	1 ♠
P	3 ♠	P	4 ♠
P	P	P	

West leads ♡ K.

T. 1: East's Ace wins.
T. 2: ♡ J led. West plays ♡ 3.
T. 3: ♡ 7 led. Declarer ruffs; West plays ♡ 10.
T. 4: ♠ K. Both follow.
T. 5: ♠ Q. East discards ♢ 8.

Analysis 64.

WEST	EAST
♠ 10 8 7 5	♠ 3
♡ K Q 10 3	♡ A J 7
◇ 10 6 4	◇ K Q 8 3 2
♣ J 2	♣ 10 8 7 6

At first, the contract looks like a laydown by dummy reversal; after five tricks this plan is out.

To give West the Clubs would mean that Diamonds are 7-1, so place the Clubs with East. In case he also has ◇ K Q (his silly signal says that he does, and unless Clubs run it is the only chance anyway), we nail him by losing squeeze-card. The sequence is ♠ J, ♣ Q, ♠ A, ♣ A K, Heart.

45. *A basic principle of squeeze defense.* Turning for a moment to the other side of the picture, let us state a general principle of squeeze defense which is invaluable, yet is not often followed, even in high-level play.

With a squeeze threatening but not yet fully established, every competent player is on the alert for a way to kill the squeeze by upsetting one of the necessary conditions. But suppose the squeeze is established, therefore certain to occur. Usually in top-flight competition, and invariably at a lower level, the victim tags docilely along like Mary's little lamb, meekly dropping his idle cards one by one and sloughing the stinger on the squeeze-trick. When this line is followed Declarer knows exactly what to do, and his success is assured.*

Instead, the defender should keep in mind this

RULE: *When you are surely in the grip of a fully established squeeze, make the key discard early.*

Of course the Rule is not always applicable. When Declarer has an accurate count on your hand, nothing can be done. And many times you cannot be sure that a squeeze is impending

---

* Quotation from an analysis in a certain daily column: "In order to have any chance whatever of defeating the contract, East must," etc.—the recommended line being to discard idle cards while they last, and make the fatal discard on the squeeze-trick. This statement should be slightly amended, to read: "In order to have no chance whatever," etc.

until too late to take effective action. But there remains an important percentage of cases where, by following this Rule, you will be able to create an ambiguous position: Declarer cannot tell with certainty what has happened, and will have to choose between two courses, with a chance—sometimes an odds-on chance—that he will go wrong.

Obviously, against a Declarer who knows your style you must "mix 'em up"—sometimes play lamb, sometimes artful dodger. The point is, don't label your play!

For a first example, see Anal. 58, third paragraph.

*Exercise 65.**

NORTH		Bidding:			
♠ A Q 9 8 7 6 3					
♡ A K 8		NORTH	EAST	SOUTH	WEST
◇ Q 7 6		1 ♠	2 ♣	2 NT	P
♣ —		3 ♣	P	3 ♠	P
		6 NT	P	P	P
SOUTH					
♠ K 5 2		West leads ♣ 4.			
♡ 10 9 5 4					
◇ A 10 4					
♣ K Q 6					

T. 1: East plays ♣ 10. King wins.
T. 2-4: Spades. East discards ◇ 9, 2, 3.
T. 5-8: Spades. East discards ♡ 2, ♣ 2, 5, J; West, ♣ 3, 7, 8, 9.
T. 9-10: Hearts. East plays ♡ 6, 7; West, ♡ 3, J.

Analysis 65.

WEST	EAST
♠ J 10 4	♠ —
♡ J 3	♡ Q 7 6 2
◇ J 8 5	◇ K 9 3 2
♣ 9 8 7 4 3	♣ A J 10 5 2

While fully aware that East might be trying to take him for a ride, Declarer after long cogitation decided that if holding a

---

* East was Mr. James C. Jackson, of Tryon, N. C.

5-4-4-0 with some strength in each suit, East would have been apt to double on the first round; so, playing East for ◇ K J and ♣ A, Declarer led the Heart as a losing squeeze-card.

Whether or not you agree with this decision is immaterial: the point is that East gave Declarer a guess, and he defeated the contract, whereas if he had followed the customary "yessir" line, he would have been a soft touch.

PROBLEMS

Problem 15*

	NORTH
♠	J 5
♡	8 4
◇	9 4 3
♣	A 7 6 4 3 2

	SOUTH
♠	A 9 3
♡	A Q 6
◇	A K Q
♣	K J 8 5

Bidding:

NORTH	EAST	SOUTH	WEST
3 ♣	P	4 NT	P
5 ◇	P	6 NT	P
P	P		

West leads ♠ K.

Plan Declarer's play.

Solution 15.

	WEST		EAST
♠	K Q 10 6 2	♠	8 7 4
♡	K 9 7 3	♡	J 10 5 2
◇	10 6 5	◇	J 8 7 2
♣	9	♣	Q 10

Unless West has the three Clubs, that suit will run. Then, after cashing the minors, Declarer will have to decide: has he executed a strip-squeeze (West holding ♡ K), or is a mere finesse required? The sequence is ♠ A, T. 1; ♣ 8 to Ace; ♣ K J; Diamonds; Clubs. In the actual play the opponents followed

* This hand was played by Mr. Don Smith, of Ann Arbor, Mich., and reported by Mr. William S. Mouser in the Detroit News.

(literally) the line of least resistance: East kept three Hearts, West two Hearts and ♠ Q. Thus Declarer had no problem.

The hand is a fine example under § 45. West can see that he must find five discards. If he nonchalantly tosses three Hearts and two Spades, there is at least a worth-while chance that Declarer will go wrong.

Problem 16.

NORTH
♠ 8 7
♡ A 9 7 2
◊ 6 3 2
♣ K 7 3 2

SOUTH
♠ A 5 2
♡ 10 4
◊ A K Q 8 5
♣ A Q 5

Bidding:

SOUTH	WEST	NORTH	EAST
1 ◊	P	1 ♡	1 ♠
2 NT	P	3 NT	P
P	Dbl.	P	P
P			

West leads ♠ Q.

T. 1: East's King wins.
T. 2: ♠ J led. Declarer ducks; West plays ♠ 3.
T. 3: Spade. West discards ♣ 4.
T. 4: ◊ A. East discards a Spade.

Solution 16.

WEST
♠ Q 3
♡ K Q J 8
◊ J 10 9 7 4
♣ 8 4

EAST
♠ K J 10 9 6 4
♡ 6 5 3
◊ —
♣ J 10 9 6

Forget the Club break—it either is or is not there. So, the only chance to be considered is that West has ♡ K Q J. But this, instead of a forlorn hope, is a fairly good prospect, because West's double is certainly based on something pretty stout in Hearts. Cash ♣ A K Q, then duck a Heart or a Diamond, according to West's discard. Of course he would toss a Heart, because this saves the day if East has ♡ 10 x x.

This is the exceptional case mentioned in § 43, where the

delayed duck succeeds with three losers in hand. The reason is this. In the usual (two-loser) case the defender must retain an extra card in the throw-in suit: this additional busy card causes the squeeze to ripen with two losers. Here, Declarer has CLE in two suits. Two Hearts and three Diamonds are enough to stop the suits, but three and four respectively are required to stave off the duck: these two extra busy cards shove the loser-count up to three.

Evidently this squeeze succeeds by virtue of bad defense, because East should realize that his partner must be crying for a Heart lead. But it is allowable to include such hands in a book for the reason that bad squeeze defense is the rule, rather than the exception, in actual play.

Problem 17.

NORTH

♠ 6 5 3
♡ Q 6
◇ A 8 4 2
♣ K Q 9 6

Bidding:

EAST	SOUTH	WEST	NORTH
P	1 NT	P	3 NT
P	P	P	

West leads ♠ Q.

SOUTH

♠ A 9 8
♡ A 8
◇ K Q 7 6
♣ A 7 5 4

T. 1: East's King wins.
T. 2: ♠ 2 led. Ace wins.
T. 3: ◇ K.
T. 4: ◇ Q. West discards ♡ 2.
T. 5: ♣ Q. West plays ♣ J.
T. 6: ♣ K. West discards ♡ 4.

Solution 17.

WEST

♠ Q J 10 7 4
♡ J 10 7 5 4 2
◇ 9
♣ J

EAST

♠ K 2
◇ J 10 5 3
♡ K 9 3
♣ 10 8 3 2

On the bridge-certainty that West holds the Spade honors, East is doomed. You merely start the process of rectifying the count by leading the Spade, T. 7. (Play it with Spades led, T. 8-9; with a Heart led, T. 9; and with a Heart led, T. 8.)

Problem 18.

NORTH
♠ Q 7
♡ 6 5 3
◇ A 6 3 2
♣ A J 8 5

SOUTH
♠ 9 4 3 2
♡ A K Q J 9
◇ K 7
♣ K 3

Bidding:

SOUTH	WEST	NORTH	EAST
1 ♡	P	2 ♣	2 ♠
3 ♡	P	4 ♡	P
P	P		

West leads ♠ 8.

T. 1: King wins.
T. 2: ♠ A led. West plays ♠ 5.
T. 3: ♠ J led. West plays ♡ 7.
T. 4: ◇ 10 led. East plays ◇ 8; King wins.
T. 5: ♡ A. Both follow.
T. 6: ♡ K. East discards ♠ 6.

Solution 18.

WEST		EAST
♠ 8 5		♠ A K J 10 6
♡ 8 7 4 2		♡ 10
◇ 10 9 5		◇ Q J 8 4
♣ 10 9 7 4		♣ Q 6 2

Until the Heart division shows up, the hand looks trivial: merely draw trumps, then ruff the Spade. But after six tricks, we must go to work.

Two methods appear at once. (a) If West has ♣ Q, a mere finesse. (b) If East has the Queen, Spade-Club simple squeeze. Since the two look equally probable, each offers a 50% chance, and we will have to choose after cashing ◇ A, ♣ K and the Hearts.

There is a third method. (c) Assume that West holds ♣ Q and play Type R double squeeze with threats R, ♠ 9; L, ♣ J; B, ◊ 6. This wins whenever (a) does; also whenever East holds ♣ Q not more than twice guarded, because the Club tops can be played and a third round ruffed. Thus (c) offers much better than an even chance.

Problem 19.*

```
        NORTH
     ♠ K 8 6 3 2
     ♡ A Q 5 3
     ◊ A 7
     ♣ Q 6

        SOUTH
     ♠ Q 9 7
     ♡ K 6
     ◊ K Q J 10 3 2
     ♣ A J
```

Bidding:

NORTH	EAST	SOUTH	WEST
1 ♠	P	2 ◊	P
3 ♡	P	4 NT	P
5 ♡	P	6 ◊	P
P	P		

West leads ♠ 5.

T. 1: East plays ♠ 10; Queen wins.
T. 2-3: ◊ A K. Both follow.
T. 4: ◊ Q. West discards ♣ 8.
T. 5-7: Diamonds. Both discard Clubs.

Solution 19.

```
     WEST                    EAST
  ♠ 5 4                   ♠ A J 10
  ♡ J 9 4                 ♡ 10 8 7 2
  ◊ 9 5                   ◊ 8 6 4
  ♣ K 10 8 5 3 2          ♣ 9 7 4
```

The key card is ♠ 4. East's last six cards are ♠ A J, three Hearts, and either ♠ 4 or a fourth Heart. If the former, throw West in with the Heart for a Club return; if the latter, lay down ♣ A to squeeze out ♠ J. But if holding ♠ 4, East would read his partner's lead as a singleton, thus would play his Ace and come back. Long odds in favor of the Club lead.

* This hand was played by Mr. William B. Woodson.

CHAPTER V

TRIPLE SQUEEZE AND REPEATING SQUEEZE

46. *The triple squeeze.* In the standard form of the two-suit squeeze, or simple squeeze, one opponent has the whole burden in two suits, and Declarer has only one loser.

In the corresponding standard form of the *three-suit squeeze,* or *triple squeeze,* one defender is solely responsible for *three suits,* and the squeeze ripens with *two losers* remaining in Declarer's hands. The reason for this last is not hard to find. Presence of two losers gives the victim an advantage of one trick, but the necessity of retaining a third stopper cancels that advantage, so that the pinch occurs, just as in simple squeeze, on the *last free winner.*

It follows from these remarks that BLUE serves for the triple squeeze with only two changes: (B) means Busy in *three* suits, (L) means only *two* Losers.

We have seen that there are other forms of the two-suit squeeze, beyond the standard form. The same is true of the three-suit squeeze. These more advanced situations, or some of them, will be studied in due course; but in this chapter we are speaking only of the primary form described above.

A word about nomenclature. The double squeeze, as the name implies, consists of two simple squeezes—one on each defender. The triple squeeze is so called because it may be viewed as equivalent to three simple squeezes.* Let the free suit be Spades. Then the sufferer is simple-squeezed in Hearts-Diamonds, Hearts-Clubs, and Diamonds-Clubs simultaneously.

* See George S. Coffin, Endplays, p. 105.

47. *Classification.* In the forthcoming text, though not always in the exercises, South will denote *the hand containing the squeeze-card* (last free winner).

We know that in simple squeeze the South hand cannot hold both threats, because there simply isn't room. For the same reason, in triple squeeze South cannot hold all three threats. That hand may, however, hold two threats, because one space is opened up by the presence of one threat opposite.

Thus all (standard) triple squeezes fall under one or another of three headings, as follows.

Case I: North (opposite the squeeze-card) holds one threat.
Case II: North holds two threats.
Case III: North holds three threats.

Since each of these cases has certain features peculiar to itself, we shall consider them separately.

Apparently, some players believe that a three-suit squeeze nearly always, if not always, produces two tricks. That this is very far from true will appear as we proceed. In studying each of the three forms, beginning with Case I in § 48, we shall first develop the conditions under which the squeeze will gain one trick. Immediately following, in § 49 for Case I, we shall note the additional conditions that are necessary if the squeeze is to "repeat," for gain of a second trick.

48. *Case I: One threat opposite the squeeze-card.* In this case, when the squeeze is reached, North has in general two idle cards, due to the presence of two threats in South's hand. When North's only entry is in one of South's suits there may be only one idle card*, but since one is plenty, no trouble arises.

Summary: With one threat opposite the squeeze-card, the triple squeeze always succeeds against either defender.

---

* Possibly some few readers, of an analytical turn of mind, might like to see the argument. Let the free suit be Spades, with South holding the Heart and Diamond threats, North the Club. (a) When North has an entry in Clubs, South's minimum holding is one Spade, the two threats, and a small Club; North holds winner and threat in Clubs plus two idle cards. (b) When North's only entry is in (say) Diamonds, South must hold one Spade, the Heart threat, threat and small in Diamonds; North holds winner and small in Diamonds, the Club threat, and one idle card. When South holds one or more winners in his own threat-suits, this in general increases the number of North's idle cards.

Exercise 66.

NORTH
♠ K 5 4
♡ A 4 3
♢ K Q 8 3
♣ 10 8 3

SOUTH
♠ A 10 6
♡ K 10 6
♢ A J 10 7 6 5
♣ Q

Bidding:

EAST	SOUTH	WEST	NORTH
P	1 ♢	2 ♣	3 ♢
P	5 ♢	P	P
P			

West leads ♣ K.

T. 1: King wins.
T. 2: ♣ J led.

Analysis 66.

WEST
♠ Q J 3
♡ Q J 8
♢ 9 2
♣ A K J 5 2

EAST
♠ 9 8 7 2
♡ 9 7 5 2
♢ 4
♣ 9 7 6 4

Since a squeeze is the only hope, a momentary thought might be to duck the second trick, in hope of setting up a simple squeeze on West. But a Spade or Heart discard leaves no threat in that suit, and a third Club lead will excise the Club threat. No simple squeeze.

The best chance is that West may hold all the invisible high cards. If so, the triple squeeze is established right now, and an easier one could hardly be conceived. Just run all the trumps, and West will buckle.

49. *The repeating squeeze: Case I.* As our next step, another highly important possibility must be developed.

As soon as one threat is unguarded, that threat becomes a new winner, and since the victim is still busy in two suits, it is obvious that under proper conditions this new winner will inflict a simple squeeze, for gain of another trick. When this happens, the sequence is called a *repeating squeeze.*

The conditions under which a three-suiter will repeat are easily discovered. In Case I—North holding one threat—if West is the target he can always escape the second squeeze merely by establishing North's threat, because that squeeze will fail for lack of (U)—both threats South, stoppers West. When East has the stoppers, (U) will be present no matter what he does, and his only chance of beating the second squeeze is by upsetting (E). Manifestly, this is impossible if North has an entry in his own suit and South an entry in one of his. But if South's only entry is in North's suit, or if he has none in any suit, East establishes North's threat, leaving South high and dry—see Example (a). And when North's only entry is in one of South's suits, East gives up that suit—Example (b).

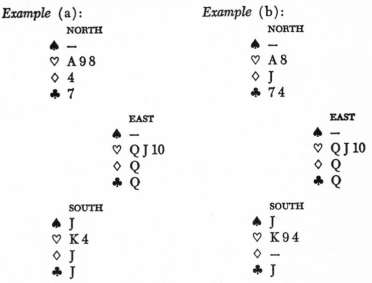

Example (a):

NORTH

♠ —
♡ A 9 8
◇ 4
♣ 7

EAST

♠ —
♡ Q J 10
◇ Q
♣ Q

SOUTH

♠ J
♡ K 4
◇ J
♣ J

Example (b):

NORTH

♠ —
♡ A 8
◇ J
♣ 7 4

EAST

♠ —
♡ Q J 10
◇ Q
♣ Q

SOUTH

♠ J
♡ K 9 4
◇ —
♣ J

Summary: When North (opposite the squeeze-card) holds one threat, a triple squeeze will never repeat against West. Against East it will always repeat if North has an entry in his own suit and South an entry in one of his; in all other cases, with rare exceptions, the second squeeze will fail.

Strictly speaking, the name *repeating squeeze* is a misnomer. The triple squeeze does not repeat, because it is all over as soon as the last free winner has been played; instead, it produces an elementary (one-loser) simple squeeze. Continuing the argument of § 46 (last paragraph), we find that the logically correct name for the phenomenon now in hand is *quadruple squeeze*, for it consists of a triple (equivalent to three simples) followed by a simple. Some authors have suggested the name *progressive squeeze*. But since "repeating squeeze" is firmly imbedded in the literature, let us use it.

Exercise 67.

NORTH
- ♠ 4
- ♡ A J
- ◇ A J 9 7 3
- ♣ A Q 9 8 3

SOUTH
- ♠ A K Q J 10 9 5
- ♡ 6
- ◇ K 6 2
- ♣ J 4

Bidding:

WEST	NORTH	EAST	SOUTH
P	1 ◇	P	2 ♠
P	3 ♣	P	3 ◇
P	3 NT	P	4 NT
P	5 ♠	P	5 NT
P	6 ◇	P	7 ♠
P	P	Dbl.	Rdbl.
P	P	P	

West leads ◇ 8.

Analysis 67.

WEST
- ♠ 8 7 3 2
- ♡ 10 9 8 5 3 2
- ◇ 8
- ♣ 6 5

EAST
- ♠ 6
- ♡ K Q 7 4
- ◇ Q 10 5 4
- ♣ K 10 7 2

North's slip of the tongue, in saying six Diamonds when he meant six Clubs, has put Declarer out on the end of a limb, where the only straw to grasp at (how is that for a mixed metaphor?) is a repeating squeeze. East's idiotic double raises some hope that he may have all the adverse point-cards; West's lead is almost surely his highest Diamond. Granted so much, the repeater is there. But watch your step!

One threat is ♡ J. If North holds either of the other two threats, East will establish South's threat, and with both threats in the lower hand, the second squeeze will fail. This says that the minor-suit threats must be ◇ 6 and ♣ J.

How about that first trick? As soon as ◇ K is spent, South has no entry, and the quarry escapes the second squeeze by surrendering the Heart. Thus the first trick must be won with the Ace.

There is one more pitfall. On the last trump, Dummy of course discards ♣ Q. Now if East parts with a Heart or a Club, the result is automatic. But if he gives a Diamond, Vienna Coup will be required for the Heart-Club squeeze: that is, Declarer must cash ♣ A, T. 9.

x   x   x   x

In general, as the Summary states, the second squeeze will fail unless North holds an entry in his own threat-suit and South in one of his. Exceptionally, the second squeeze will succeed when North, though holding no entry in his own suit, has entries in *both* of South's suits and South has entries in *two*—any two— of the three threat-suits. Then, no matter what East does, the requisite entries will be in hand for the second squeeze.

Exercise 68.

	NORTH
♠	A 7 2
♡	Q 8
◊	A J 7 5
♣	K 7 4 3

Bidding:

WEST	NORTH	EAST	SOUTH
P	1 ◊	1 ♡	2 ♣
P	3 ♣	P	4 NT
P	5 ♡	P	7 NT
P	P	Dbl.	P
P	P		

	SOUTH
♠	K 10 3
♡	A
◊	K Q 10 8 6 4
♣	A 10 6

West leads ♡ 4.

T. 1: East plays ♡ 10.

Analysis 68.

	WEST		EAST
♠	9 6 5 4	♠	Q J 8
♡	9 7 5 4 2	♡	K J 10 6 3
◊	2	◊	9 3
♣	9 8 5	♣	Q J 2

If East has the missing pictures, this crazy contract can be made. Both North and South have entries in both of South's threat-suits, so that no matter which of these is surrendered by East, Condition (E_2) will be in effect for the second squeeze.

x   x   x   x

One important constituent of the present problem remains to be pointed out. Fairly often, as regards the second squeeze, the defender is confronted with the bitterest kind of pseudo, sometimes under such circumstances as to make correct play all but impossible. Thus in some cases the squeeze actually will repeat when, according to our theory above, it does not rate to do so.

A striking example is furnished by Ex. 66. West can see that he is squeezed in three suits if Declarer's six majors are exactly ♠ A 10 x, ♡ K 10 x. Seldom if ever in match play would West discard ♣ A, and a cold *never* in rubber, because this discard hands Declarer his contract, while a Spade or a Heart keeps bright hope alive at the risk of a contemptible 20 points. And if anything but the Ace is thrown, the squeeze repeats.

Exercise 69.*

	NORTH		Bidding:			
	♠ 9 2					
	♡ 10 6 5 2		EAST	SOUTH	WEST	NORTH
	◇ Q 6 3		P	1 ♠	2 ◇	P
	♣ A 8 6 5		P	4 ♠	Dbl.	P
			P	P		

	SOUTH
	♠ A K Q 10 8 6 5 3
	♡ K 4
	◇ 5
	♣ K 2

West leads ◇ K.

T. 1: East plays ◇ 2.
T. 2: ♣ 10 led. East plays ♣ 4; King wins.

Analysis 69.

	WEST			EAST
	♠ —			♠ J 7 4
	♡ A Q 7			♡ J 9 8 3
	◇ A K J 9 4			◇ 10 8 7 2
	♣ Q 10 9 7 3			♣ J 4

After seven trumps Dummy had remaining ◇ Q and ♣ A 8 6; West, ♡ A, ◇ A and ♣ Q 9. By discarding ◇ A West can hold the hand to one overtrick. But he elected to throw

* This hand was played by Mr. H. Sanford Brown, of Detroit, and reported by Mr. Frank S. Eaton in the Detroit Free Press.

the Heart on the chance that East might have the King, where-upon South's King inflicted the second squeeze.

50. *Case II: Two threats opposite the squeeze-card.* Here, just as in § 48, we are examining only the triple squeeze—nothing to do with the question of repetition.

When North has an entry in either (or of course each) of his own suits, presence of one threat South provides North with one idle card, available for discard on the squeeze-trick, so that the squeeze is valid against either adversary. But suppose that North's only entry is in South's suit: if South has a winner in one—any one—of the three threat-suits, that winner makes room for an idle card North. Finally, if North's only entry is in South's suit and South has no winner in any threat-suit, North has no idle card: the squeeze succeeds against West but fails against East. (Compare § 14.)

The failing case would seldom occur in play.

Summary: When North (opposite the squeeze-card) holds two threats, the triple squeeze always succeeds against West, and always against East with one rare exception.

Exercise 70.

NORTH		Bidding:			
♠ A J 9 5		NORTH	EAST	SOUTH	WEST
♡ 9 7 5 4 3		P	2 ♣	5 ◇	P
◇ —		P	Dbl.	P	P
♣ 9 7 4 3		P			
SOUTH		West leads ♣ 8.			
♠ 3 2					
♡ K					
◇ A K Q J 10 6 5 3 2					
♣ 10					

T. 1: ♣ J wins.
T. 2: ♣ A led.

Analysis 70.

WEST		EAST
♠ 8 7 4		♠ K Q 10 6
♡ 10 6 2		♡ A Q J 8
◇ 9 8 7 4		◇ —
♣ 8 6 2		♣ A K Q J 5

Thanks to East's open-handed generosity in not returning a Spade, the contract is a laydown if East holds ♡ A and ♠ K Q —not unlikely on his two-bid.

You will surely agree that this triple squeeze is as easy, in plan and play, as any simple squeeze that could be constructed.

Moral: When you hold a gigantic power-house opposite a washout, begin very early to think of squeeze defense!

Exercise 71.

NORTH
♠ J 10 6
♡ J 4 3
◊ K Q 8 6
♣ K 9 2

SOUTH
♠ A K Q 7 3 2
♡ K
◊ 10 9 5
♣ A 5 4

Bidding:

NORTH	EAST	SOUTH	WEST
P	P	1 ♠	P
2 ◊	P	3 ♠	P
4 ♠	P	P	P

West leads ◊ 4.

T. 1: Queen to East's Ace.
T. 2: ◊ 2 led. West ruffs.
T. 3: ♣ 8 led. Dummy plays ♣ 2, East ♣ 10.

Analysis 71.

WEST
♠ 9 5 4
♡ A 10 9 6 5 2
◊ 4
♣ 8 7 6

EAST
♠ 8
♡ Q 8 7
◊ A J 7 3 2
♣ Q J 10 3

Since West's ♣ 8 is doubtless top of nothing, East has the minors. If also holding ♡ A, he is subject to a triple squeeze with threats ♡ K, ◊ 8, ♣ 9. But if holding the Ace he would have shoved out a higher Diamond, T. 2, calling for a Heart return: therefore, West probably has ♡ A.

Of course you don't care where the Ace is. But it's lucky you didn't play carelessly to the first two tricks!

This hand is designed to remind you that the standard three-suit squeeze is to be *added* to the list of two-loser squeezes given in § 43 (last paragraph)—not substituted for that list. In other words: where you have two losers and no triple squeeze is present, there are two other lines of play to be investigated.

51. *The three-suit* Vienna Coup. The two-suit Vienna Coup (§ 11) has its three-suit counterpart. For Case II—North holding two threats—the set-up is exactly the same as in simple squeeze: East is the quarry, South has or will have no entry in any of the three suits, North has one or more winners in South's suit. Then, those winners must be cashed before the squeeze is reached: this is the *three-suit Vienna Coup.* Of course the reason is precisely the same as in two-suit play: *to avert the blocking of South's threat.*

RULE: *In triple squeeze, when North (opposite the squeeze card) holds two threats, East is the defender, South has no entry in any threat-suit, and North has one or more winners in South's threat-suit, cash those winners before the squeeze-trick.*

This Coup is comparatively rare, even in Case II. While it may conceivably arise in Case I, the contingency is too remote to be worth considering.

Note that the Vienna Coup of Ex. 67 had nothing to do with the three-suit squeeze, which was already in hand; instead, it was nothing more than our old friend of simple-squeeze days, necessary in order to produce the second, or simple, squeeze. The three-suit Coup, on the other hand, is an essential ingredient of the triple squeeze.

If we are to be hair-splittingly accurate, that word "always," used in the Summary of § 48, must be trimmed by half the thickness of a hair. It is easy to lay out a hand where the three-suit Vienna Coup is required, but cannot be executed because South has no re-entry: of course in that event the squeeze fails. But since the odds against your ever holding such a hand are prohibitive, suppose we let "always" stand.*

A similar remark applies in § 50.

---

* It would be an over-statement to say that "always" must *always* be avoided, and that "never" must *never* be used; yet both words are dangerous, and should not be employed unless one is very sure of his ground.

Exercise 72.

NORTH		Bidding:			
♠ J 10 6 3					
♡ 8 3		EAST	SOUTH	WEST	NORTH
◊ 7 6		P	1 ◊	P	2 ♣
♣ A K Q J 9		P	3 NT	P	6 NT
		P	P	P	

SOUTH
♠ A 7 4
♡ A K 9
◊ A K Q 9 5
♣ 10 2

West leads ♡ Q.

T. 1: King wins.
T. 2: ◊ A.
T. 3: ◊ K. East discards a Heart.

Analysis 72.

WEST	EAST
♠ K Q 2	♠ 9 8 5
♡ Q J 10 6	♡ 7 5 4 2
◊ J 10 8 4 3	◊ 2
♣ 7	♣ 8 6 5 4 3

Of course a first-trick duck is out of the question, for if Diamonds are 4-2, one trick will have to be lost in that suit.

When Diamonds fail, look for a squeeze. No Heart-Diamond simple, for lack of (U). As the only hope, give West ♠ K Q. Then, he is subject to a triple squeeze. Watch it! South, opposite the squeeze-card, has a winner in North's suit (Spades), and North has no winner in any threat-suit: unless we cash ♠ A (Vienna Coup) ahead of the second Club, the triple squeeze will develop engine trouble.

52. *The repeating squeeze: Case II.* It is a simple matter to discover the conditions under which the second squeeze will occur in Case II, because the reasoning parallels that of § 49. You may verify the

Summary: When North (opposite the squeeze-card) holds two threats, a triple squeeze will never repeat against East. Against

*West it will always repeat if South has an entry in his own suit
and North in one of his; in all other cases, with rare exceptions,
the second squeeze will fail.*

Exercise 73.

	NORTH
♠	A 9 6 5 3
♡	6 2
◇	3 2
♣	Q 10 9 8

	SOUTH
♠	K 7 2
♡	A Q
◇	A K Q J 10 6 5
♣	A

Bidding:

WEST	NORTH	EAST	SOUTH
1 ♡	P	P	2 ♡
3 ♡	3 ♠	P	4 NT
P	5 ◇	P	6 NT
P	P	P	

West leads ♠ Q.

Analysis 73.

	WEST		EAST
♠	Q J 10 8	♠	4
♡	K J 10 8 7 4	♡	9 5 3
◇	—	◇	9 8 7 4
♣	K 7 2	♣	J 6 5 4 3

In rubber bridge the hand is routine. Win, return a Spade and duck, to set the Spade finesse; or, if you prefer, duck the first trick to establish the practically proved Spade-Heart squeeze. But in match play something better is required. Win, T. 1, and run the Diamonds. If East has ♣ K, West will discard all his Clubs, and the Spade throw-in, T. 11, will compel him to lead a Heart for contract. But if West has ♣ K, as indicated by his bid, he is in the grip of a repeater for an overtrick.

53. *Case III: Three threats opposite the squeeze-card.* When North holds all three threats, the squeeze always succeeds against West. Against East it always fails, for the obvious reason that North must discard a threat on the squeeze-trick, thereby releasing East's guard.

For the same reason—that one threat will have been discarded—the squeeze cannot possibly repeat under any circumstances.

Exercise 74.

NORTH
♠ A K Q 3
♡ 10 7 6
◇ 3 2
♣ K 8 3 2

Bidding:

SOUTH	WEST	NORTH	EAST
1 ◇	Dbl.	Rdbl.	2 ♣
3 ◇	P	3 ♠	P
4 ◇	P	5 ◇	P
6 ◇	P	P	P

SOUTH
♠ 6 5 2
♡ A 5
◇ A K Q 10 7 6 5
♣ 5

West leads ♡ K.

T. 1: Ace wins.
T. 2: Diamond. Both follow.

Analysis 74.

WEST	EAST
♠ J 10 9 7	♠ 8 4
♡ K Q J 4 3	♡ 9 8 2
◇ 8	◇ J 9 4
♣ A Q 9	♣ J 10 7 6 4

The hand literally plays itself. Poor West cannot even indulge in any deception.

x x x x

The practical importance of Case III is slight, for two reasons. First, it is comparatively rare in play. Second, even when it is present, very often some other line of play will seem to offer a better chance of success. Therefore, there will be no further reference to Case III in this book.

54. *The double threat.* It may happen that Declarer's holding in one threat-suit is such that if that suit is given up by the defender, two tricks will be established at once. Such a threat is called a *double threat*, to distinguish it from the simple or one-trick threats with which we have dealt hitherto.

It has seemed best not to mention the double threat previously, in order to avoid discussing too many subjects at once. Nevertheless this weapon is a highly useful adjunct to the triple squeeze. Not infrequently, when the conditions for repetition are wanting, a double threat can be dug up, to produce that second trick.

In Case I, let North hold *a double threat accompanied by an entry in its own suit.* Now, return to § 49. We found that West "can always escape the second squeeze merely by establishing North's threat." But here, this strategy would hand Declarer two tricks at once. The only alternative is to establish one of South's threats, whereupon the lead of that threat immediately inflicts the simple squeeze. That is, West can take his choice—heads you win, tails he loses.

In Case II—North holding two threats—give South *a double threat with an entry in its own suit.* Here also it is easily seen that the defender—either one—is invariably out of luck.

There remain two other possibilities: the two-trick threat has no entry in its own suit; or, that threat lies in the hand containing two threats. Almost always in these cases, the double threat is no better than a simple threat: that is, if the second member of the double threat were replaced by a worthless card, the net result—success or failure as the case might be—would be unaffected.

Summary: When the lone threat—North's in Case I, South's in Case II—is a double threat accompanied by an entry in its own suit, the squeeze always gains two tricks against either defender. In all other cases, with rare exceptions, the double threat is merely equivalent to a simple threat.

Exercise 75.

	NORTH		Bidding:			
♠	K 6 4 3					
♡	A K Q 5		EAST	SOUTH	WEST	NORTH
◇	Q 2		P	1 ♠	P	2 ♡
♣	J 7 4		P	3 ♣	P	4 ♠
	SOUTH		P	4 NT	P	5 ◇
♠	A Q J 10 2		P	5 NT	P	6 ♡
♡	6 2		P	7 ♠	P	P
◇	A		P			
♣	A K 6 5 3		West leads ◇ J.			

T. 1: East plays ◇ 8.
T. 2: Spade. East discards ◇ 5.

Analysis 75.

	WEST			EAST	
♠	9 8 7 5		♠	—	
♡	J 4 3		♡	10 9 8 7	
◇	J 10 9 4 3		◇	K 8 7 6 5	
♣	9		♣	Q 10 8 2	

In view of the Spade division, there is a fine chance that East holds all the stoppers. The hand is about as difficult as patronizing a vending machine. Just deposit your nickel—five Spades—and out pops the contract. One tiny point: one Club should be cashed ahead of the last Spade, on the chance that ♣ Q is single.

Exercise 76.*

	NORTH		Bidding:			
♠	A Q 5 2					
♡	A Q 7 5		SOUTH	WEST	NORTH	EAST
◇	5 4		2 ♣	P	2 ♠	P
♣	8 7 5		3 ◇	P	3 ♡	P
	SOUTH		3 NT	P	4 NT	P
♠	6		5 ♡	P	5 NT	P
♡	6		7 NT	P	P	Dbl.
◇	A K Q 7 3		P	P	P	
♣	A K Q J 6 2		West leads ♠ J.			

* This hand was played by Mr. Harold S. Hemrick.

T. 1: Ace wins. East plays ♠ 4.
T. 2: Club. Both follow.
T. 3: Club. West discards ♡ 2.

Analysis 76.

WEST	EAST
♠ J 10 9 8 7	♠ K 4 3
♡ 10 9 8 3 2	♡ K J 4
♢ 8 2	♢ J 10 9 6
♣ 3	♣ 10 9 4

West discarded two Diamonds and East one, for a spread.

When West refuses, T. 3, East can see that he will have to find three discards. If he throws ♡ J 4 and ♠ 3 in that order (§ 45) and West keeps his Diamonds, they can at least make Declarer hesitate. East can help further by dropping his Nine on the first Diamond lead.

Exercise 77.

NORTH
♠ K 10 2
♡ Q 10 9 8
♢ K J
♣ K Q 4 3

Bidding:

WEST	NORTH	EAST	SOUTH
P	1 ♣	1 ♢	2 ♠
4 ♢	4 ♠	P	7 ♠
P	P	P	

West leads ♢ 10.

SOUTH
♠ A Q J 8 5 4 3
♡ A 7 4 2
♢ —
♣ A 5

T. 1: East plays ♢ Q; Declarer ruffs.
T. 2: Spade. East discards a Diamond.

Analysis 77.

WEST	EAST
♠ 9 7 6	♠ —
♡ 6 5	♡ K J 3
♢ 10 9 6 4 3 2	♢ A Q 8 7 5
♣ 8 6	♣ J 10 9 7 2

In his wild shot for a top board, South has climbed out on the end of a twig. For his bid, East is very likely to hold the Heart honors, and with West holding three Spades plus lots of

Diamonds, East undoubtedly has the Club length. If so, the triple squeeze is in force with threats ◊ K, ♣ 4, ♡ 7. But with North holding two threats, the squeeze will never repeat against East. No hope!

But look! Holding so many Spades and Diamonds, West probably has no more than two Hearts: if so, the closed hand has a double threat.

Following Dummy's third Heart discard East also will give a Heart, because this saves the day if West's Hearts are as good as 7 x or 6 x x.

55. *Double threat divided.* Although it is much less common than the situation discussed in § 54, a possibility worth keeping in mind is that the two members of a double threat may be divided between Declarer's two hands.

Exercise 78.

```
        NORTH
     ♠ K J 7
     ♡ A 9 5 4 3
     ◊ K 6 5 2
     ♣ 9


        SOUTH
     ♠ Q 10 9 8 4
     ♡ 10 6
     ◊ A Q 7
     ♣ Q 6 3
```

Bidding:

SOUTH	WEST	NORTH	EAST
P	1 NT	P	P
2 ♠	P	3 ♠	P
4 ♠	Dbl.	P	P
P			

West leads ♣ K.

T. 1: King wins. East plays ♣ 2.
T. 2: ♠ A.
T. 3: Spade. East follows.
T. 4: Club ruff.
T. 5: ◊ A.
T. 6-8: Spades.

Analysis 78.

```
        WEST                    EAST
     ♠ A 5                   ♠ 6 3 2
     ♡ K Q J                 ♡ 8 7 2
     ◊ J 9 8 4               ◊ 10 3
     ♣ A K 10 8              ♣ J 7 5 4 2
```

West sees that he can hold Declarer to his contract by discarding Diamonds; but the contract can be defeated if East has ♡ 10. Unquestionably West would abandon Hearts, establishing the divided double threat for an overtrick.

56. *The double threat in simple squeeze.* In addition to the three typical simple squeezes (§§ 5, 12, 13), variant forms are possible. For one such, see the hand below. In triple squeeze the double threat is a common phenomenon. In simple squeeze it is rare indeed: in fact, this hand is the only one of its kind that this writer recalls having seen, from play.

Exercise 79.*

NORTH
♠ Q J
♡ K 7 6 5
◊ A K 3 2
♣ K 7 6

SOUTH
♠ K 10 9 8
♡ A Q
◊ J 7 6 5
♣ A Q 2

Bidding:

SOUTH	WEST	NORTH	EAST
1 NT	P	6 NT	P
P	P		

West leads ♣ 10.

T. 1:   East plays ♣ 3. Queen wins.
T. 2:   ♠ 8 led. East's Ace wins.
T. 3:   ♡ 10 led. Ace wins; West plays ♡ 2.
T. 4-5: Spades. Both follow.
T. 6:   Spade. East discards ♣ 8.

Analysis 79.

WEST	EAST
♠ 5 4 3 2	♠ A 7 6
♡ J 3 2	♡ 10 9 8 4
◊ 8 4	◊ Q 10 9
♣ 10 9 5 4	♣ J 8 3

After six tricks the indications are that East held four Hearts and three Diamonds: if so, he is doomed. On the Spades, Dummy has discarded Diamonds. Now Declarer cashes the

---

* This hand was played by Mrs. Lorraine Heinrick, of Detroit, and reported by Mr. Frank S. Eaton in the Detroit Free Press.

Clubs. If East gives a Heart, the result is obvious; if he yields a Diamond, South cashes the Diamond tops, returns to ♡ Q and makes the good Diamonds.

This hand is highly interesting, not only as a playing problem, but from the theoretical standpoint as well. With ◊ 5, ♣ 3 traded, is BLUE present? No. (L) and (U) are OK. (E) is present for the Diamond threat, but if that entry (♡ Q) is used and the Diamond threat cashed, North's ♡ K will go to sleep, for no net gain. That is: with ◊ 5, ♣ 3 traded, East can discard a Diamond without costing his side anything, which means that he is not "Busy in two suits." But as the cards lie, BLUE (variant form) is in hand. If East establishes the *double threat*, sacrifice of the Heart winner leaves a net gain of one trick.

It is also interesting to note that with the East-West hands interchanged, this would be an ordinary simple squeeze of the second type (§ 12). West leads ♡ 10; West wins the Spade and leads another Heart; Declarer finishes the Spades, discarding a Club and a Diamond; now the third Club puts the bee on West.

57. *Multiplicity of double threats.* Hands containing two double threats are rare indeed.[*] The following hand—the only one of its kind that we have ever seen or heard of, from play[**]— contains *three double threats*.

Exercise 80.

NORTH
♠ Q J 5
♡ A K 9 6 4
◊ A K J 9 2
♣ —

SOUTH
♠ A K 3 2
♡ J 7
◊ 7 6
♣ A K Q 10 9

Bidding:

WEST	NORTH	EAST	SOUTH
P	1 ♡	P	2 ♣
P	3 ◊	P	4 NT
P	5 ♡	P	5 NT
P	6 ♡	P	7 NT
P	P	P	

West leads ♠ 10.

[*] See George S. Coffin, Endplays, p. 103.
[**] Declarer was Mr. Carlos Palmer, of Ann Arbor, Mich. The hand occurred in a rubber bridge game in December, 1955.

T. 1: Jack wins. East plays ♠ 6.
T. 2: ♠ Q. East discards ♡ 2.

Analysis 80.

	WEST		EAST
♠	109874	♠	6
♡	103	♡	Q852
◊	853	◊	Q104
♣	762	♣	J8543

At first check there are two mildly promising chances: Clubs
unbalanced with the Jack short, or Diamonds 3-3 with the Queen
at the left. After two tricks the triple squeeze—always a possibility, of course—looms up more prominently. Declarer cashes
two Hearts and a Diamond to reduce the danger of ambiguity,
then finishes the Spades.

To the student of bridge theory the hand is one of the most
interesting in this book. You must be sure to see that all three
double threats are "effective": that is, if any one were replaced
by a simple threat, East could kill the hand by establishing
the simple threat. Also, if Dummy held so much as one Club,
each of the red threats would be "merely equivalent to a simple
threat."

x x x x

The celebrated hand following, known as "The Great Vienna
Coup," was propounded in Vienna around the middle of the
nineteenth century as a double-dummy problem in whist. South,
on lead with Clubs as trumps, is supposed to take thirteen
tricks. To translate this into bridge terms, merely have West
lead a Club to South's seven Notrump.

Exercise 81.

NORTH	Contract
♠ J 10 3	
♡ A K Q J 3	7 Notrump by South.
◇ 5 2	
♣ 7 4 2	West leads ♣ 8.

SOUTH
♠ A Q
♡ 2
◇ A Q 7 6 4 3
♣ A K Q 3

T. 1-3: Clubs break 3-3.

Analysis 81.

WEST	EAST
♠ K 6	♠ 9 8 7 5 4 2
♡ 10 9 7 6 5	♡ 8 4
◇ J 10 8	◇ K 9
♣ 8 6 5	♣ J 10 9

As the only chance, assume that ◇ K is on side. Then, if Hearts run and the Spade-Diamond stoppers are together, the hand makes by simple squeeze. If Hearts fail, the only chance is a triple squeeze. In either case, ♠ A must be cashed (Vienna Coup) before crossing the table.

This hand contains two double threats—Spade, Diamond— but is not a genuine specimen of two-double-threater, because the play proceeds in the same way and leads to the same result, with the Spade replaced by a simple threat. To see this, merely discard a Spade on the fourth Club, regardless of what West has done. This is just one more example of the fact that when a double and a simple threat lie in the same hand, the former is no better than a simple threat.

West leads a Club because required to do so by the conditions of the original problem. In play he probably would lead a Heart, spilling all the beans. But if he leads a Diamond, we discover in another way that the Spade double threat is counterfeit. Now, on the fourth Club Declarer discards a Spade willy-nilly, yet his play remains intact.

Exercise 82.

NORTH	Bidding:			
♠ Q J 9				
♡ A K 9 8 3	NORTH	EAST	SOUTH	WEST
◇ A K 9 5 3	1 ♡	P	1 ♠	P
♣ —	3 ◇	P	4 NT	P
	5 ♡	P	5 NT	P
SOUTH	6 ♡	P	7 NT	P
♠ A K 5 3 2	P	P		
♡ 7 2				
◇ 7 6	West leads ♡ Q.			
♣ A K Q 10				

T. 1: King wins. East plays ♡ 4.
T. 2: ♠ Q. West discards ♡ 5.
T. 3: ◇ K. East plays ◇ 10, West ◇ 2.

Analysis 82.

WEST	EAST
♠ —	♠ 10 8 7 6 4
♡ Q J 10 5	♡ 6 4
◇ Q J 10 2	◇ 8 4
♣ J 8 5 4 3	♣ 9 7 6 2

Here is a hand containing two genuine double threats, for if either of the reds were a simple threat, West could escape by establishing that threat. (Trade from North's hand two Hearts for East's Diamonds or two Diamonds for East's Hearts.)

58. *Squeeze on the first trick.* The statement is sometimes made that a squeeze may culminate as early as the second trick, the implication being clear that no squeeze can happen on the first trick. Just for fun, suppose we investigate.

As regards the two-suit squeeze, the argument runs as follows. If in any suit Declarer holds six winners plus a small card, the suit will surely run. Thus the maximum number of winners that he can hold in a threat-suit is five. Hence, the maximum number of busy cards in the defender's hand, in any threat-suit, is six: five to follow suit on Declarer's five winners plus a sixth to kill the threat. It follows that in two threat-suits the maximum number of busy cards is twelve, which leaves the defender an idle card to play on the first trick. Consequently, no simple squeeze can occur on the first trick.

It is, however, the easiest job imaginable to construct three-suit squeezes climaxing on the first trick, although apparently no such hand is on record from play.

Example (a):

```
              NORTH                Bidding:
              ♠ 4
              ♡ A K Q J 10 4       NORTH   EAST   SOUTH   WEST
              ◇ —                  2 ♡     P      2 ♠     P
              ♣ A K Q J 10 3       3 ♣     P      3 ◇     P
                                   3 ♡     P      3 ♠     P
    WEST                EAST       4 ♣     P      4 ◇     P
  ♠ K Q J 7 6 5      ♠ —           6 ♣     Dbl.   6 ◇     Dbl.
  ♡ 3                ♡ 9 8 7 6 5 2 6 ♡     Dbl.   6 ♠     Dbl.
  ◇ J 9 7 5 3 2      ◇ A           P       P      6 NT    Dbl.
  ♣ —                ♣ 9 8 7 5 4 2 P       P      Rdbl.   P
                                   P       P
              SOUTH
              ♠ A 10 9 8 3 2
              ♡ —                  West leads ♠ K.
              ◇ K Q 10 8 6 4
              ♣ 6
```

East cogitates. If Declarer holds ♠ A, a Heart or Club discard solidifies the contract. Since if the contract makes he is assured of a bottom anyway, East discards his Ace on the chance that West, who doubled Diamonds, has the King.

When asked about the bidding, South replied: "No comment." But you must admit she played the hand well—an overtrick!

Example (b):

NORTH
♠ A J 10 9 8 3
♡ 7
♢ A K Q 5 2
♣ 7

Contract

7 Notrump by South.

West leads ♠ K.

WEST
♠ K Q 7 5 4 2
♡ 4
♢ J 9 3
♣ 8 6 3

EAST
♠ —
♡ 10 9 8 5 3
♢ 8 7 6 4
♣ J 10 9 2

SOUTH
♠ 6
♡ A K Q J 6 2
♢ 10
♣ A K Q 5 4

Etaoin shrdlu!

PROBLEMS

Problem 20.*

	NORTH	Contract
♠	A 6 4 3 2	6 Hearts by South.
♡	K J	West leads ♡ 5.
◊	K 2	
♣	10 9 4 2	

	SOUTH
♠	K J 5
♡	A Q 10 9 4
◊	Q 10 4
♣	A Q

T. 1: King wins.
T. 2: ♠ 2 led. East plays Queen; King wins.
T. 3: ♡ A. Both follow.
T. 4-5: Hearts. West discards ♣ 6, ◊ 3.
T. 6: ◊ 4 led. Dummy plays King; East's Ace wins.
T. 7: ♣ 3 led. Ace wins.

Solution 20.

WEST		EAST	
♠	10 9 8 7	♠	Q
♡	5 3	♡	8 7 6 2
◊	J 7 5 3	◊	A 9 8 6
♣	K 8 6	♣	J 7 5 3

Due to Declarer's accurate guess in refusing the Club finesse, after seven tricks a standard triple squeeze is set up, with threats ♠ 6 4 (double threat), ◊ 10, ♣ Q. In the play, West gave up first Diamonds, then Clubs. Note that if Declarer makes the mistake of discarding a Spade on the Hearts, West can escape by abandoning Spades.

* This hand was played by Mr. Sam Seplowin, of Chicago, and reported by Mr. Frank S. Eaton in the Detroit Free Press. The bidding is not available.

Problem 21.

NORTH
♠ K 10 3 2
♡ 10
◇ K 9 6 5 2
♣ K Q 6

Bidding:

NORTH	EAST	SOUTH	WEST
1 ◇	P	2 ♣	P
2 ♠	P	3 NT	P
6 NT	P	P	P

SOUTH
♠ A 5
♡ K 9 6
◇ A Q 3
♣ A 10 5 4 2

West leads ♡ 7.

T. 1: East plays ♡ Q. King wins.
T. 2: ◇ A. East discards ♡ 2.
T. 3: ♣ Q. Both follow.
T. 4: ♣ K. West discards a Diamond.
T. 5-7: Clubs. West discards ♡ 8 J and ♠ 7.
T. 8: ♠ A. West plays ♠ J.

Solution 21.

WEST	EAST
♠ J 9 7	♠ Q 8 6 4
♡ A J 8 7	♡ Q 5 4 3 2
◇ J 10 8 7 4	◇ —
♣ 8	♣ J 9 7 3

North "learned bridge" just last month, and she thinks bidding is such fun!

After eight tricks: West is clearly in the jaws of a repeater. Cash ♠ K, dropping the Queen, whereupon ♠ 10 will inflict the Heart-Diamond squeeze, for an overtrick.

Don't be so piggish! You know that chap West—he would steal his grandmother's false teeth and pawn them for cigarette money. You lead a Heart.

Evidently the contract is assured after five tricks, on the bridge-certainty that West has ♡ A J. West's only chance is to make the key discard (♡ J) early and bolster it with some monkey business in Spades, in hope of imbuing South with delusions of grandeur.

Problem 22.

	NORTH
♠	K Q 10
♡	A 9 6 5
◊	Q 10
♣	K 10 6 3

	SOUTH
♠	J 8 7 5 2
♡	K J
◊	9 7 4 3
♣	A 9

Bidding:

WEST	NORTH	EAST	SOUTH
1 NT	P	P	2 ♠
P	4 ♠	P	P
P			

West leads ♠ 6.

T. 1: East follows.
T. 2: ◊ Q led. East plays ◊ 2; West, ◊ K.
T. 3: ◊ J led. East plays ◊ 5.
T. 4: ♠ A led. East follows.
T. 5: Spade led. East discards ◊ 6.

Solution 22.

	WEST		EAST
♠	A 9 6	♠	4 3
♡	Q 10 8	♡	7 4 3 2
◊	A K J 8	◊	6 5 2
♣	Q J 8	♣	7 5 4 2

On the bidding, there is a good chance that East has a Yarborough. If so, West will crumble on the last Spade.

This hand exhibits the exceptional case mentioned in § 52 (Summary). South holds an entry in each of North's suits: thus, no matter what West does, the second entry-condition (§ 12) will be in effect for the second squeeze.

If South commits the bush-league blunder of parting with ♠ 10, T. 1 or T. 4, the hand can be defeated, with East's two trebly-guarded Sevens playing the stellar role. (We leave it to you.)

Problem 23.

NORTH			
♠ 854			
♡ A K Q 10 8 7			
◊ —			
♣ A 7 6 5			

Bidding:

WEST	NORTH	EAST	SOUTH
P	1 ♡	P	3 ◊
P	4 ♡	P	4 NT
P	5 ♡	P	7 NT
P	P	P	

SOUTH
♠ A J 6
♡ 6 5
◊ A K Q J 10 5 4
♣ Q

West leads ♠ 10.

T. 1: East plays ♠ Q.
T. 2: Diamond. Both follow.
T. 3: Diamond. East plays ♠ 2.

Solution 23.

WEST	EAST
♠ 10 9 7	♠ K Q 3 2
♡ 9	♡ J 4 3 2
◊ 9 8 7 3 2	◊ 6
♣ 9 8 4 3	♣ K J 10 2

Neglect as usual the trivial case—Heart run. Then, the only chance seems to be Spade-Heart squeeze—undoubtedly against East. But this squeeze will fail because it is impossible to cash ♣ A—free winner—and then return.

Hold it! There is a chance after all. If we discard ♣ A and East holds ♣ K, he will be subject to a triple squeeze. Will this squeeze gain two tricks? Obviously yes.

Evidently this is another case where two losers are better than one (review Ex. 58).

Problem 24.

NORTH
♠ A K 8 2
♡ 6 5 3
◊ 8 6 5
♣ J 8 3

SOUTH
♠ Q 6 3
♡ A K 9 7
◊ 1 0 9 4 3
♣ A K

Bidding:

NORTH	EAST	SOUTH	WEST
P	P	1 ♣	P
1 ♠	P	1 NT	P
P	P		

West leads ◊ 2.

T. 1: East's Ace wins.
T. 2: ◊ J led. West plays ◊ 7.
T. 3: ♠ J led.

Solution 24.

WEST
♠ 7 5
♡ J 4
◊ K Q 7 2
♣ 9 6 5 4 2

EAST
♠ J 10 9 4
♡ Q 10 8 2
◊ A J
♣ Q 10 7

There is probably nothing to the hand except to take the contract and go home, but it can cost nothing to try. The first duty, clearly, is to lose some tricks. So, win with the Queen, T. 3, and lead a Diamond. The average West would cash his other Diamond, but this West, being a squeeze-player himself, leads a Spade. You win, cross in Clubs, and push out the Diamond (losing squeeze-card). East, hoping to hold you to one overtrick at most, would contribute another Heart, establishing the concealed double threat. Any other play by East would lead to the same result.

CHAPTER VI

ADVANCED THREE-SUIT SQUEEZES

59. *Preliminary survey.* We have now finished our study of the basic or typical forms of three-suit squeeze, viz. those forms in which Declarer has *two losers* remaining, and proceed to consider some positions that may be less familiar to the average reader.

If your time is limited, you may omit this chapter without serious damage to your game. While it is true that any one of the forms treated might confront you tomorrow, nevertheless the combined frequency of all of them is not high. This means that the space devoted to this subject is somewhat out of proportion to its practical importance. It has seemed worth while to take that space, for three reasons. First, some of the situations in prospect have never before been systematically studied, so far as can be determined. Second, a number of them are so keenly interesting, merely as problems in analysis, that surely some readers will enjoy studying them for their own sake, apart from any thought of their playing value. Third and most important: if you should encounter one of these forms and are able to recognize and handle it, you are quite likely to score a clean top, even against good competition.

The first part of the chapter will be devoted to the three-suit strip-squeezes (three losers or more), the latter part to one-loser squeezes.

Perhaps this is the spot for a general remark. It may be that the reader becomes weary of this incessant harping on "number of losers." But anyone who does not realize that *the loser-count*

155

is the central feature in all squeeze play, from the simple squeeze up, should go back to the foot of the class and start all over again. "How many losers do I have? How many can I stand? If I can't reduce my loser-count, what squeezes (if any) are available with the number I have now?" These questions should spring to mind instantly, just as soon as you begin to consider the possibility of a squeeze.

60. *The three-suit strip-squeeze: vulnerable stopper.* Suppose that one defender is solely responsible for three suits, with at least *one stopper vulnerable.* Say also that Declarer has three or more losers in hand. The first thought would be to duck down to one of the plays already in our repertoire; but for any one of a variety of reasons, this might be inadvisable or even impossible. Then, Declarer resorts to *three-suit strip-squeeze.* Just as in §§ 38-39, the plan is to effect a throw-in that will ultimately force a lead from the vulnerable stopper.

Exercise 83.

	NORTH	EAST	SOUTH	WEST	NORTH
♠	K 7	1 ◊	4 ♡	P	P
♡	A 4 2	P			
◊	8 7 6 4 3				
♣	A Q 2		Bidding:		

	SOUTH	
♠	J 3	West leads ◊ J.
♡	K Q J 9 8 7 6	
◊	A 10	
♣	9 8	

T. 1: East plays ◊ 2. Ace wins.

Analysis 83.

	WEST		EAST
♠	Q 10 9 8 6 5	♠	A 4 2
♡	10 5 3	♡	—
◊	J	◊	K Q 9 5 2
♣	7 5 3	♣	K J 10 6 4

That East probably has ♣ K is indicated in two ways: by his bid, and by his play of ◊ 2, T. 1. Thus if he blanks his

King, Declarer will go up with the Ace. And unless he blanks the King, the Diamond throw-in will nail him. Nothing to do but run all the trumps.

Note that there are four losers.

Exercise 84.

NORTH	Bidding:
♠ J 4 2	
♡ 9 5 3	
◇ A K 9 8	
♣ Q 10 4	

SOUTH	WEST	NORTH	EAST
P	1 ♡	P	P
1 NT	P	P	P

West leads ♡ 6.

SOUTH
♠ Q 9 7
♡ K 10 8
◇ Q 7 5 2
♣ A J 2

T. 1: East plays Queen. King wins.
T. 2-3: Diamonds. Both follow.
T. 4: Diamond. West discards ♣ 3.
T. 5: Diamond. West discards ♡ 2; East, ♠ 3.

Analysis 84.

WEST	EAST
♠ A K	♠ 10 8 6 5 3
♡ A J 7 6 4 2	♡ Q
◇ 6 4	◇ J 10 3
♣ K 7 3	♣ 9 8 6 5

West's Heart discard shows that he is in straits. While Declarer cannot read the situation with certainty, the Heart throw-in is clearly suggested. Although there are seven losers, the squeeze functions with precision and dispatch.

61. *Correcting the count: three losers.* In three-suit stripsqueeze, when the defender is unable to retain a card of exit you may have any number of losers in hand, from three up (compare § 38). But when that card will have to be squeezed out, you must have *only three losers* (compare § 39).

The truth of these statements is easily proved. The standard three-suit squeeze (Chap. V) matures with two losers. Here the victim must keep an exit open, which puts an extra busy card in his hand and ripens the squeeze one trick earlier. To prove the possibility of failure with more than three losers, a single example is sufficient: see Ex. 85. (Of course other examples are easily found.)

In the standard (two-loser) triple squeeze the location of threats is restricted in two ways: there is not room for all three in the same hand with the squeeze-card, and the squeeze will fail if all three lie at the right of the busy defender (§ 53). In the vulnerable-stopper strip-squeeze there are no restrictions: all three threats and the squeeze-card may lie in either hand, due of course to the fact that the presence of an extra loser opens up an extra space. See, for example, Ex. 85.

Exercise 85.

NORTH	Bidding:
♠ 6 4 3	
♡ A Q J 9 7 6	
◇ J 2	
♣ Q 7	

EAST	SOUTH	WEST	NORTH
1 ♠	Dbl.	P	3 ♡
4 ♠	4 NT	P	P
P			

SOUTH	
♠ A 8	
♡ K 8 4 3 2	
◇ A 9 5	
♣ A 6 5	

West leads ♠ 2.

T. 1: East plays ♠ 9. Declarer ducks.
T. 2: Spade. West plays ♣ 4.

Analysis 85.

WEST	EAST
♠ 2	♠ K Q J 10 9 7 5
♡ 10 5	♡ —
◇ 10 8 6 4 3	◇ K Q 7
♣ J 10 9 8 4	♣ K 3 2

South, feeling that he is being gypped out of a vulnerable game by a non-vulnerable East, decides to shoot the works.

Since West's lead is undoubtedly a singleton, the usual reason for ducking is not present. But with all those Spades and nothing much else, East would have pre-empted originally. Thus he has a strong hand, probably including all the invisible high cards, which means that a three-suit strip-squeeze is ahead. Although he can see no advantage in so doing, just on general principles Declarer loses the first trick (Anal. 16, last sentence). Now the last Heart neatly closes the exit.

NORTH
♠ 6 4
♡ J
◇ J 2
♣ Q 7

WEST
♠ —
♡ —
◇ 10 8 6
♣ J 10 9 8

EAST
♠ Q J
♡ —
◇ K Q 7
♣ K 3

SOUTH
♠ 8
♡ —
◇ A 9 5
♣ A 6 5

Suppose that South, not knowing his strip-squeezes, wins the first trick. Now, this is the end position. On the last Heart East blithely sheds another Spade, then makes a graceful exit on the third Diamond.

These are tricky situations. A close look is required in order to see the difference between Exs. 83 and 85. In the latter, the first trick may be ducked with safety, and unless this is done the squeeze will fail. In the former, if Declarer ducks "on general principles," West will respond to his partner's ◇ 2 by leading a Club, and the hand dissolves. But in this case four losers do no harm.

x   x   x   x

In the two-suit problem (§ 39) you have one solid suit; in each of two other suits you have a card (the threat) higher than anything that the weak defender can produce; but there is a fourth suit—an *escape suit*. In that suit the victim is very apt to hold an exit card, and unless you duck down to two losers he will be able to keep that card.

In the present problem you have one solid suit, and *in each of the other three suits* you have a threat higher than anything held by the victim's partner: in other words, there is no "escape suit." Thus the first thought might be that no exit would be possible in any case. That this is not true is shown by Ex. 85. The loophole is this. In one threat-suit (Diamonds above) the defender holds *enough high cards to kill the threat*, and has in addition, in that suit, a possible card of exit. But with ♠ 3 traded for ◇ 3 in Ex. 85, it would be perfectly safe to win the first trick. (Play it.)

In the two-suit problem the failing case—that is, the case where you must correct the count or come a cropper (§ 41)— is quite common.* Here, on account of the peculiar condition just stated—"enough high cards," etc.—the failing case is comparatively rare.

62. *The three-suit strip-squeeze: delayed duck.* Like the vulnerable-stopper squeeze, the delayed-duck squeeze also has its three-suit counterpart. Just as in § 43, the three requisites are CLE—*companion, lead, entry.* Also, while you may or may not hold the master card in the throw-in suit, you must hold the master in at least one of the other threat-suits; for if not, on getting in the opponent could run off his full quota of tricks at once.

We have seen (§§ 60-61) that with rare exceptions the three-suit vulnerable stopper squeeze succeeds regardless of the number of losers. The same is true of the three-suit delayed duck, and for the same reason, viz. that there is no "escape suit." The exceptional case, where the squeeze will fail unless you correct the count, will be taken up in § 64.

* Here and in all similar contexts the word "common" means, of course, common among plays of the particular type under consideration. No endplay —not even the simple squeeze—is common in the broad sense of that word.

Exercise 86.

NORTH
♠ 7 6
♡ J 8
◇ A K Q 7 2
♣ Q 8 3 2

Bidding:

EAST	SOUTH	WEST	NORTH
1 ♠	Dbl.	P	3 ◇
P	3 NT	P	P
P			

SOUTH
♠ A 10 2
♡ A 9 4
◇ 5 4 3
♣ A K 10 5

West leads ♠ 8.

T. 1: East's Jack wins.
T. 2: ♠ K led. Ace wins; West follows.
T. 3: ♣ A. Both follow.
T. 4: ♣ Q. East discards ♡ 7.

Analysis 86.

WEST	EAST
♠ 8 5 4	♠ K Q J 9 3
♡ 10 6 5 3 2	♡ K Q 7
◇ 8	◇ J 10 9 6
♣ J 9 7 6	♣ 4

East's bid, very light anyway, seems to call for ♡ K Q. You have (presumably) eleven winners. Thus by staying off the first trick you fix the Spade-Heart simple squeeze.

Of course it may be that neither minor will run. If West has both, your play makes no difference; but if East has four Diamonds he is subject to a delayed duck. You will be unable to determine this fact, in time to use it, unless the second Diamond lead comes from the closed hand. This means that a Diamond must be laid down, T. 5. The third Club, T. 6, extorts a Spade from East; thus when West refuses Diamonds the duck is safe. (Play it with no Diamonds, and with two Diamonds, preceding the third Club.)

Note that this is a four-loser squeeze; also that if Declarer carelessly wins the first trick, the squeeze—now with five losers —is still in force.

63. *Repeated duck.* The extraordinary hand following—believed to be the only one of its kind on record, from play*—illustrates a type of exceptional case that we have not previously developed.

*Exercise 87.**

NORTH
♠ A K J
♡ K Q 5 4 3
◇ 10 9 6
♣ 6 3

SOUTH
♠ 9 7 4
♡ A
◇ 8 7 4 3
♣ A K Q 8 4

Bidding:

NORTH	EAST	SOUTH	WEST
1 ♡	P	2 ♣	P
2 ♡	P	2 NT	P
3 NT	P	P	P

West leads ♠ 2.

T. 1: King wins. East plays ♠ 8.
T. 2: ♡ A.
T. 3: ♠ A. East plays ♠ 3.
T. 4: ♡ K. South discards a Club.
T. 5: ♡ Q. East discards ◇ J.

Analysis 87.

WEST
♠ 10 6 5 2
♡ J 10 9 8 2
◇ 5 2
♣ J 7

EAST
♠ Q 8 3
♡ 7 6
◇ A K Q J
♣ 10 9 5 2

Declarer, taking East at his word, abandons all thought of the Spade finesse, and runs his major-suit winners on the off-chance that something will turn up. Something does. While it is no certainty, South chooses to believe that East has the three Diamond tops plus four Clubs. So, discard the Club threat, T. 5, and hit East with the *triple delayed duck*: that is, lead Diamonds three times to establish the fourth.

* For the same type of situation, but in a highly artificial hand, see an article by Mr. Paul M. Hummell, of University, Ala.: Bridge World, Sept., 1953.

* This hand was played by Mr. Sam Seplowin, of Chicago, and reported by Mr. William S. Mouser in the Detroit News.

That three ducks were possible is remarkable enough; even more remarkable is the fact that the situation could be recognized in time to use it.

An instance of the double delayed duck, also from play, will be presented later.

x   x   x   x

It should be obvious that this phenomenon—repeated duck—may occur also in two-suit strip-squeeze (§ 43). For a striking example, merely trade ♠ Q J in Ex. 87. Now East is busy in two suits only, yet the operation of the squeeze is unaffected.

64. *The guaranteed case: three losers.* We know (§ 43) that the two-suit delayed duck is sure-fire with two losers, and may fail with more than that number. Thus we should expect to find that the three-suit squeeze is certain to succeed with three losers, and may fail with four or more. That this is the fact is easily shown. Since the argument parallels that of § 61, it may be omitted.

Exercise 88.

<table>
<tr><td colspan="5">NORTH</td></tr>
<tr><td colspan="5">♠ J 6</td></tr>
<tr><td colspan="5">♡ 5 4 2</td></tr>
<tr><td colspan="5">◇ K Q 10 7 4 3</td></tr>
<tr><td colspan="5">♣ 8 2</td></tr>
</table>

Bidding:

WEST	NORTH	EAST	SOUTH
P	P	1 ♡	Dbl.
P	3 ◇	3 ♡	3 NT
P	P	4 ♡	4 NT
P	P	P	

SOUTH
♠ A 5 2
♡ A 8
◇ A J 6 5 2
♣ A 10 6

West leads ♡ 9.

T. 1: East plays ♡ 10; Declarer ducks.
T. 2: ♡ J led. West plays ♡ 3.

Analysis 88.

WEST	EAST
♠ 10 9 8 7 4	♠ K Q 3
♡ 9 3	♡ K Q J 10 7 6
◇ 8	◇ 9
♣ 9 7 5 4 3	♣ K Q J

In view of East's ferocious bidding, there is a possibility that he held six Hearts and has all the black pictures: if so, we are in. The last Diamond extorts a Club, whereupon ♣ 10 can be set up. You must be sure to see that had the first trick been taken, the squeeze would have failed.

Note that the card pinched out is neither an exit card nor a surplus winner—merely a potential winner. No matter—all is grist that comes to this mill! (Anal. 60, last paragraph.)

65. *The two-trick gainer.* We know that in an important percentage of cases the pure three-suit squeeze (Chap. V) will gain two tricks. The same is true of the strip-squeezes. This may happen in any one of several ways. (a) The defender may unguard one of his stoppers, whereupon (under proper conditions) the new winner inflicts a two-suit strip-squeeze. Or, say that Declarer effects a delayed duck, creating one trick in the throw-in suit. (b) The defender may be vulnerable in each of the other suits, so that his return gives a second trick; or (c) Declarer may have held a double threat (§ 54) in the throw-in suit, so that the throw-in sets up two tricks at once.

All three of these cases are illustrated, according to West's discard, by the truly remarkable hand following.

Exercise 89.°

NORTH				
♠ K 10 7				
♡ A K Q J 10 8				
◊ 9 2				
♣ 9 4				

Bidding:

SOUTH	WEST	NORTH	EAST
1 ◊	P	1 ♡	P
2 ♣	P	3 ♡	P
5 ♣	P	6 ♡	P
6 NT	Dbl.	P	P
P			

SOUTH
♠ 5
♡ 9
◊ A K Q 10 5
♣ A Q J 10 6 3

West leads ♡ 7.

T. 1:   East follows.

T. 2-3: Hearts. Both follow.

T. 4-5: Hearts. West discards ♣ 5, ♠ J; East, ♠ 2, 3.

° This hand was played by Mr. Don Oakie, of San Francisco, and reported by Mr. William S. Mouser in the Detroit News.

Analysis 89.

	WEST	EAST
♠	A Q J	♠ 9 8 6 4 3 2
♡	7 4 2	♡ 6 5 3
◊	J 8 7 4	◊ 6 3
♣	K 8 5	♣ 7 2

From West's double it is morally certain that he has ♠ A and ♣ K, and very possibly a Diamond stopper as well. The closed hand discards ♣ 3, 10, J, Q, T. 2-5. After five tricks it looks as if West really is protecting something in Diamonds. So, on the last Heart, South pitches ◊ 10; West drops ♠ Q. Now the Spade throw-in does the work. Whether West returns a Diamond or a Club, Dummy has an entry to make his Spade.

Notice that the throw-in produces two Spade winners—item (c) above. However, the second Spade is unnecessary, because the Diamond return makes the Nine a winner—item (b). In fact, with ♠ Q J 10 traded for East's ♠ 4 3 2, the play and the result would be the same. Finally, if West discards a Diamond, the fourth Diamond winner completes the Spade-Club strip-squeeze—item (a).

It detracts not at all from the sparkling sheen of Declarer's performance to remark that this hand is tailor-made for our defensive Rule (§ 45). A glance at the table shows West that he will have to find three discards. If he throws ♣ 8 5 and ♠ Q in that order, it would seem that even this Declarer has his work cut out for him. West has one unmarked card—is it ♠ J or ♣ 7? But one question must be referred to higher authority. Dear Emily Post: Would it be proper for West to squirm *just a little* before dropping his Queen?

If there ever was a "constructed-looking" hand, this is surely it. Among many other strange features, two doubleton Nines, each playing a vital role! Had the hand been presented without reference to its origin, the reader would say with a shrug: "All very nice, except that it would never happen." But anything and everything will happen in bridge, if you just stick around!

x   x   x   x

Beside the items (a), (b), (c) listed above, there is a fourth way whereby a second trick may sometimes be gained. (d) With three losers in hand, Declarer effects a delayed duck. This loses a trick and creates a winner, thus at one stroke reducing the loser-count to one; whereupon, granted proper placement of threats and entries, the victim will be subject to a simple squeeze.

Exercise 90.

	NORTH		
♠	A Q 7 6 3		
♡	5 2		
◇	10 5 4		
♣	K 7 5		

Bidding:

WEST	NORTH	EAST	SOUTH
3 ♡	P	P	4 ♡
P	5 ♠	P	6 NT
P	P	P	

	SOUTH
♠	K 8 4
♡	A K
◇	A K 6 3
♣	A Q 4 2

West leads ♡ Q.

T. 1: East plays ♡ 10.
T. 2: Spade. West discards ♡ 3.
T. 3-4: ♣ K Q. Both follow.
T. 5: Heart. East discards a Spade.

Analysis 90.

	WEST		EAST
♠	—	♠	J 10 9 5 2
♡	Q J 9 8 7 6 4 3	♡	10
◇	9 8 2	◇	Q J 7
♣	9 6	♣	J 10 8 3

After two tricks, the best chance is that East has four Diamonds and three Clubs. In that event the Heart followed by the long Club will compel East to discard (a) a second Diamond, establishing the double threat for an overtrick, or (b) a Spade, whereupon the delayed duck will function. (Play it with ◇ 9, ♣ J traded.)

After five tricks it seems likely that East held three Diamonds and four Clubs. Then, we are home provided East's Diamonds include the two pictures. Duck a Spade, T. 6, and use the new Spade winner to inflict the Diamond-Club simple squeeze.

Evidently the second half of this two-trick gainer is pseudo. If East yields a Club, T. 5, Declarer will have no recourse but to finish the Clubs, squeezing Dummy: East discards whatever Dummy discards.

Note that unless Declarer wins the first Spade with the King, he himself assures the demise of the second squeeze.

Exercise 91.

NORTH
- ♠ 10 9 7
- ♡ A 7
- ◇ A Q J 6
- ♣ K J 6 5

SOUTH
- ♠ A 5 4 3
- ♡ Q 6 5
- ◇ K 10 4
- ♣ A 10 3

Bidding:

WEST	NORTH	EAST	SOUTH
1 ♠	Dbl.	P	2 NT
P	3 NT	P	P
P			

West leads ♠ K.

T. 1: East plays ♠ 8. King wins.
T. 2: ♠ Q led. East discards ◇ 2.

Analysis 91.

WEST
- ♠ K Q J 6 2
- ♡ K J 9
- ◇ 5
- ♣ Q 9 8 7

EAST
- ♠ 8
- ♡ 10 8 4 3 2
- ◇ 9 8 7 3 2
- ♣ 4 2

Since his bid was very light at best, it seems safe to give West ♡ K and ♣ Q. If his Clubs are exactly Q xx, we have ten tops. In case we pass the second trick, to set up a Spade-Heart simple squeeze, no dividends: both threats—♠ 5, ♡ Q —in the lower hand. But if we take the second trick and run the minors, West's last three cards will be ♠ J and ♡ K x, for a perfect toss-in.

Better look a bit further, though. West may have Club length, in which event there are only nine winners. By ducking the second trick we establish a standard triple squeeze with threats ♠ 5, ♡ Q, ♣ 6. Will this squeeze repeat? No, because West will throw his Club stopper on the seventh trick (last Diamond).

Better look a bit further. If we win the second trick and run the Diamonds, a delayed duck will be present provided West blanks his ♠ J, with threat ♠ 5, companion ♠ 4, lead ♠ 10, entry ♣ A; and since each of the other stoppers is vulnerable, a two-trick gain will result. But of course West will throw a Club on the last Diamond, whereupon the play proceeds as if he had held only three Clubs in the first place. That is: the second-trick win, followed by the Diamonds, produces five odd on the one assumption that West's bid was sound.

We know that in two-suit play, two losers may be better than one. Stepping up the loser-count as usual, we should expect to find that in three-suit play three losers may be better than two. This hand exhibits that fact.

66. *Triple squeeze with one loser.* We know that the standard triple squeeze matures with two losers still in Declarer's hand. It might seem that the one-loser triple squeeze would be merely equivalent to a simple squeeze: if the defender is unable to maintain his fences on two fronts, what matter whether or not he is busy on a third front?

The above generalization, plausible on its face, will not stand inspection. (It would hold, of course, in all cases where the simple squeeze is actually established or establishable.) The fact is that the one-loser three-suit squeeze has many applications. Some of these will be presented here and in § 67; but the most useful of all must be deferred to Chap. VII, where we shall find that this squeeze is the very backbone of a large family of highly important endplays.

There is good reason to feel sure, in advance of any investigation, that the one-loser triple squeeze will be useful on occasion, by this argument. The standard (two-loser) squeeze is completed by the last free winner. Here, with only one loser, the squeeze will occur one trick earlier, on the *next-to-last* free winner, which opens up another space in Declarer's hand. Anyone who has developed the slightest "feeling" for squeeze play knows without being told that this extra degree of freedom is bound to be a lifesaver in some cases.

Exercise 92.

NORTH
♠ K 7 4 3
♡ A Q 9 6 2
◊ A J
♣ 7 3

SOUTH
♠ A Q 5
♡ K J
◊ Q 5 2
♣ A K Q J 9

Bidding:

SOUTH	WEST	NORTH	EAST
2 NT	P	3 ♡	P
3 NT	P	4 NT	P
5 ♡	P	5 NT	P
7 NT	P	P	P

West leads ◊ 10.

T. 1: Ace wins. East plays ◊ 7.
T. 2: ♡ K.
T. 3: ♡ J. West plays ◊ 3.
T. 4: ♠ A. West plays ♠ 6; East, ♠ 2.
T. 5: ♣ A. Both follow.
T. 6: ♣ K. East discards ◊ 4.

Analysis 92.

WEST	EAST
♠ 9 6	♠ J 10 8 2
♡ 7	♡ 10 8 5 4 3
◊ 10 9 8 6 3	◊ K 7 4
♣ 10 8 6 5 2	♣ 4

A word about the bidding. North's second Blackwood assures South that there is no Ace off the hand, and he goes all the way on the strength of his great Club suit. Observe that thirteen tricks would be solid, but for the two bad divisions.

After six tricks, it is highly unlikely that West stops Spades (check it), but East very easily may. If so, there is no elementary squeeze in the hand: no Spade-Heart for lack of (U), no Heart-Diamond for lack of (E), no Spade-Diamond because it is impossible to cash the free winners without destroying (E). But the one-loser three-suiter brings succor: East will perish on the *next-to-last* Club top, at which stage Dummy still has an idle card.

The hand is unusual in that Declarer has no solid suit.

Exercise 93.

NORTH	Bidding:
♠ K 10 7	
♡ A K Q J 10 8	
◇ 9 2	
♣ 9 4	

SOUTH	WEST	NORTH	EAST
1 ◇	P	1 ♡	P
2 ♣	P	3 ♡	P
5 ♣	P	6 ♡	P
P	Dbl.	6 NT	P
P	P		

SOUTH
♠ 5
♡ 9
◇ A K Q 10 5
♣ A Q J 10 6 3

East leads ♠ 9.

T. 1: West's Ace wins.
T. 2: West leads ♡ 2.

Analysis 93.

WEST	EAST
♠ A Q J	♠ 9 8 6 4 3 2
♡ 7 4 2	♡ 6 5 3
◇ J 8 7 4	◇ 6 3
♣ K 8 5	♣ 7 2

This is Ex. 89 with North coming to his own rescue. Now, the outcome depends on East's lead. The case of present interest arises when a Spade is led.

If West carelessly returns a Spade, the simple squeeze is easily executed. But no great acumen is required of West to see that the only possible return is a Heart, because this cuts Declarer's communications. It is now impossible to cash the tops in either minor suit and then return to the closed hand:

---

* Use of this method in the present instance was suggested by Dr. Ben Dushnik.

therefore, no Spade-Diamond or Spade-Club squeeze. And the Diamond-Club fails because both threats are in the lower hand. But the one-loser three-suiter runs like a clock. (Play it.)

Note that the device adopted in Prob. 24 can be used here as an equally good alternative process:* discard on the Hearts all of South's Clubs except a small one. This converts the hand into a standard repeating squeeze: a case where two losers are not better than one, but just as good.

x x x x

One important difference between Exs. 92, 93 may have escaped your notice. In Ex. 92, the squeeze-card (*next-to-last* Club top) extracts Dummy's last idle card, so that on the last Club Declarer will have to discard one of the threats; in Ex. 93 Dummy has an idle card still in hand, available for play on the *last* Heart.

At double dummy this distinction would be trivial; in actual play it may be vital, in this way. When Declarer has to throw a threat-card on the last free winner, as in Ex. 92, serious ambiguity may still be present (though not, of course, in that particular hand); when the extra idle card is available, as in Ex. 93, the luckless victim *will have been squeezed twice* before Declarer has to make up his mind, and the danger of ambiguity is usually nil. To see the point more clearly, compare Exs. 89, 93. The fact was pointed out that in Ex. 89 foresighted discarding by West will give Declarer the meanest kind of guess, with the odds probably against his guessing right. But in Ex. 93, suppose that West does embark on a career of deception by discarding ♣ 8 5 in that order. That last Heart comes down, Dummy discards an idle Diamond—and what is West to do now, poor thing?

It is a nice exercise—left to the reader—to write out the conditions under which that extra idle card will be present.

67. *The simple guard squeeze.* Suppose that all conditions for simple squeeze are present except that (E) is lacking. It may be that in a third suit the victim has to keep certain cards *to protect his partner from a finesse.* Then, that third suit may provide the needed entry.

Example:

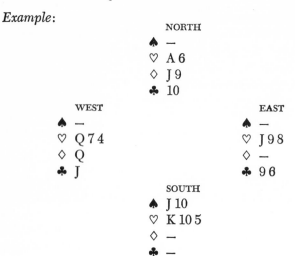

NORTH
♠ —
♡ A 6
◇ J 9
♣ 10

WEST
♠ —
♡ Q 7 4
◇ Q
♣ J

EAST
♠ —
♡ J 9 8
◇ —
♣ 9 6

SOUTH
♠ J 10
♡ K 10 5
◇ —
♣ —

On the next-to-last Spade West can discard a Heart, but the last ruins him. Note that East's ability to help in Hearts provides West with an extra idle card, because his Queen has to be kept only once guarded. It follows that this squeeze, unlike those of § 66, pinches on the *last free winner.*

This type of one-loser triple squeeze is called a guard squeeze, for the obvious reason that one defender guards his partner against a finesse.* More precisely, it is a *simple guard squeeze,* because only one opponent is squeezed.

68. *The standard forms.* There are only two simple guard squeeze positions that rate to be called typical, or standard. In the following formulation, South is assumed to hold the squeeze-card.

TYPE I: *East is the defender. A simple squeeze is present except that North has no entry in either threat-suit. In a third suit North holds a finessing combination which will be established unless East retains certain cards. This squeeze will fail unless South has a winner remaining in his own threat-suit when the squeeze is reached.*

TYPE II: *West is the defender. A simple squeeze is present except that North has no entry in either threat-suit. In a third*

---

* Since one opponent is responsible for two suits and carries half the load in a third, why not call this the two-and-a-half-suit squeeze?

suit North holds winner-and-small, and in that suit West must retain certain cards to protect his partner against a finesse by South.

It would seem that the guard-squeeze possibility is especially easy to overlook. When all conditions for simple squeeze are present except that (E) is lacking, do not fail to look for the possibility of an entry in that third suit.

Exercise 94.

NORTH
♠ A 10 6 5 4 3
♡ 7 6 2
◇ A J 9 7
♣ —

SOUTH
♠ K Q
♡ A K Q J 10 4
◇ 6 3
♣ A K J

Bidding:

SOUTH	WEST	NORTH	EAST
2 ♡	P	2 ♠	P
3 ♣	P	3 ◇	P
3 ♡	P	4 ♡	P
4 NT	P	5 ♡	P
7 NT	P	P	P

West leads ♠ 9.

T. 1: East plays ♠ 2.
T. 2: Spade. West discards a Club.

Analysis 94.

WEST
♠ 9
♡ 9 8 3
◇ Q 5 4 2
♣ 10 7 6 5 3

EAST
♠ J 8 7 2
♡ 5
◇ K 10 8
♣ Q 9 8 4 2

There are several simple-squeeze prospects, but for one reason or another all will fail. (Check it.) However, East is known to have at least one high Diamond, for if holding both West would have opened the suit. In case East also has ♣ Q, he is strapped in the hot seat right now. On the last two Hearts East would throw Clubs, because this saves the day if West has ♣ J xx.

A better way to play the hand would be to run all the Hearts at once, T. 2-7, because this might possibly elicit a helpful discard, and cannot do any harm (§ 35).

By cashing the two Clubs ahead of the last Heart (try it), you discover the truth, and come to realize the importance, of that last sentence in the statement of Type I. In all such spots as this, if South has no winner remaining in his own threat-suit, the number of busy cards held by North will equal the number held by East, and since North has to discard first, he will be squeezed. But if South has a winner still in hand, this gives East an additional busy card and makes room for an idle card in North's hand.

Exercise 95.

NORTH			
♠ A K 8 6			
♡ 10 2			
◊ 8 5 4 2			
♣ A 7 2			

Bidding:

NORTH	EAST	SOUTH	WEST
1 ♣	P	1 ♡	1 ♠
Dbl.	P	4 ♡	P
P	P		

SOUTH
♠ 9
♡ A K Q J 6 4
◊ J 7
♣ K 9 5 4

West leads ◊ K.

T. 1: East plays Ace.
T. 2: Diamond returned. Queen wins.
T. 3: ♠ Q led. King wins.
T. 4: Diamond ruff. East discards a Spade.
T. 5: ♡ 10. West discards a Spade.

Analysis 95.

WEST	EAST
♠ Q J 10 3 2	♠ 7 5 4
♡ —	♡ 9 8 7 5 3
◊ K Q 10 9 3	◊ A 6
♣ Q 10 3	♣ J 8 6

There seems to be little hope of the overtrick. West has the Spades and Diamonds, but the Spade-Diamond simple squeeze is out—neither threat accompanied by an entry. However, the hand is worth playing out on the chance that West has the three Club honors, in which event the next-to-last Heart will slay him.

To expect that West will hold all the high Clubs is asking a great deal, and more than is needed. If he holds any two of those cards, he is in the grip of a "two-and-a-half-suit" squeeze, and will buckle on the last Heart. Evidently no risk is involved in taking the finesse, T. 12, because West's last two cards are known.

Exercise 96.

NORTH	Bidding:			
♠ A Q				
♡ K 8 5 3	SOUTH	WEST	NORTH	EAST
◇ A K Q 9 3	1 ♠	P	3 ◇	P
♣ K Q	3 NT	P	4 NT	P
	5 ♡	P	5 NT	P
SOUTH	6 ◇	P	7 NT	P
♠ K 10 8 7 5	P	P		
♡ A 10 2				
◇ J	West leads ♣ J.			
♣ A 9 7 5				

T. 1: East follows.
T. 2: Club. East discards ♡ 4.
T. 3: ◇ J.
T. 4-5: ♠ Q A. Both follow.
T. 6: ◇ Q. Both follow.
T. 7: ◇ K. South discards a Heart, West a Club.

Analysis 96.

WEST	EAST
♠ 6 2	♠ J 9 4 3
♡ Q 7 6	♡ J 9 4
◇ 7 6	◇ 10 8 5 4 2
♣ J 10 8 6 3 2	♣ 4

After 6½ tricks it is known that East (if either) stops Diamonds, so assume it. If West stops Spades the hand will fail (check it), so give East that suit also. Now, no Spade-Diamond squeeze for lack of entry. But if East has any two of the three high Hearts, he will be guard-squeezed by the last Club. Note that if Declarer slops out ♠ K ahead of ♣ A, he waves goodby to one grand slam.

On the seventh trick South could have discarded ♣ 9 instead of ♡ 10. But *not* that priceless ♡ 2!

In Squeeze Play the statement is made that "BLU never squeezed anybody"; yet in these hands BLU did squeeze somebody. But of course not really, because (E) was there all the time. We just didn't recognize him at first—he looked so different in his new suit.

x x x x

A word in summary. The only time when you need to look for a simple guard squeeze is when all conditions for simple squeeze are present except that *a necessary entry is lacking.* It is easy to construct layouts where the necessary entry is present and where a guard squeeze is also present; but these turn out to be merely simple squeezes played the hard way. Thus the sphere of usefulness of the guard squeeze is restricted to the case stated.

69. *An exceptional case.* Let us look at a hand.

Exercise 97.

NORTH
♠ A K 10
♡ A K Q J 6 5 4
◇ 6 2
♣ 7

SOUTH
♠ —
♡ 8 7 3
◇ A K 10 5 4
♣ A J 10 4 2

Bidding:

NORTH	EAST	SOUTH	WEST
2 ♡	P	3 ◇	P
3 ♡	P	4 NT	P
5 ♡	P	5 NT	P
6 ♡	P	7 NT	P
P	P		

West leads ♣ K.

T. 1: East plays ♣ 3.
T. 2-4: Hearts. West discards ♣ 5, 6, 8.
T. 5-7: Hearts. West discards ♠ 2, 5, ◇ 7;
           East, ♣ 9, ♣ 3, 4.

Analysis 97.

WEST
♠ Q J 9 5 2
♡ —
◇ Q 8 7
♣ K Q 8 6 5

EAST
♠ 8 7 6 4 3
♡ 10 9 2
◇ J 9 3
♣ 9 3

South's wild lunge for a top has changed a boring laydown into an interesting hand. If West has the Spade-Diamond pictures, he is ripe for the harvest. Better than that: if he has the Spades and one Diamond, the guard squeeze will nip him.

<pre>
                          NORTH
                        ♠ A K 10
                        ♡ A
                        ◊ 6 2
                        ♣ —

        WEST   EAST
      ♠ Q J 9   ♠ 8 7 6
      ♡ —   ♡ —
      ◊ Q 8   ◊ J 9 3
      ♣ K   ♣ —

                          SOUTH
                        ♠ —
                        ♡ —
                        ◊ A K 10 5
                        ♣ J 10
</pre>

What happened? With all requisites for guard squeeze apparently present, how come it went bad?

As follows. Say that one player stops two suits and guards his partner in a third. If the number of Declarer's winners in the guard-suit equals the number of cards in that suit that must be retained by the defender, the squeeze is there; but *if the former number exceeds the latter,* the excess provides room for an extra idle card in the defender's hand, and the squeeze fails.

In this hand, the remedy is obvious: merely cash a Diamond, T. 2. But note that with ◊ 2 traded for a small black card, the hand cannot be made.

While this exceptional case is not common in play, one should always keep an eye open for it. When you hold in the guard-suit two tops and a middle card opposite two small, *cash one of the tops* before using up your entries.

x x x x

The next play in logical order would be the "double guard squeeze." But since this play is closely related to the compound squeeze, its discussion will be more easily followed after we have studied that squeeze (Chap. VII).

70. *A four-loser squeeze.* We know that two losers may be better than one (Ex. 58, Prob. 24), also that three may be better than two (Ex. 91). It will now be shown that in rare instances *four losers are better than three.*

Exercise 98.

	NORTH		
♠	A J 2		
♡	8 6		
◇	K Q 10 9 4		
♣	K Q 8		

Bidding:

WEST	NORTH	EAST	SOUTH
P	1 ◇	1 ♡	1 ♠
P	2 ♠	P	3 NT
P	P	P	

	SOUTH
♠	K 7 6 4
♡	A 7 3 2
◇	A 6 3
♣	A 2

West leads ♡ 5.

T. 1: East plays ♡ 9.

Analysis 98.

	WEST		EAST
♠	10 9 5	♠	Q 8 3
♡	5 4	♡	K Q J 10 9
◇	5	◇	J 8 7 2
♣	J 10 9 7 5 4 3	♣	6

That East stops Diamonds is more than normally unlikely in view of his length in Hearts, and West cannot stop the suit, even with five. (Of course the Ace should be played first, to guard against this contingency.) Thus eleven tricks are probably solid, with two chances for a twelfth—Spade finesse, or Spade-Heart simple squeeze if East appears to hold the Queen. Better duck the first trick to set the squeeze.

Any chump can take twelve tricks if Diamonds run and East has ♠ Q. Suppose we stop thinking à la novice and try to crash the big time. If the Spade-Heart squeeze is present, the two-loser strip-squeeze (§ 39) will serve exactly as well as the elementary form, so no gain can result from the duck.

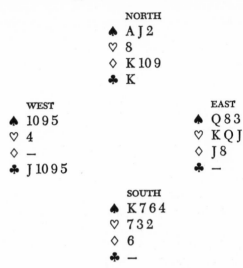

NORTH
♠ A J 2
♡ 8
◇ K 10 9
♣ K

WEST
♠ 10 9 5
♡ 4
◇ —
♣ J 10 9 5

EAST
♠ Q 8 3
♡ K Q J
◇ J 8
♣ —

SOUTH
♠ K 7 6 4
♡ 7 3 2
◇ 6
♣ —

Any chance of loss? Yes: though unlikely, it is possible that East has all three suits. In that event the hand is three-suit strip-squeeze, for ten tricks if you duck, eleven if you hang tight to those four precious losers. (Play it.)

The basic requirement for hands of this type is easily discovered: the hand containing *the last free winner* must have remaining a card of the enemy's suit, for the throw-in. Above, with ◇ 4 traded for ♡ 4, or ♠ 4 for ♣ 4, the duck would do no harm.

Every raw beginner would win that first trick as a matter of course—why lose a trick that you are able to win? It is amusing to note that while Declarer is not "thinking à la novice," he plays à la novice by winning the first trick.

PROBLEMS

Problem 25.

NORTH			
♠ J 7			
♡ 10 7			
◇ A K 6 5 2			
♣ K Q 4 2			

Bidding:

NORTH	EAST	SOUTH	WEST
1 ◇	P	2 NT	P
3 NT	P	P	P

West leads ♡ Q.

SOUTH
♠ A 6 3
♡ K 4 2
◇ Q 9 3
♣ A 8 7 6

T. 1: East's Ace wins.
T. 2: ♡ 6 led. West's Jack wins.
T. 3: ♠ 10 led. East plays Queen; Ace wins.
T. 4: Club. Both follow.
T. 5: Club. West discards a Spade.
T. 6: Diamond. Both follow.

Solution 25.

WEST	EAST
♠ 10 9 8 5 4	♠ K Q 2
♡ Q J 9 8 5 3	♡ A 6
◇ 7	◇ J 10 8 4
♣ 3	♣ J 10 9 5

After three tricks: West's shift, when one more lead would have established Hearts, indicates that he has no stopper or entry of any kind. So, assume that East stops both minors. Then, his last ten cards are ♠ K, four Diamonds, four Clubs, and one other: this last will be stripped out or squeezed out by the lead of ♡ K, T. 7.

However, careful play is required. Unless the first two Clubs are won by K Q, Dummy will be squeezed by the Heart. Also, the first Diamond must be won with the Queen, so that if and when West refuses Diamonds, there will be time to effect the duck. Finally, if you play ♠ J, T. 3, and East happens to hold a small Spade, he will escape by slipping ♠ K under ♡ K.

Observe that this is another hand (compare Ex. 88) where you fail unless you duck down to three losers.

Problem 26.[*]

NORTH	Bidding:			
♠ 8 3 2				
♡ A J	WEST	NORTH	EAST	SOUTH
◇ A K Q 7 3	1 ♠	2 ◇	P	2 NT
♣ Q 4 3	P	3 NT	P	P
	P			

SOUTH
♠ A K 9 5
♡ 9 8 6 2
◇ 8 2
♣ J 10 7

West leads ♡ 4.

T. 1: Jack wins.
T. 2-3: Diamonds. Both follow.
T. 4-5: Diamonds. West discards ♣ 5, ♠ 4.
T. 6: East leads a Heart.
T. 7: Diamond. West discards ♠ 6.

Solution 26.

WEST	EAST
♠ Q J 6 4	♠ 10 7
♡ K Q 5 4	♡ 10 7 3
◇ 9 4	◇ J 10 6 5
♣ A K 5	♣ 9 8 6 2

On the last Diamond South discards ♡ 9. West drops a Spade on the chance that Declarer has only A K remaining. And now Declarer has a problem. West holds ♠ Q J, ♡ K Q, ♣ A. Is his other card a Spade, or ♣ K? If the former, lead a Club;

[*] This hand was played by Mr. Robert Cole, of Dayton, Ohio, and recorded by Mr. William B. Woodson, who was so indiscreet as to hold West's cards.

if the latter, a Spade. Without ♣ K the opening bid would have been very light, so Declarer leads a Spade.

Suppose instead that West discards a Heart, T. 7. Now Declarer leads a Club (delayed duck). West cashes ♡ K, then leads a Spade; Declarer wins and ducks a second Club.

Problem 27.

NORTH
♠ A Q 3
♡ 8 6 5 2
◇ A 10 3
♣ A J 3

Bidding:

WEST	NORTH	EAST	SOUTH
1 ♡	Dbl.	P	2 ♠
P	3 ♠	P	4 ♠
P	P	P	

SOUTH
♠ K J 10 6 4 2
♡ Q 4 3
◇ K 8 5 4
♣ —

West leads ♡ K.

T. 1: East plays ♡ J.
T. 2: ♡ A. East discards ♣ 2.
T. 3: ♡ 7 led. East ruffs.
T. 4: Spade.

Solution 27.

WEST
♠ 5
♡ A K 10 9 7
◇ J 9 2
♣ K Q 6 5

EAST
♠ 9 8 7
♡ J
◇ Q 7 6
♣ 10 9 8 7 4 2

West probably holds ♣ K Q, but no Heart-Club squeeze for lack of (E). As the next best, hope that West holds ◇ Q J: then, a Heart-Diamond simple squeeze. Cash ♣ A, then run the trumps, discarding the Clubs. As the cards lie, no squeeze.

Once more, don't play so fast! The Diamond threat is the Eight, not the Ten. The Ten gives you one chance—that West has Q J. Using the Eight, you have three chances—West holding Q J, Q 9, or J 9. Discard ◇ 10 on the fifth Spade, then feed West that last Spade.

Problem 28.

	NORTH
♠	6 5 4 2
♡	9 6 4 2
◊	K 6 2
♣	J 5

	SOUTH
♠	A 10
♡	A K Q J 5
◊	A J 5
♣	A Q 6

Bidding:

WEST	NORTH	EAST	SOUTH
1 ♠	P	P	2 ♠
4 ♠	P	P	4 NT
P	P	P	

West leads ♠ K.

T. 1: East discards ♣ 2.

Solution 28.

	WEST
♠	K Q J 9 8 7 3
♡	7
◊	Q 8 7
♣	K 9

	EAST
♠	—
♡	10 8 3
◊	10 9 4 3
♣	10 8 7 4 3 2

On West's bidding, there is a fine chance that he has ♣ K and ◊ Q. If so, we have him. Duck, T. 1; run the Hearts; cross in Diamonds and toss him in, for contract. But this is no good: most tables will play the hand in Hearts, for a laid-down five.

Can we make five Notrump? Easily, if West has the two key cards. Merely win the first trick, keeping ♠ 10 available for the throw-in. No matter how he wriggles and squirms, West will take only two tricks. (Check it.)

Note that this hand is essentially identical with Ex. 98. Don't waste those beautiful losers!

Problem 29.

	NORTH
♠	K 10 2
♡	10 9 7 4 2
◇	7
♣	K 10 8 5

Bidding:

EAST	SOUTH	WEST	NORTH
P	1 ♣	P	1 ♡
P	3 NT	P	P
P			

	SOUTH
♠	A 7
♡	A J 8
◇	A K Q J 10 2
♣	6 2

West leads ♣ Q.

T. 1: King wins. East plays ♣ 7.
T. 2: Diamond. Both follow.

Solution 29.

	WEST		EAST
♠	Q J 4	♠	9 8 6 5 3
♡	K Q	♡	6 5 3
◇	6 5	◇	9 8 4 3
♣	A Q J 9 4 3	♣	7

In view of his own holding in Clubs, the original bid looks to West like exactly what it is—a lead-inhibitor. So he lays down his Queen, with excellent prospect (as he thinks) of establishing the whole suit at once.

Hoping that his partner has ♡ J, West discards a Heart on the last Diamond, setting up the hidden double threat. And now the last Heart puts West through the wringer again, for seven. Evidently the last two-thirds of this three-trick gainer is pseudo, because a Spade discard, T. 7, holds the hand to five.*

* For a squeeze gaining three tricks against any defense see Clyde E. Love, Bridge World, April, 1954.

CHAPTER VII

THE COMPOUND SQUEEZE

71. *An introductory example.* Let us look at a hand.

Exercise 99.

	NORTH			
♠	A 5 4			
♡	10 2			
◇	K 8 5 3 2			
♣	A K 2			

Bidding:

WEST	NORTH	EAST	SOUTH
P	1 ◇	P	2 ♠
P	3 ♠	P	4 NT
P	5 ♡	P	5 NT
P	6 ♡	P	7 NT
P	P	P	

	SOUTH
♠	K Q J 9 8 3 2
♡	A J
◇	A 4
♣	10 7

West leads ♡ 9.

T. 1: East plays ♡ Q. Ace wins.
T. 2: ♠ A.
T. 3: ♠ K. East discards a Heart.
T. 4-5: Spades. Both discard Hearts.
T. 6: Spade. West discards a Heart; East, ♣ 3.
T. 7: Spade. West discards ♣ 4; East, ♣ 5.

Analysis 99.

	WEST		EAST
♠	10 6	♠	7
♡	9 8 7 4	♡	K Q 6 5 3
◇	Q 9 6	◇	J 10 7
♣	Q 8 6 4	♣	J 9 5 3

185

With twelve tricks solidly assured, South decides to try for a clean top. When he sees the Dummy, he is glad that he dared.

A player who is skilled in elementary squeeze play sees almost at a glance that a squeeze is in hand if Diamonds are unevenly divided and East has ♡ K. In case East has the Diamonds, Heart-Diamond simple; if West has Diamonds, Type R double.

Our present Declarer, however, is made of sterner stuff. He sees that if East holds ♡ K a squeeze is certainly present and can certainly be inflicted, *against any adverse distribution or defense whatsoever*. That you come to realize the truth of this statement, beyond doubt or question, is a necessary first step toward the reading of this chapter. A strict proof will be forthcoming presently.

NORTH
♠ —
♡ 10
◊ K 8 5 2
♣ A K 2

WEST
♠ —
♡ 8
◊ Q 9 6
♣ Q 8 6 4

EAST
♠ —
♡ K
◊ J 10 7
♣ J 9 5 3

SOUTH
♠ 9 8 3
♡ J
◊ A 4
♣ 10 7

Let us look first at East's problem. He sees that West holds both minor Queens, for if holding one of those cards, Declarer would spread the hand. After five tricks, East knows that Declarer holds three Spades, ♡ J, and ◊ A. If his other three cards include two small Diamonds, leaving West with Q x only, a Diamond discard would be fatal. But since South cannot have more than three Clubs, West has at least Q x x, so that two of East's Clubs may be safely thrown. Unquestionably East would discard as above.

Now to Declarer's problem after seven tricks. Each adversary can be trusted to know that the closed hand has remaining no winners except ◊ A and a Spade. Therefore, the holder of four Diamonds would see that one could be safely thrown: the fact that no Diamond has appeared is strong evidence that the suit is 3-3. If so, East can no longer stop Clubs, which means Type R double squeeze with threats R, ♡ J; L, ♣ 2; B, ◊ 8. Cash the Clubs, return to ◊ A—quick, Watson, the needle!

To prove with mathematical certainty that (granted ♡ K East) a squeeze is present, against any distribution or any defense, is the easiest task imaginable. We have already noted that an elementary squeeze is in hand if Diamonds are unevenly divided; the same would be true, of course, if Clubs are 6-2 or worse. There remains the case where both minor suits are stopped by both adversaries. Now, East is busy in three suits. We know (§ 66, third paragraph) that a one-loser triple squeeze pinches on the *next-to-last* free winner. On the sixth Spade East will perforce surrender his stopper in either Diamonds or Clubs. Instantly there emerges a typical double squeeze, with the last Spade for squeeze-card, just as if East had never held a stopper in the suit that he has now abandoned. Had East yielded in Diamonds instead of Clubs, the only difference would have been in the sequence of winners: one Club (on general principles), ◊ K A, Spade.

As always in such spots, a word of caution. With presence and execution of the squeeze guaranteed, still Declarer's success is not guaranteed, because he may (sometimes with good excuse) go wrong at the fork—may pick the wrong suit as having been abandoned by East. More about this as we go along.

72. *The compound squeeze.* The broad class of squeezes to be discussed in this chapter may be described in general terms as follows.

Declarer has *only one loser* remaining. He holds threats in three suits. One of these threats is *stopped by one defender only*, with the threat lying *over the stopper*; the other two threats are stopped by both adversaries. Under these conditions the holder of three stoppers will be forced out of one suit by the next-to-last free winner (one-loser triple squeeze). This creates a typical double squeeze, granted the necessary entry conditions, no matter which suit has been abandoned under the triple squeeze.

Since this play is compounded of a triple followed by a double squeeze, let us name it the *compound squeeze.**

We know that ambiguity—uncertainty as to what has happened when the fork is reached—may in some cases cloud the picture, even in simple squeeze (§ 15). It is probably true that this trouble is more serious in compound squeeze than in the elementary forms, for an obvious reason: it is seldom possible to probe deeply into the adverse holdings in the two doubly-defended suits. Nevertheless, in the great majority of cases, Declarer can by close reasoning make his choice with high prospect of success. And even a 50-50 guess is better than nothing!

73. *Two fundamental requirements.* Let us begin by pointing out two conditions that are necessary for every compound squeeze. The first has been noted already, but is worth re-stating for emphasis.

I. *In every compound squeeze, Declarer must hold one threat stopped by one defender only, with the threat lying over the stopper.*

II. *In every compound squeeze, each of the doubly-stopped threats must be accompanied by an entry in its own suit.*

Proof of I: After the triple squeeze, the hand must have reduced to an ordinary double squeeze. Now we know (§ 22) that in every double squeeze at least one threat must lie over the stopper. If all three threats were stopped by both adversaries, each could retain his stopper (or stoppers) against the threat (or threats) lying at his right, and the double squeeze would fail. Therefore, there must be one singly-stopped threat, and that threat must lie over the stopper.

Proof of II: We know that in every double squeeze, the B threat must be accompanied by an entry in its own suit. But here, either of the doubly-defended suits may become the B suit, according to the discard on the triple squeeze: therefore, each of the two threats must be so accompanied.

---

* A triple squeeze is equivalent to three simples (§ 46); a double squeeze consists of two simples. Quintuple squeeze?

Of course I and II, though *necessary*, are not *sufficient*. That is, without those conditions, no squeeze; with them, perhaps a squeeze. The additional requisites differ in various cases: the two above (together with the one-loser requirement) are the only ones applying to *all* compound squeezes.

Exercise 100.*

NORTH	Bidding:			
♠ A 8 7 5 2				
♡ A 7 5	WEST	NORTH	EAST	SOUTH
◊ K 4 3	P	1 ♠	P	3 ♡
♣ 5 4	P	4 ♡	P	4 NT
	P	5 ♡	P	5 NT
SOUTH	P	6 ◊	P	7 NT
♠ K 4	P	P	P	
♡ K Q 10 9 4 2				
◊ A 8	West leads ♠ Q.			
♣ A K 6				

T. 1: East plays ♠ 3. King wins.
T. 2: ♡ K. Both follow.

Analysis 100.

WEST	EAST
♠ Q J 10 6	♠ 9 3
♡ J	♡ 8 6 3
◊ Q 6 5 2	◊ J 10 9 7
♣ Q 9 7 3	♣ J 10 8 2

As the only chance, assume that West held four Spades: then, I is in hand. Each of the doubly-stopped threats—◊ 4, ♣ 6— is accompanied by an entry: II is right.

This hand is of a less simple type than Ex. 99, in that the double squeeze will be of either Type R or Type B_2, at West's whim. But in another respect it is simpler than Ex. 99, because the entire Heart suit can be run off ahead of the fork. For practice, suppose you pause after five tricks and make sure that

* This hand was played by Mr. William B. Woodson.

the requisite entries are in hand, no matter which way the cat jumps.

```
                    NORTH
                 ♠ A 8 7
                 ♡ —
                 ◇ K 4 3
                 ♣ 5 4

    WEST                            EAST
 ♠ J 10                          ♠ —
 ♡ —                             ♡ —
 ◇ Q 6 5                         ◇ J 10 9 7
 ♣ Q 9 7                         ♣ J 10 8 2

                    SOUTH
                 ♠ 4
                 ♡ 9 4
                 ◇ A 8
                 ♣ A K 6
```

74. *Classification.* From now on, let the singly-stopped threat be called the *basic threat*. This term is introduced not merely for brevity, but also to keep constantly before us the fact that the holding of such a threat is the basic requirement for every compound squeeze.

Quite evidently, the two doubly-defended threats will be in one hand with the basic threat opposite; or, the doubly-defended threats will be divided between Declarer's two hands. This suggests the division of all compound squeezes into two classes, to be known as Type R and Type L.

TYPE R COMPOUND SQUEEZE: *The two doubly-stopped threats lie in one hand. The double squeeze will be of Type R, with the basic threat as the R threat.*

TYPE L COMPOUND SQUEEZE: *The two doubly-stopped threats are divided between Declarer's two hands. The double squeeze will be of Type R or Type B, according to the triple-squeezee's choice of discard, with the basic threat as the L threat in either case.*

Note that Ex. 99 is Type R; Ex. 100, Type L.

The above is a slight over-simplification, in that certain exceptions are possible. Such cases are excluded until further notice (§ 84).

75. *The restricted and unrestricted forms.* From a different point of view, all compound squeezes may be divided into two classes on an entirely different basis.

In every compound squeeze, the triple squeeze is inflicted by the *next-to-last* free winner. In many hands the fork is reached at that point: before making his next play, Declarer must decide as best he can which suit has been given up by the triply-busy defender, and plan his play accordingly. (See Ex. 99.) However, in another large group of hands it is possible to *cash the entire free suit* before making the decision. (See Ex. 100.) Let us call these two groups *restricted* and *unrestricted* respectively.

The two forms differ in two important respects.

(a) In the restricted form, the free suit must lie always in the one-threat hand; in the unrestricted, that suit may lie in either hand. (Proofs later.)

(b) In the restricted form, ambiguity is frequently present in some—perhaps in great—degree; in the unrestricted this danger is usually slight, because that *last* F is a real abrasive. Look again at Ex. 100.

Sorry to have to introduce so much terminology, but if you are to recognize compound squeezes quickly and play them accurately, a knowledge of these two classifications—Type R and Type L, restricted and unrestricted—would seem to be necessary.*

With comparatively rare exceptions, all compound squeezes fall into one or another of four standard forms. Let us proceed to examine the four cases in detail. Throughout the text (but not necessarily in the exercises), South will denote the hand *containing only one threat.*

76. *Type R compound squeeze, unrestricted.* Say that South holds the basic threat (stopped by East only), with the ambiguous (doubly-defended) threats opposite. Then (§ 74), the

---

* A few great experts, by sheer card genius, can think their way through each individual problem as it arises, with no rules to go by; but the vast majority, including your author, lack that ability.

double squeeze will be of Type R, with the basic threat as R threat. The entire play of the unrestricted form is covered by the following statement.

CASE I: *Type R compound squeeze, unrestricted. When South holds the R threat (stopped by East only) accompanied by an R winner, together with an entry in one of the three threat-suits, the free suit may lie in either hand, and the entire free suit may be run off. Next, cash North's R and L tops; then cross the table and lead the final squeeze-card (last R winner).*

Exercise 101.*

	NORTH	Bidding:			
	♠ A 9 7 2				
	♡ 6 5 4 2	EAST	SOUTH	WEST	NORTH
	◊ 8 3	P	2 ◊	3 ♠	3 NT
	♣ A 9 6	P	4 NT	P	5 ♡
		P	5 NT	P	6 ♣
	SOUTH	P	6 ◊	P	P
	♠ 3	P			
	♡ A 7				
	◊ A K Q J 9 7 5	West leads ♠ K.			
	♣ K 5 4				

T. 1: Declarer ducks. East plays ♠ 8.
T. 2: ♠ Q led. East plays ♠ 5; Declarer ruffs.

Analysis 101.

WEST	EAST
♠ K Q J 10 6 4	♠ 8 5
♡ K 10	♡ Q J 9 8 3
◊ 4 2	◊ 10 6
♣ Q 10 3	♣ J 8 7 2

On the bridge-certainty that East cannot stop Spades, the Type R compound squeeze is proved, with ambiguous threats ♡ 7, ♣ 5. Since the R (Spade) threat is accompanied by an R winner, and there is a side entry (♣ A), the entire free suit may be cashed, reducing West to rags and tatters.

* See an article by this writer, Bridge World, July, 1953.

Exercise 102.

NORTH
♠ A 4 2
♡ 8
♣ A K Q J 5
◊ A 8 3 2

SOUTH
♠ J 9 7 5
♡ A K 5 4 3
◊ K 7
♣ 9 2

Bidding:

NORTH	EAST	SOUTH	WEST
1 ♣	1 ♡	Dbl.	P
3 ♣	P	3 NT	P
P	P		

West leads ♡ 6.

T. 1: East's ♡ 9 wins.
T. 2: East's ♡ Q wins. West plays ♡ 2.
T. 3: Heart. Declarer wins; West discards ♠ 3.
T. 4-5: Clubs. Both follow.

Analysis 102.

WEST	EAST
♠ Q 8 6 3	♠ K 10
♡ 6 2	♡ Q J 10 9 7
◊ J 9 4	◊ Q 10 6 5
♣ 10 8 7 6	♣ 4 3

If East has both Spade pictures, a Spade-Heart simple—no! (E) is lacking. If West has both Spades, a Type B₁ double squeeze; but this is unlikely on the bidding.

Who cares about *Spades?* The R threat (Heart) is accompanied by an R winner, and there is a side entry. Finish the Clubs.

77. *Type R compound squeeze, restricted.* Say now that South holds the R threat (basic threat, stopped by East only), but the conditions of Case I are not satisfied. This may happen in either of two ways, (a) or (b) below, with (a) the more common.

CASE II: *Type R compound squeeze, restricted. When South holds the R threat (stopped by East only) (a) unaccompanied by an R winner, or (b) accompanied by one R winner with small opposite and no entry in either of the ambiguous suits, South must hold the free suit. After the triple squeeze, cash*

North's R and L tops; then recross the table and lead the last F winner.

For a Type R double squeeze, we know (§ 23) that the final squeeze-card must be the last of the F-R group.* In (a), the R threat is not accompanied by an R winner; in (b), South's R winner must be used for re-entry. Thus in either case the last F must be reserved for final squeeze-card, which means that the compound squeeze is always of the restricted form. Further, in Type R double squeeze the final squeeze-card must lie in and be led from the one-threat hand, which means that South must hold the free suit. After the triple squeeze, it must be possible to cash North's R and L tops and then recross the table, to lead the last F.

For a first example under (a), review Ex. 99.

Exercise 103.

NORTH
- ♠ 9 8 4
- ♡ 7
- ◇ A 7
- ♣ A K J 8 7 6 4

SOUTH
- ♠ A J 5
- ♡ A K 5
- ◇ K 6 4 3
- ♣ Q 9 5

Bidding:

EAST	SOUTH	WEST	NORTH
P	1 NT	P	3 ♣
P	3 NT	P	4 NT
P	5 ♡	P	5 NT
P	6 ♡	P	7 NT
P	P	P	

West leads ♠ K.

T. 1: East plays ♠ 2. Ace wins.
T. 2: Club. Both follow.
T. 3: Club. East discards ♡ Q.
T. 4-6: Clubs. West discards ♠ 3, ♡ 3, 4; East, ♡ 2, ♠ 6, 7.
T. 7: Club. East discards ◇ 2; South, ♠ J; West, ♠ Q.

Analysis 103.

WEST
- ♠ K Q 10 3
- ♡ 9 6 4 3
- ◇ J 10 5
- ♣ 10 3

EAST
- ♠ 7 6 2
- ♡ Q J 10 8 2
- ◇ Q 9 8 2
- ♣ 2

* With exceptions so rare as to be negligible.

As the only hope, assume firmly that West has ♠ 10. Then, the basic threat is in hand—♠ 9.

After seven tricks the squeeze is as good as proved. West would not discard ♠ Q unless also holding the Ten; since East surely has ♡ J 10 x remaining, West cannot stop Hearts. Cash ♡ A K, return to ◊ A and turn the screw.

Exercise 104.

NORTH
♠ A J 8 7
♡ A K 6 3
◊ J 2
♣ 8 6 5

Bidding:

NORTH	EAST	SOUTH	WEST
1 ♠	P	3 ◊	P
3 ♡	P	4 NT	P
5 ♡	P	5 NT	P
6 ◊	P	P	P

SOUTH
♠ 2
♡ 5 4
◊ A K Q 10 7 5
♣ A K 4 3

West leads ♣ 2.

T. 1: East plays ♣ Q.

Analysis 104.

WEST	EAST
♠ K 9 3	♠ Q 10 6 5 4
♡ Q 8 7 2	♡ J 10 9
◊ 8 6	◊ 9 4 3
♣ J 9 7 2	♣ Q 10

West's lead looks like a fourth-best: if so, the duck is safe, and it will correct the count for a squeeze. There is no compound squeeze because the singly-stopped threat (Club) lies under the stopper, but there are other possibilities. One is to ruff a couple of Spades, succeeding by main strength if either adversary holds K Q doubleton or K Q x, and by Spade-Club simple squeeze if West has five Spades.

A more promising plan is to ruff a Heart, establishing the Heart-Club simple squeeze if West has four Hearts; but even this is less than an even chance because of the Club division.

While the Heart play succeeds as the cards lie, it would be a very bad way to play the hand. Unquestionably the right method is to win, cash the other Club and lead a third Club, intending to ruff the fourth. This succeeds unless Clubs are 5-1 (which is contraindicated) or Diamonds 5-0.

Exercise 105.

NORTH	
♠ A Q 6	
♡ A K 5	
◊ A 10 8	
♣ A J 3 2	

SOUTH	
♠ K J 9 7 5 3 2	
♡ 7	
◊ 5 4	
♣ K 9 6	

Bidding:

WEST	NORTH	EAST	SOUTH
P	2 NT	P	3 ♠
P	4 ♠	P	4 NT
P	5 ♣	P	5 NT
P	6 ◊	P	7 ♠
P	P	P	

West leads ♣ 8.

T. 1: East plays ♣ 7.

Analysis 105.

WEST	EAST
♠ 10 8 4	♠ —
♡ J 8 6 2	♡ A 10 9 4 3
◊ K J 9 3	◊ Q 7 6 2
♣ 8 5	♣ Q 10 7 4

After winning the first trick, with the Ace of course, you run six Spades. It seems likely that West would discard ◊ 9 on the fourth Spade, whereupon East abandons Diamonds, and the double squeeze is Type R with threats R, ♣ 9; L, ◊ 10; B, ♡ 5. Evidently this hand illustrates Case II (b).

The hand has a peculiar feature which is worth noting for its theoretical interest. As soon as East trims down to one Diamond, South's ◊ 5 qualifies as a threat against West, and the squeeze may be played as Type B_2 with threats R, ◊ 5; L, ♣ 9; B, ♡ 5.

78. *An exceptional case.* In Case II (b), the requirement is that South hold one R winner with small opposite. When the small card opposite is lacking, so that South has no entry in any threat-suit, there is still one chance. If the free suit is *evenly divided* between the two hands, and if it is possible to win the last trick in that suit in the one-threat hand, that last F winner

furnishes the means of return, with the last R winner still available for final squeeze-card.

Exercise 106.

NORTH	Bidding:
♠ A K 6 3	
♡ A K 9 6	
◇ 9	
♣ A Q 7 4	

NORTH	EAST	SOUTH	WEST
1 ♠	P	2 ◇	P
2 ♡	P	3 NT	P
6 NT	P	P	P

SOUTH
♠ 8 2
♡ 10 5
◇ A K Q 7 3
♣ K 5 3 2

West leads ♣ J.

T. 1: Ace wins. East plays ♣ 6.
T. 2: ◇ 9 led. East's 10 wins.
T. 3: ♠ Q led. West plays ♠ 10. King wins.
T. 4: ♣ Q. Both follow.
T. 5: ♣ K. East discards ♠ 4.
T. 6: ◇ A. Both follow.
T. 7: ◇ K. West discards ♠ 5.

Analysis 106.

WEST	EAST
♠ 10 9 7 5	♠ Q J 4
♡ J 7 4 2	♡ Q 8 3
◇ 8 2	◇ J 10 6 5 4
♣ J 10 9	♣ 8 6

After seven tricks, only three Spades are out. If East has two of the three, then West has discarded a Spade in order to keep five Hearts, which doesn't make sense. You cash the Spade, return in Clubs and administer the Diamond.

79. *Elementary squeeze played as a compound squeeze.* In elementary squeeze play it may happen that only a simple squeeze is present, but with no way to tell whether East or West is to be pulverized. Then, granted proper conditions, Declarer solves the problem *by playing the hand as a double squeeze* (§ 24).

Needless to say, a similar situation may arise at our present level, and in fact is very common. That is: your holding in one of the ambiguous suits—perhaps in both of those suits—is such that only one defender can stop the suit, but with no way to locate the stopper. Then, granted the requisite conditions, you merely *play the hand as a compound squeeze*.

Exercise 107.

NORTH
♠ 4 2
♡ 3 2
◇ K 10 9 8 2
♣ A K Q 5

SOUTH
♠ A K J 3
♡ A K 6
◇ Q J 6
♣ 7 4 3

Bidding:

WEST	NORTH	EAST	SOUTH
P	1 ◇	P	2 ♠
P	3 ♣	P	4 NT
P	5 ◇	P	6 NT
P	P	P	

West leads ♣ 2.

T. 1: Queen wins. East plays ♣ 9.
T. 2: ◇ Q to West's Ace.
T. 3: Club. East plays ♣ J.
T. 4: ◇ J. Both follow.
T. 5: Diamond. West discards a Heart.
T. 6: Diamond. Each discards a Heart.

Analysis 107.

WEST
♠ Q 10 9
♡ J 8 7 5
◇ A 7
♣ 10 8 6 2

EAST
♠ 8 7 6 5
♡ Q 10 9 4
◇ 5 4 3
♣ J 9

The difficult part of compound squeeze play lies in weighing the evidence when the crux is reached. Here, West's discards mean little, because he might easily have held two Spades and five Hearts. The deciding factor is East's discard, T. 6. If West can still stop Hearts, then East has thrown a Heart from a holding of five Spades and three Hearts, which sounds unlikely. So Declarer cashes the Hearts, returns in Clubs and leads the Diamond.

80. *Type L compound squeeze, unrestricted.* Say now that North holds the basic threat (stopped by West only), with the ambiguous threats divided between Declarer's two hands. Then (§ 74), the double squeeze will be of Type R or Type B, with the basic threat as L threat in either case.

CASE III: *Type L compound squeeze, unrestricted. When North holds the L threat (stopped by West only), with the ambiguous threats divided, and South's threat is accompanied by two winners in its own suit with small opposite, the free suit may lie in either hand, and the entire free suit may be cashed. After the triple squeeze, the conditions for both Type R and Type B, double squeeze must be present.*

Exercise 108.

	NORTH			
♠	A 10 7 2			
♡	J 4 3			
◇	7			
♣	A K 5 3 2			

Bidding:

WEST	NORTH	EAST	SOUTH
P	1 ♣	P	2 ◇
P	2 ♠	P	3 ◇
P	3 NT	P	4 NT
P	5 ♡	P	5 NT
P	6 ◇	P	7 ◇
P	P	P	

	SOUTH
♠	J 5
♡	A K 2
◇	A K Q J 10 8 2
♣	9

West leads ♣ Q.

T. 1: King wins. East plays ♣ 6.
T. 2: ♣ A. East plays ♣ 7, West ♣ 4.
T. 3: Club ruff. East plays ♣ 8, West ♣ 10.
T. 4-5: Diamonds. Both follow.
T. 6: Diamonds. East plays ♠ 9.
T. 7: Diamond. West plays ♠ 6, East ♠ 3.
T. 8-9: Diamonds. West plays ♠ 8, Q, East ♡ 6, 7.

Analysis 108.

	WEST		EAST
♠	Q 8 6	♠	K 9 4 3
♡	10 8 5	♡	Q 9 7 6
◇	6 5 3	◇	9 4
♣	Q J 10 4	♣	8 7 6

After three tricks it is proved (for bridge purposes) that West has the Club, so that the necessary basic threat is in hand. The ambiguous threats—♠ 10, ♡ 2—are divided, and South's threat is accompanied by two tops. The only question is, will West abandon Spades or Hearts? This question answers itself after nine tricks, and ♠ A neatly completes the Type B₂ double squeeze. Had West kept Spades instead of Hearts, ♡ A K would have been laid down to complete the Type R double squeeze.

Evidently the basic threat could be set up equally well by ruffing a Club, T. 2, leaving the Ace in Dummy. If it seemed to you that in leading the Ace Declarer ran a needless risk (Clubs might be 6-1), then you should look further at the hand, because this is the key play. Say that a low Club is led for the ruff, T. 2. As the cards lie, East would still signal in Spades (they *will* do it), whereupon West would abandon Spades (they *will* do it); after the Diamonds Declarer crosses to ♠ A and completes the Type B₂ double squeeze by leading ♣ A. But if West understands compound squeeze play he will keep his Spades, whereupon the Type R double squeeze cannot be executed. (Play it.)

To play this and similar hands correctly, you have to keep in mind the fact that in Type L compound squeeze—ambiguous threats divided—either Type R or Type B double squeeze may eventuate. So, call on your knowledge of double-squeeze technique to determine a sequence which will keep both types in hand. Now we know (§ 23) that in Type R double squeeze, if South holds neither a B winner nor the last L, then all L's *must* be cashed while South has remaining an F or R *entry*, in addition to the final squeeze card. This means, in Ex. 108, get rid of that L winner!

Exercise 109.

	NORTH			
	♠ A 8 3			
	♡ Q 10 8 6			
	◇ A K 7			
	♣ J 8 7			

Bidding:

SOUTH	WEST	NORTH	EAST
1 ♡	1 ♠	3 ♡	P
4 ♣	P	4 ♠	P
5 ♣	P	5 ◇	P
6 ♡	P	P	P

SOUTH

♠ J 6
♡ A K 9 7 5 2
◇ 4 2
♣ A K 4

West leads ♠ K.

T. 1: Duck.
T. 2: ♠ Q led. Ace wins.
T. 3: ♡ A. Both follow.
T. 4: ♡ Q. West discards ♠ 4.
T. 5: Heart. East discards ♠ 7; West, ♠ 9.
T. 6-8: Hearts. West discards ♣ 2, 3, 5; East, ◇ 3, 6, 8.

Analysis 109.

WEST	EAST
♠ K Q 10 9 4	♠ 7 5 2
♡ J	♡ 4 3
◇ Q 10 5	◇ J 9 8 6 3
♣ 9 5 3 2	♣ Q 10 6

A Club lead, T. 2, would change the hand from "unrestricted" to "restricted," which is always undesirable (more about this later). Thus South drops ♠ J, T. 1, to make it safe for West to continue Spades.

After the Hearts Declarer cashes the Clubs or the Diamonds to complete the Type R or Type B_2 double squeeze, according as West has preserved Diamonds, East Clubs, or vice versa.

81. *Type L compound squeeze, restricted.* Let the conditions be the same as in Case III, except that South's threat is accompanied by *only one winner* in its own suit.

CASE IV: *Type L compound squeeze, restricted. When North holds the L threat (stopped by West only), with the ambiguous threats divided, and South's threat is accompanied by only one winner in its own suit, South must hold the free suit, and the decision must be made after the next-to-last free winner. After the triple squeeze, the conditions for both Type R and Type B₁ double squeeze must be present.*

The reason why South must hold the free suit is this. West can always produce a Type B_1 double squeeze if he so wishes, and we know (§ 28) that a Type B_1 squeeze will fail unless the last F winner is in the same hand with the B threat.

Exercise 110.

	NORTH			
♠	K 7 5 2			
♡	A K 6			
◇	Q 6			
♣	K Q 5 4			

Bidding:

SOUTH	WEST	NORTH	EAST
1 ♠	P	3 ♠	P
4 ◇	P	4 ♡	P
4 NT	P	5 ♣	P
5 NT	P	6 ♠	P
7 ♠	P	P	P

	SOUTH
♠	A Q J 10 4 3
♡	8
◇	A 7
♣	A 8 3 2

West leads ♣ J.

T. 1: Declarer wins. East plays ♣ 6.
T. 2-4: Spades. East discards ♡ 9, 3, 4.

Analysis 110.

	WEST		EAST
♠	9 8 6	♠	—
♡	10 5 2	♡	Q J 9 7 4 3
◇	J 9 3	◇	K 10 8 5 4 2
♣	J 10 9 7	♣	6

Of course you assume that West stops Clubs. If you let the first trick ride to the Ace, the decision will have to be made after the third Spade. Since West can be trusted to give up Hearts, the squeeze will be RFL (§ 28) with threats R, ♡ 6; L, ♣ 5; B, ◇ 7. This means that the Hearts must be cashed now. But as soon as the Heart tops are played, West (if he knows his way around) will keep his last Heart, making Hearts the B suit: automatic failure for lack of a B winner.

Instead, you must win the first trick in Dummy and run five Spades. West will throw Hearts, whereupon RFL says Hearts, ♣ A, Spade, ♣ K.

If by any chance West yields Diamonds, keeping his Hearts, the Type R double squeeze is easily executed. (Play it.)

Exercise 111.*

	NORTH	Bidding:			
	♠ K 6 4 3				
	♡ A 3	WEST	NORTH	EAST	SOUTH
	◊ J 9 6 4 2	P	P	P	3 NT
	♣ 10 5	P	7 NT	P	P
		P			
	SOUTH				
	♠ A 10 5	West leads ♣ 3.			
	♡ K Q 8 4				
	◊ A K 3				
	♣ A K 6				

T. 1: ♣ 3, 10, J, A.
T. 2: Diamond. Both follow.
T. 3: Diamond. West's Queen drops.
T. 4: ◊ J. West discards ♣ 2.
T. 5: Diamond. East discards ♣ 4, West ♣ 7.

Analysis 111.

	WEST		EAST
	♠ J 9 7		♠ Q 8 2
	♡ J 7 2		♡ 10 9 6 5
	◊ Q 8		◊ 10 7 5
	♣ Q 8 7 3 2		♣ J 9 4

As the only chance, play East for the Hearts. Some counting is required. After four tricks it is known that East held three Diamonds, three Clubs, and (by assumption) four Hearts. Thus if East were to discard a Spade, T. 5, the double squeeze would be Type R with threats R, ♠ 6; L, ♡ 8; B, ♣ 6. The sequence

---

* This hand was played by Dr. Ben Dushnik. Unfortunately, the bidding is available.

would be Hearts, ♠ A K, Diamond. But the Club discard produces a Type B_1 squeeze with threats R, ♣ 6; L, ♡ 8; B, ♠ 6. The sequence is ♣ K, ♡ A, Diamond, Hearts.

The especially interesting feature of the hand is this. Both in Type R and Type B_1 (a) double squeeze (one of which is to eventuate here), we cash the L winners early. But this is compound squeeze. Say that the Hearts are run, T. 4-6: that is, before East has committed himself. Now, *unless* Declarer cashes the Club, T. 7, East can defeat the hand by merely throwing Clubs (check it). And *if* the Club is cashed, T. 7, the hand will fail provided East keeps his Club and West hangs tight to his Spades. It's 100-1 that they wouldn't, but the stuff is there. This produces the unusual result that when the Type B_1 squeeze develops, the final squeeze-card must be the last L instead of the customary F (Rule, § 28).

82. *Compound squeeze defense.* Chances for the defense to kill the squeeze are relatively more frequent in compound than in elementary squeeze play because, due to the greater number of conditions required for the squeeze, Declarer is subject to attack on more fronts.

In the following hands correct defense, with no double-dummy reasoning, will foil Declarer's villainous schemes.

Exercise 112.*

NORTH
♠ J 9 8 7
♡ A K 8
◇ K 4 3
♣ A K 6

SOUTH
♠ 6 5
♡ Q J 9 6 5 2
◇ 10 6 2
♣ 7 5

Bidding:

WEST	NORTH	EAST	SOUTH
1 ♣	Dbl.	P	1 ♡
Dbl.	P	2 ♣	P
2 ◇	2 ♡	P	3 ♡
P	4 ♡	P	P
Dbl.	P	P	P

West leads ♠ K.

* This hand was played by Mrs. Al Shanbrom, of Detroit, and reported by Mr. Frank S. Eaton in the Detroit Free Press.

T. 1: East plays ♠ 2.
T. 2: ♠ Q. East plays ♠ 3.
T. 3: ◊ A led. East plays ◊ 8.
T. 4: ◊ 5 led. King wins; East plays ◊ 9.
T. 5: ♡ K. Both follow.
T. 6: ♡ A. West discards ♣ 2.
T. 7: Spade ruff. Both follow.

Analysis 112.

WEST	EAST
♠ A K Q 4	♠ 10 3 2
♡ 7	♡ 10 4 3
◊ A Q 7 5	◊ J 9 8
♣ Q J 4 2	♣ 10 9 8 3

The indications are that the Diamond tops are divided: if so, no squeeze. But Declarer kept the flag flying by running off her Hearts, and was richly rewarded—on the next-to-last West discarded his Diamond! Whereupon the last Heart completed the double squeeze.

Actually, West's problem is not too hard. He can see that the last Heart will force him out of Clubs, so as the only hope give East a Club stopper. Then, the only squeeze is Spade-Diamond simple, which will fail for lack of (E).

Let us take a moment to fit the hand into our general theory. The basic threat is ♠ J with ambiguous threats divided: A Type L compound squeeze, but with the fatal flaw that the Diamond is not accompanied by an entry. So, if West keeps his Diamond, making ◊ 10 the B threat, the squeeze fails.

Exercise 113.*

NORTH
♠ J 7 6
♡ A K 10 9 2
◇ 9 6 4
♣ 6 5

Bidding:

SOUTH	WEST	NORTH	EAST
1 ♠	Dbl.	2 ♠	3 ♣
P	P	3 ♡	P
3 ♠	P	P	P

SOUTH
♠ A K 9 4 2
♡ 3
◇ A J 10 3
♣ 4 3 2

West leads ♣ A.

T. 1: East plays ♣ K.
T. 2: ♣ 8 led. East's Nine wins.
T. 3: ◇ 5 led. West's Queen wins.
T. 4: ◇ 8 led. East plays ◇ 2; Ten wins.
T. 5-6: ♠ A K. West plays ♠ 8, Q; East, ♠ 3, 5.
T. 7: ♠ J. West discards ♡ 4.
T. 8: Diamond led. East discards ♣ 10; Ace wins.

Analysis 113.

WEST	EAST
♠ Q 8	♠ 10 5 3
♡ Q 6 5 4	♡ J 8 7
◇ K Q 8 7	◇ 5 2
♣ A 8 7	♣ K Q J 10 9

East's discard of ♣ 10 marks West with the Seven, so that the only squeeze possibility is Heart-Diamond simple, requiring West to hold both Heart pictures. But on the next-to-last Spade West discards his Club! Whereupon the last Spade completes the Type B₂ double squeeze.

There is much to be said for a Club lead, T. 3, because if West's Spades are as good as Q x, a Dummy ruff sets up East's Ten. West's Diamond lead, insuring the contract, is also highly unfortunate. The point of interest to us is that the overtrick could still be stopped. East's ♣ 10 discard shows West that Declarer still has a Club. West can see that he will be squeezed

---

* This hand was played by Mr. Al Shanbrom, of Detroit, and reported by Mr. Frank S. Eaton in the Detroit Free Press.

out of Hearts by the last Spade. If East has to defend Clubs, he also will fail in Hearts. But if West keeps his Club, no squeeze.

Evidently in this Type L compound squeeze the flaw is that the basic threat, ♣ 4, lies under the stopper, ♣ 7. As soon as that stopper is discarded, the sun breaks through.

Exercise 114.

NORTH
♠ 6 3
♡ A 10
◇ K Q J 10 8 5
♣ K 6 3

EAST
♠ J 9 8 5 2
♡ J 8 4
◇ 3 2
♣ 7 4 2

Bidding:

SOUTH	WEST	NORTH	EAST
1 ♣	P	1 ◇	P
2 NT	P	4 NT	P
5 ♠	P	5 NT	P
6 ♡	P	7 NT	P
P	P		

West leads ◇ 7.

T. 1: Ace wins.
T. 2: Diamond. West plays ◇ 6.
Select East's four discards for the Diamond run.

Analysis 114.

WEST
♠ Q 7 4
♡ Q 9 6 3 2
◇ 7 6
♣ Q 10 9

SOUTH
♠ A K 10
♡ K 7 5
◇ A 9 4
♣ A J 8 5

Declarer takes a dim view of the Club finesse, because he suspects that West had his reasons for not leading anything but a Diamond. However, there is a fully established compound squeeze, Type R unrestricted, in case West has four Clubs.

The whole deal is visible to East. West has three Queens,

for with one Queen in hand Declarer would have thirteen tops. (Possible exception, ♡ K Q doubleton: but in that event, probably nothing to worry about.) In case South's Notrump jump is strictly a book bid, East can even determine that South's nineteenth point is ♣ J; but no matter. East must keep ♡ J to prevent a first-round finesse of the Ten; he must keep three Spades on the chance that West has only Q x; but his main job is to keep tight grip on those power-packed Clubs.

83. *Some general principles of defense.* The following, while it is only a small fraction of what could be written on the subject, does list a few cardinal principles of defense which should always be kept in mind.

Point 1: Do not try to hang onto a suit that you will surely be forced out of, at the expense of surrendering a possibly valid stopper in another suit. Example: Anal. 112, second paragraph.

Point 2: Never forget that in squeeze defense, just as surely as in offense, cards that look hopelessly insignificant may play the star's role. Example: East's Clubs, Ex. 114.

Point 3: Do not be overawed by a high card until you have determined whether that card actually plays a role. Example: In Ex. 114, East can see that Dummy's only possible threat is in Clubs, which means that he (East) holds a sure stopper. On the bidding, Declarer is believed to hold ♣ J, but who cares?

Point 4: When your partner advertises a stopper in a certain suit, do not jump to the conclusion that you can always afford to discard that suit, for two reasons. First: If Declarer can depend upon you always to abandon the suit where your partner holds a stopper, his task in reading the situation, when the decision-point is reached, is greatly simplified. Second: In some cases your partner's stopper will ultimately be squeezed out, so that the load will fall on you. Example: In Ex. 113 the fact that East is rolling in Clubs does not release West's all-important ♣ 7.

Point 5: Do not signal possession of a stopper unless the information will be of more help to your partner than to Declarer. Quite often, Declarer's choice of plays would be very uncertain, but for the fact that an eager-beaver opponent has given the show away by a foolish signal. This admonition applies to bridge in general, not merely to squeeze play: an admonition which should be memorized by everyone at an early stage of his bridge education, yet which many never learn.

Exercise 115.

NORTH
♠ 5 4 2
♡ A 8 7
◇ 8 7 4
♣ 10 9 6 3

Bidding:

SOUTH	WEST	NORTH	EAST
2 ♣	3 ♠	P	P
4 ◇	P	4 ♡	P
7 NT	P	P	P

EAST
♠ 6 3
♡ J 10 6 5 3
◇ J 10 5 3
♣ 5 2

West leads ♠ K.

Plan East's defense.

Analysis 115.

WEST
♠ K Q J 10 9 8 7
♡ Q 9 4
◇ 9 2
♣ 7

SOUTH
♠ A
♡ K 2
◇ A K Q 6
♣ A K Q J 8 4

Give Declarer six Clubs, since otherwise there is probably nothing to fear. Then, your Heart stopper will be forced out. Your partner may hold a Heart stopper, but that too will go if he has to defend Spades. But look! If West's pre-empt was a book bid—Rule of Two and Three—South's Ace is blank, the Spade threat is Dummy's Five, and you have a stopper. If you keep that stopper, the squeeze will fail.

Declarer cashes five Clubs and three Diamonds. When the sixth Club comes out, West must do a trifle of counting. If holding ♡ K East would have advertised (this is not one of those cases coming under Point 5); therefore East has ♡ J 10 remaining. He has ◊ J. His fourth item is either ♠ 6 or a laundry ticket. So West sloughs his last Spade, and the curtain falls.

x x x x

In our opinion, the simpler forms of compound squeeze are hardly more difficult, as regards Declarer's play, than some forms of double squeeze. But in undertaking to attain real proficiency in compound squeeze defense, you are faced with one of the most exacting tasks in bridge. Of the many reasons for this, let us mention one. In double squeeze, each opponent is busy in two suits. In compound squeeze, one opponent is busy in three suits, often *without realizing that fact* until too late—perhaps with no one at the table realizing it, even after the hand is over. In Ex. 115, with East playing ♠ 6 to the first trick, it is conceivable that four good players could hold a post-mortem without discovering that the contract should have been defeated. See also Exs. 113, 114.

Let us play one more hand.

Exercise 116.

NORTH
♠ A K
♡ 10 9 5 4
◊ A 8 6 4
♣ A 10 3

EAST
♠ 5
♡ K Q 7 2
◊ K 10 3
♣ Q J 8 6 2

Bidding:

WEST	NORTH	EAST	SOUTH
P	1 ◊	P	2 ♠
P	3 ♠	P	4 ♠
P	5 ♠	P	6 ♠
P	P	P	

West leads ♣ 9.

T. 1: Ace wins. South plays ♣ 4.
T. 2: Heart. South's Ace wins.
T. 3: Spade. West follows.
T. 4: Heart ruff.
T. 5: Spade. West follows.
T. 6: Heart ruff.
T. 7-9: Spades. West discards ♣ 5, ◊ 2, 5.

Analysis 116.

```
          WEST
          ♠ 9 4
          ♡ J 8 6 3
          ◇ J 9 7 5 2
          ♣ 9 5
```

```
                    SOUTH
                    ♠ Q J 10 8 7 6 3 2
                    ♡ A
                    ◇ Q
                    ♣ K 7 4
```

If holding ♣ K x originally, Declarer would have won the first trick with the King: thus he has remaining one Spade, one Diamond, and ♣ K x. If East parts with his Heart, the Type R double squeeze will run on rollers. But if each defender keeps his Heart, making Hearts the B suit, the squeeze will fail for that old, familiar reason—no B winner. (Compare Ex. 29.)

84. *The alternate-threat squeeze.* It is time to consider the non-typical hands mentioned in § 74 (last paragraph).

Example:

```
                    NORTH
                    ♠ K Q 8 7 4
                    ♡ A 10 9 5 4
                    ◇ J
                    ♣ A 8
```

```
     WEST                              EAST
     ♠ J 10 9 6                        ♠ A 3 2
     ♡ Q 8 7 6                         ♡ K J
     ◇ 7 6                             ◇ 9 8 3
     ♣ Q 10 5                          ♣ J 9 6 3 2
```

```
                    SOUTH
                    ♠ 5
                    ♡ 3 2
                    ◇ A K Q 10 5 4 2
                    ♣ K 7 4
```

To South's six Notrump West leads ♠ J; East wins and returns ◇ 9. The hand looks like Type L restricted compound squeeze (§ 81) with L (basic) threat ♠ 8, ambiguous threats ♡ 10, ♣ 7. We must be prepared for both Type R and Type B₁ double squeeze. In case West gives Clubs, the Type R double squeeze works out perfectly: six Diamonds, ♣ A, ♠ K, ♣ K, Diamond. But if West keeps his Clubs, the double squeeze is Type B₁ with threats R, ♡ 10; L, ♠ 8; B, ♣ 7. "The last R must precede the last F," and it can't be done: no squeeze.

But look! With West down to one Heart, ♡ 3 is a competent threat against East. With ♡ 3 as the threat, the Type R double squeeze is in hand: cash the last Diamond, discarding ♡ 10, then North's tops.

This hand is an example of a specific type of compound squeeze which might be called the *alternate-threat squeeze*. It is evidently a hybrid between Type R and Type L compound squeeze. With ♡ 10 as the threat, the compound squeeze is Type L restricted, succeeding if West keeps Hearts, failing if he keeps Clubs. With ♡ 3 as the threat, the compound squeeze is Type R unrestricted, succeeding if West keeps Clubs, failing if he keeps Hearts. Due to the presence of the alternate threat, Declarer is able to pick the winning route in either case.

If the hybrid form is to develop, the basic threat must be accompanied by at least one winner (♠ K above), to serve as final squeeze card in case the alternate threat has to be used. In the two-threat suit (Hearts above) nothing more is needed than winner and small opposite two small. Since these requirements are modest indeed, it might seem that the hybrid ought to be comparatively common in play.

The stringency lies elsewhere. At the moment when Declarer takes control, *South's hand is tightly packed with busy cards*, and is in fact cut to a very precise pattern: this accounts for the relative rarity of the alternate-threat variant. In support of the italicized statement, we point out that in the Example, if East returns a Spade the closed hand will be squeezed on the second trick. (Oh sure—East could and should wreck the machine by ducking the first trick. But isn't the going rough enough without that?)

We have had previous instances (Exs. 31, 105, and doubtless others) where an "alternate threat" was present. But in those cases this feature was of theoretical interest only, because a single threat would suffice. In the present problem, unless both threats are in hand the squeeze can be defeated.

Although not too common in play, as a problem in analysis the alternate-threat squeeze is one of the most fascinating in our repertoire. If you do not agree, please omit Exs. 117-120.

Exercise 117.*

<table>
<tr><td>NORTH</td><td>Contract:</td></tr>
<tr><td>♠ K 5 2</td><td rowspan="2">6 Notrump by South.
West leads ♡ J.</td></tr>
<tr><td>♡ 10 8</td></tr>
<tr><td>◇ 7 2</td><td></td></tr>
<tr><td>♣ A K Q 6 3 2</td><td></td></tr>
</table>

SOUTH
♠ A 8
♡ A K 9 5 2
◇ A 8 4
♣ J 5 4

T. 1: East plays ♡ 4. King wins.
T. 2-3: Clubs. Both follow.
T. 4: Club. East discards ◇ 3; West ◇ 10.
T. 5-6: Clubs. East discards ◇ 9, J; West, ♠ 4, 6.

Analysis 117.

<table>
<tr><td>WEST</td><td>EAST</td></tr>
<tr><td>♠ Q 9 7 6 4</td><td>♠ J 10 3</td></tr>
<tr><td>♡ J 3</td><td>♡ Q 7 6 4</td></tr>
<tr><td>◇ Q 10 6 5</td><td>◇ K J 9 3</td></tr>
<tr><td>♣ 10 7</td><td>♣ 9 8</td></tr>
</table>

Unless the original lead is a false card, it insures the contract by Heart finesse, but Declarer plays for the overtrick. The hand

* This hand was played by Dr. Paul F. Zweifel, of Schenectady, N. Y., and reported by this writer in the Bridge World, Nov., 1955. The bidding is not available.

looks like a Type L restricted compound squeeze with L (basic) threat ♡ 5, ambiguous threats ♠ 5, ◇ 8. After six tricks it is clear that East has broken Diamonds, so that the double squeeze is Type B₁ with threats R, ◇ 8; L, ♡ 5; B, ♠ 5. The last R must precede the last F, and this is impossible: no squeeze.

Take another look! With East down to one Diamond, Dummy's Seven is a competent threat. On that basis the double squeeze is Type R with threats R, ♡ 5; L, ◇ 7; B, ♠ 5. Last Club, Heart finesse, Diamond, Heart.

Note that the "tight" hand—North in this instance—has no idle card.

Exercise 118.*

```
            NORTH
        ♠ A 10 7 2
        ♡ A 7 5
        ◇ A K Q 6
        ♣ 3 2

            SOUTH
        ♠ K 9 6
        ♡ 6 4
        ◇ 9 5
        ♣ A K Q 10 7 5
```

Bidding:

SOUTH	WEST	NORTH	EAST
2 NT	P	7 NT	P
P	P		

West leads ◇ 4.

T. 1: Queen wins. East plays ◇ 2.
T. 2-3: Clubs. Both follow.
T. 4: Club. Dummy discards ♠ 2; East, ♡ Q.
T. 5: Club. West discards ◇ 3; Dummy, ♡ 5; East, ♡ 2.
T. 6: Club. West discards ♡ 8.

Analysis 118.

```
        WEST                        EAST
    ♠ Q 8 4                     ♠ J 5 3
    ♡ K 8                       ♡ Q J 10 9 3 2
    ◇ J 8 7 4 3                 ◇ 10 2
    ♣ 9 6 4                     ♣ J 8
```

*This hand was played by Mr. Harold S. Hemrick, and reported by Mr. Hemrick in the Bridge World, June, 1957.

After 5½ tricks Declarer reads West for three Spades, ♡ K and three Diamonds. Now, the first thought might be that the Type L compound squeeze has produced a Type B₁ double squeeze with threats R, ♡ 7; L, ◊ 6; B, ♠ 9. But this squeeze will bog down for the same reason as in the previous hands. However, the alternate threat ♡ 6 comes to the rescue, making the double squeeze Type R with threats R, ♡ 6; L, ◊ 6; B, ♠ 10. Discard ♡ 7 on the fifth Club; cash the red tops; return to ♠ K and shove out the Club.

Due to the presence of an alternate threat in Spades as well as in Hearts, another way to play the hand would be to discard ♠ 10, T. 6; lead the last Club, T. 7, discarding the Heart. Now the double squeeze is Type R with threats R, ◊ 6; L, ♡ 6; B, ♠ 9.

The phenomenon of alternate threats in two suits is possible only in case Declarer has two winners remaining in the third threat-suit. In Ex. 117, this feature would be present if ◊ 4 were traded for ♠ 4.

Just to keep an eye on our theory, note that if the first method is to be used, the extra winner in Diamonds makes room for one idle card—a Spade—in the tight hand; but under the second method, again that hand has no idle card.

It would seem that West could make the going very rugged by taking the other tine of the alternate-threat fork—that is, by pitching a Spade on the fifth Club (§ 83, Point 4). Now, does West have still in hand two Spades and ♡ K x, or three Spades and ♡ K?

x x x x

The rigidity of form of this hybrid squeeze will stand out more clearly if we compare these last two hands suit by suit, with Ex. 118 to be played by the first method above. The solid suits are by chance identical. In Spades, each hand has a winner and small opposite winner and two small (in Ex. 118, there is an idle Spade in each hand). In the alternate-threat suit—Diamonds and Hearts respectively—each hand has two winners and small (with one idle in Ex. 117), opposite one small. That is: these two hands are as alike as two baseballs.

Exercise 119.

	NORTH
♠	A K 3
♡	6 4 2
◇	K 8
♣	A K Q 6 5

Bidding:

EAST	SOUTH	WEST	NORTH
P	1 ◇	P	3 ♣
P	3 ◇	P	3 ♠
P	3 NT	P	4 NT
P	5 ♡	P	7 NT
P	P	P	

	SOUTH
♠	7 6 5
♡	A 7 3
◇	A Q J 10 3
♣	J 9

West leads ♠ 2.

T. 1: King wins. East plays ♠ 10.
T. 2: ◇ K. Both follow.
T. 3: Diamond. West discards ♡ 9.
T. 4-5: Diamonds. West discards ♠ 8, 9.

Analysis 119.

	WEST			EAST
♠	J 9 8 2		♠	Q 10 4
♡	K 9 5		♡	Q J 10 8
◇	2		◇	9 7 6 5 4
♣	10 8 7 3 2		♣	4

There is no squeeze if East stops Clubs, for lack of a basic threat; but after five tricks it is as good as proved that West (if either) has that suit. The standard threats are R, ♠ 3; L, ♣ 6; B, ♡ 7; but this RFL squeeze would require discard of the Club threat without having tested the suit. Turning to the alternate threat ♠ 7, we have a Type R double with threats R, ♣ 6; L, ♠ 7; B, ♡ 7. Cash the last Diamond, discarding the Spade; run the blacks. With North holding three L (Club) tops, South has room for two Club spots: since he has only one, there must be an idle card somewhere, and here it is—a Heart.

This hand is just another baseball, except in the minor point that at double dummy the Type L compound squeeze (using ♠ 3 as the threat) could be executed. This of course is due to South's possession of a re-entry in Clubs.

Exercise 120.

	NORTH		Bidding:			
♠	10 7 6 2					
♡	A 10 2		NORTH	EAST	SOUTH	WEST
◇	K 8 4		1 ♣	P	2 ♠	3 ♡
♣	A K 7		3 ♠	P	4 ◇	P
			4 ♡	P	4 NT	P
	SOUTH		5 ◇	P	5 NT	P
♠	A K Q J 8 5 3		6 ♡	P	7 ♠	P
♡	—		P	P		
◇	A 5 3					
♣	5 4 3		West leads ♡ K.			

T. 1:   East plays ♡ 5. Declarer ruffs.
T. 2-3:   Spades. West discards ♡ 3, 4.
T. 4-6:   Spades. West discards ♡ 7, 9, ♣ 2; East, ♣ Q,
          ♡ 6, 8.

Analysis 120.

	WEST		EAST	
♠	—	♠	9 4	
♡	K Q J 9 7 4 3	♡	8 6 5	
◇	Q J 2	◇	10 9 7 6	
♣	10 9 2	♣	Q J 8 6	

The first thought might be to use Dummy's Seven as the Club threat. If West yields Diamonds, the Type R double squeeze with threats R, ◇ 5; L, ♡ 10; B, ♣ 7 will go through easily. But after six tricks it appears that West has given up his Club stopper, and the Type B$_1$ double squeeze with threats R, ♣ 7; L, ♡ 10; B, ◇ 5 will fail (check it). So, turn to the alternate threat ♣ 5. Cash the last Spade, discarding ♣ 7; etc.

In a large tournament some would shoot for a top with 7 NT. This contract fails because Declarer is squeezed on the first trick. If he discards a Club and West surrenders Clubs, the Type B$_1$ squeeze with threats R, ♣ 7; L, ♡ 10; B, ◇ 5 will fail as noted above. And if Declarer discards a Diamond, West discards Diamonds, making ♣ 5 the B threat: failure for the obvious reason that there is no winner accompanying the B threat.

"This contract fails." It is true that West is groping in the dark, and even a great expert might easily fail to find the correct defense; yet the fact remains that the squeeze is pseudo.

Do you wonder that the alternate-threat squeeze strikes our fancy?

85. *The double guard squeeze.* First,* let us look at

Example (a):

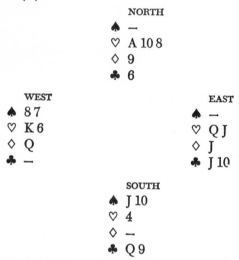

NORTH
♠ —
♡ A 10 8
♦ 9
♣ 6

WEST
♠ 8 7
♡ K 6
♦ Q
♣ —

EAST
♠ —
♡ Q J
♦ J
♣ J 10

SOUTH
♠ J 10
♡ 4
♦ —
♣ Q 9

Say that South knows the location of the outstanding minors. Then, he sees a Type R restricted compound squeeze with basic threat ♣ 9, failing because the Diamond threat is not accompanied by an entry. However, if East holds two of the Heart honors, he is in trouble. On ♠ J he discards a Heart; on the last Spade he can take his choice. Another Heart discard establishes the finesse; a Diamond discard sets up the Heart-Diamond simple squeeze on West. Do not fail to see that with ♡ J, 6 traded, there is no squeeze.

A fundamental requirement: *the R threat must be accompanied by an R winner,* because this is the only way to make room for an idle card North, for discard on the last free winner. With ♣ Q replaced by a Spade, one of East's Clubs is released

* Before proceeding, you are advised to review §§ 67-69.

for discard on the second Spade, whereupon the third Spade pinches North.

Example (b):

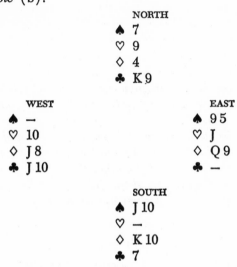

NORTH
♠ 7
♡ 9
◇ 4
♣ K 9

WEST
♠ —
♡ 10
◇ J 8
♣ J 10

EAST
♠ 9 5
♡ J
◇ Q 9
♣ —

SOUTH
♠ J 10
♡ —
◇ K 10
♣ 7

In case the Diamond pictures are divided, Declarer sees a Type L restricted compound squeeze with the basic threat ♣ 9, but lacking the vital requisite of a Heart entry. However, on the last Spade West will have to discard his Heart stopper in order to guard his partner against the Diamond finesse, whereupon the Club inflicts the Heart-Diamond simple squeeze on East.

The play now in hand, consisting of a simple guard squeeze on one opponent followed by a simple squeeze on the other, or (at the defender's option) a successful finesse, is called a *double guard squeeze*. Like its brother the simple guard, it pinches on the *last free winner*.

The need of double guard squeeze arises when a compound squeeze is present except that a necessary entry is missing (compare § 67). This suggests the division of all double guard squeezes into two classes, according as the compound squeeze in question is Type R or Type L.

Due to the multiplicity of entry requirements that may be

present in compound squeeze, the double guard squeeze may occur in a variety of situations. The statements following cover the two cases that seem most likely to occur in play. South as usual is the hand containing one threat—basic (R) threat in Type R, an ambiguous threat in Type L.

Note that Example (a) is Type R; Example (b), Type L.

Type R double guard squeeze: A Type R compound squeeze is present except that one of North's threats is not accompanied by an entry. In the other ambiguous suit East must retain certain cards to protect his partner against a finesse. This squeeze will fail unless South has an R winner remaining.

Type L double guard squeeze: A Type L compound squeeze is present except that North's ambiguous threat is not accompanied by an entry. In one of the other threat-suits North holds an entry, and in South's threat-suit West must retain certain threat cards to protect his partner against a finesse.

Exercise 121.

NORTH
♠ 6 5 2
♡ A 10 9 3
♢ 6 5 3
♣ 8 7 4

SOUTH
♠ A
♡ K 2
♢ A K Q J 8 4
♣ A K Q 2

Bidding:

SOUTH	WEST	NORTH	EAST
2 ♢	3 ♠	P	P
4 ♣	P	4 ♢	P
4 NT	P	5 ♢	P
7 NT	P	P	P

West leads ♠ K.

T. 1: East plays ♠ 3.
T. 2: Diamond. Both follow.
T. 3: Diamond. West discards ♠ 4.

Analysis 121.

WEST
♠ K Q J 10 9 8 4
♡ J 8 4
♢ 7
♣ 6 3

EAST
♠ 7 3
♡ Q 7 6 5
♢ 10 9 2
♣ J 10 9 5

On the bidding, Declarer gives East stoppers in three suits. If in Hearts East has both honors or any five, the easiest kind of Heart-Club simple squeeze. If both defenders stop Hearts, a Type R compound with R (basic) threat ♣ 2, ambiguous threats ♠ 6, ♡ 10, except that the Spade has no entry; but East will have to guard in Hearts.

In case Declarer "tries the suit" by cashing the three Clubs ahead of the last Diamond, retribution will be swift and sure. Instead, he should finish his chores before touching Clubs at all (§ 35).

If East drops ♠ 7, T. 1, the hand is merely a Type R double squeeze with B threat ♡ 10, succeeding no matter how the Hearts are placed.

Exercise 122.

NORTH
♠ A 9 2
♡ K J 2
◇ K 8 5
♣ 7 6 3 2

Bidding:

NORTH	EAST	SOUTH	WEST
P	P	1 ◇	3 ♣
3 ◇	P	5 ◇	P
P	P		

SOUTH
♠ 8 5 4
♡ A 9 5
◇ A Q J 10 7 4 2
♣ —

West leads ♣ K.

T. 1: East plays ♣ 5. Declarer discards a Spade.
T. 2: ♠ Q led. Declarer ducks; East plays ♠ 7.
T. 3: ♠ J led. Ace wins; East plays ♠ 3.

Analysis 122.

WEST	EAST
♠ Q J 10	♠ K 7 6 3
♡ Q 7 4 3	♡ 10 8 6
◇ —	◇ 9 6 3
♣ A K Q 10 8 4	♣ J 9 5

The next five tricks are routine. T. 4: Club ruff. T. 5-7: ◇ A Q K. T. 8: Club ruff (§ 10). Now, if East has both Heart honors, failure. If West has both, Heart-Club simple squeeze. If the Hearts are divided, Type L compound squeeze with L (basic) threat ♣ 7, except that the Spade has no entry; but the guard squeeze brings succor. On the last two trumps Dummy discards ♡ J and the basic threat; West can do whatever makes him happiest.

It might be helpful if we emphasize the principle of play illustrated above:

In every Type L double guard squeeze, when the squeeze on West is complete, North discards the basic threat.

As the cards lie, above, Declarer can make his contract by the mere finesse of ♡ J, but this would be a sorrowful way to play the hand. The squeeze succeeds if West has either of the Hearts: why adopt a method that requires him to hold a particular one?

Past question, many opportunities for skillful end play go completely unnoticed. Here, if Declarer makes his contract by finessing the Jack, even a good foursome might never realize that the hand had been dismembered.

Exercise 123.

	NORTH			
♠	—			
♡	A J 9 5 4 3			
◇	A K 9 3			
♣	8 7 3			

Bidding:

NORTH	EAST	SOUTH	WEST
1 ♡	P	3 ♣	P
3 ◇	P	4 NT	P
5 ♡	P	5 NT	P
6 ◇	P	7 NT	P
P	P		

	SOUTH
♠	A K 9
♡	8
◇	6 2
♣	A K Q 10 6 5 4

West leads ◇ J.

T. 1: King wins. East plays ◇ 5.
T. 2: Club. Both follow.
T. 3: Club. West discards ♠ 2.
T. 4: Spade. West plays ♠ 4; East, ♠ Q.

Analysis 123.

WEST	EAST
♠ 10 8 5 4 2	♠ Q J 7 6 3
♡ K 10 2	♡ Q 7 6
◇ J 10 8 7	◇ Q 5 4
♣ 2	♣ J 9

Declarer lays down the Spade in hope of getting some information, and he succeeds. As the only hope, give East ♠ J 10. East has one Heart picture, for if holding both West would have opened that suit. (a) If East has both Hearts, Spade-Heart simple squeeze: cash ◇ A, Clubs. (b) If the Hearts are divided, Type R compound squeeze with R (basic) threat ♠ 9, failing for this reason: after East has identified Suit L by his discard on the last Club, it will be necessary to cash North's L winner, then return in order to lead ♠ K, and South has no re-entry. However, the day is saved by the fact that East will have to guard in both reds.

What are the chances? Well, we are assuming that East held a (probably long) Spade suit headed by Q J 10. If also holding ♡ K Q behind the Ace, plus ◇ Q, he would probably have inserted a bid. So, the vote goes to (b): just finish the Clubs.

As the cards lie, the squeeze is pseudo; but East has made it almost impossibly difficult for West, and almost all Wests would abandon Spades. East has said, "partner, you may throw Spades freely, because I can handle that suit"—the truth being that East can defend both reds but is helpless in Spades.

Evidently this hand does not come under our italicized statement (§ 85), because South rather than North is the hand lacking a vital entry. (Those statements, you recall, cover only the commonest cases.)

x   x   x   x

Quite obviously, the situation described in § 69 may arise in the present problem.

Exercise 124.

NORTH
♠ 5 3
♡ A K 6 2
◊ A K 10 9
♣ 10 7 4

Bidding:

NORTH	EAST	SOUTH	WEST
1 ♡	P	2 ♠	P
3 ◊	P	4 NT	P
5 ♡	P	5 NT	P
6 ♡	P	6 ♠	P
P	P		

SOUTH
♠ A Q J 10 7 6
♡ J 4
◊ 8
♣ A K 3 2

West leads ◊ 2.

T. 1: King wins. East plays ◊ 3.
T. 2: ♠ 5, 9, Q, K.
T. 3: ◊ 4 led. Ace wins.
T. 4-6: Spades. East discards ♣ Q, ♡ 7, 8.
T. 7: ♣ K. West plays ♣ 5; East, ♣ 9.

Analysis 124.

WEST	EAST
♠ K 8 4 2	♠ 9
♡ 10 5 3	♡ Q 9 8 7
◊ Q 7 4 2	◊ J 6 5 3
♣ 6 5	♣ Q J 9 8

After seven tricks the indications are that East holds ♡ Q 10, Q 9 or 10 9, ◊ J x, ♣ J 8. If so, he is elected. The compound squeeze is Type R with R (basic) threat ♣ 3, faulty in that the Diamond threat is not accompanied by an entry: this fault is repaired by the fact that East will have to guard in Hearts. Watch it! One of those Hearts must be cashed (§ 69), and of course the blocking Jack removed. Then, Diamond ruff; Spade; Club.

NORTH
♠ —
♡ A K 6
◇ 10 9
♣ 10

WEST
♠ —
♡ 10 5 3
◇ Q 7
♣ 6

EAST
♠ —
♡ Q 9
◇ J 6
♣ J 8

SOUTH
♠ 7 6
♡ J 4
◇ —
♣ A 3

It is a measure of the progress in bridge technique that many end positions, promulgated years ago as difficult double-dummy problems, now are solvable at the bridge table, provided Declarer follows established principles of play. Double-dummy addicts will recognize this layout as the famous "Whitfield Six."[*]

x x x x

Since the guard squeeze—either simple or double—is far from common in play, it might seem that we have devoted an excessive amount of space to this device. However, no less an authority than Mr. Terence Reese has stated his belief that guard-squeeze positions occur with some frequency, but are apt to be missed. Our own experience, though much less extensive than that of Mr. Reese, would point to the same conclusion. At any rate, you must surely agree that the guard squeeze would be one of the easiest of all endplays to overlook.

86. *Compound squeeze with two losers.* By this time we have two facts clearly in mind. (a) The compound squeeze consists of two halves: first a triple squeeze, then an elementary squeeze. (b) The typical compound squeeze occurs with only one loser remaining.

[*] See H. G. Freehill, The Squeeze at Bridge, p. 121.

With a compound squeeze in prospect and two losers still in hand, it may happen that an early duck is not feasible. Then, under favorable conditions Declarer makes use of the following property. The standard triple squeeze is a two-loser squeeze, which means that the first half of the compound can be executed at once—that is, without a duck. After the triple has occurred, the picture may be so changed that it is possible to lose a trick in order to set the elementary squeeze.

This kind of thing seems most likely to occur in hands where *all four suits are stopped.* In the typical case where two of the four are doubly stopped, you have a sort of super-compound squeeze which can lead to a variety of interesting alternatives.

Exercise 125. °

```
          NORTH
      ♠ A K 8 5
      ♡ K 9 3
      ◇ K Q
      ♣ Q 7 4 3

          SOUTH
      ♠ Q 6 3
      ♡ A 6
      ◇ A 8 4 3
      ♣ A K 5 2
```

Bidding:

SOUTH	WEST	NORTH	EAST
1 NT	P	6 NT	P
P	P		

West leads ♣ J.

T. 1:   East plays ♣ 6; King wins.
T. 2-3: Diamonds. Both follow.
T. 4-5: ♠ K Q. Both follow.
T. 6:   ♠ A. West discards ◇ 9.
T. 7:   ♣ A. East discards ♡ 4.
T. 8:   ♣ Q. East discards ♡ 8.

Analysis 125.

```
      WEST                    EAST
   ♠ 7 2                   ♠ J 10 9 4
   ♡ 10 7 5 2             ♡ Q J 8 4
   ◇ 9 7 2                ◇ J 10 6 5
   ♣ J 10 9 8            ♣ 6
```

° This hand was played by Mr. Irving Deuter, of Detroit, and reported by Mr. William S. Mouser in the Detroit News.

East undoubtedly has Diamonds stopped. Unless he is false-carding, he has two Heart honors. If so, lead of the Club (losing squeeze-card) to the ninth trick will complete the guard squeeze.

It detracts not at all from the brilliance of Declarer's play to point out an alternative method. Run through the first eight tricks as above. Now, East is believed to have a Spade and two Diamonds remaining, therefore only two Hearts. If so, lead of the Spade, T. 9, will set the Heart-Club simple squeeze on West. Note that this method succeeds even if East's ♡ 8 is a false card (trade ♡ J, 7); it would also have worked with ♡ 9, 2 traded.

Exercise 126.

```
        NORTH              Bidding:
      ♠ A K 5 2
      ♡ A 6 5          SOUTH  WEST  NORTH  EAST
      ◇ 6 5 3 2         1 ♣    P    1 ♠    P
      ♣ Q 6             1 NT   P    3 NT   P
                        P      P
        SOUTH
      ♠ 10 4           West leads ◇ J.
      ♡ K 8 4
      ◇ Q 8 7
      ♣ A K J 5 3
```

T. 1: East's Ace wins.
T. 2: ◇ K led. West plays ◇ 4.
T. 3: ♣ 10 led. West plays ♣ 4; Queen wins.
T. 4: ♣ K. East plays ♣ 9; West discards ♡ 7.
T. 5: ♣ A. West discards ♠ 3.
T. 6: ♣ J. West discards ♠ 6.
T. 7: ◇ Q. East discards ♡ 2.

Analysis 126.

```
        WEST                    EAST
      ♠ J 8 6 3              ♠ Q 9 7
      ♡ Q 10 7 3            ♡ J 9 2
      ◇ J 10 9 4            ◇ A K
      ♣ 4                    ♣ 10 9 8 7 2
```

The mistake to avoid is ducking too soon, say after five tricks: instead, extort every last drop of information. After seven tricks the picture looks clear. West, reading his partner's ♣ 9 as signalling a Spade stopper, has abandoned Spades; East has responded to West's ♡ 7 by giving up Hearts. Lead ♣ 5 and discard another Spade, to set the red-suit squeeze on West. Or, if you so please, cross in Hearts—not Spades—and lead the Diamond, discarding a Heart, to set the black-suit squeeze on East.

A triple squeeze is equivalent to three simples (§ 46). Since this hand produces two triples followed by a simple, it might be called the *septuple squeeze*.

PROBLEMS

Problem 30.*

	NORTH
♠	J 9 6
♡	A 9 4 2
◇	9
♣	A 10 9 8 3

	SOUTH
♠	A K 7
♡	K
◇	A K J 10 7 6 5 3
♣	7

Bidding:

EAST	SOUTH	WEST	NORTH
P	1 ◇	P	1 ♡
P	4 NT	P	5 ♡
P	5 NT	P	6 ♣
Dbl.	7 NT	P	P
P			

West leads ♣ 6.

T. 1:   Ace wins. East plays ♣ K.
T. 2-3:   Diamonds. Both follow.

Solution 30.

	WEST
♠	10 8 2
♡	J 8 7 5 3
◇	4 2
♣	6 4 2

	EAST
♠	Q 5 4 3
♡	Q 10 6
◇	Q 8
♣	K Q J 5

After three tricks: if West holds Spades as good as 8 x x, no squeeze because all three threats lie under the stoppers. Thus

* This hand was played by Mr. Leonard P. Zdara, of Newark, O.

the only chance of a genuine squeeze is Spade-Club simple, arising if East holds ♠ Q 10 8 or any five. A much more promising prospect is that gorgeous pseudo compound, because those six remaining Diamonds will really apply the heat. In the actual play, both discarded Spades; but note that with West holding only three Spades, as soon as he discards one Spade the returns are in—Spade-Club simple established.

Can the hand be defended? Yes, if West takes time to draw all the available inferences. There is certainly no hope unless East has a high Heart and a high Spade. Then, three of Declarer's four majors are ♠ A K (or A Q—just as good) and a high Heart. If his other card is a Heart, West is not in the picture; but if Declarer has a spot Spade, West can kill the hand. Of course he pays no attention to Dummy's ♠ J.

Difficult? Certainly—it's compound squeeze defense!

Problem 31.

NORTH	Bidding:			
♠ J 6				
♡ A K Q J 3	EAST	SOUTH	WEST	NORTH
◇ 9 7	P	1 ◇	P	1 ♡
♣ A K Q J	P	1 ♠	P	3 ♣
	P	3 NT	P	4 NT
SOUTH	P	5 ♡	P	5 NT
♠ A K 8 4	P	6 ♡	P	7 NT
♡ 6 2	P	P	P	
◇ A K 6 4 3				
♣ 7 4	West leads ♡ 9.			

T. 1: East plays ♡ 5.

Solution 31.

WEST	EAST
♠ Q 9 2	♠ 10 7 5 3
♡ 10 9 8 7 4	♡ 5
◇ 10 8 5	◇ Q J 2
♣ 10 5	♣ 9 8 6 3 2

The lead places ♡ 10 with East; East's Five gives West the Four. Thus Hearts will surely run, and the hand is a spread.

However, since "no harm can possibly be done thereby," let's run the Clubs first. When the fact develops that East held five Clubs, defeat is certain in case East stops Hearts, because West will sit over both of South's threats. But if West stops Hearts, he is sunk.

As the cards lie, West would discard two Diamonds. Now, if he can still stop Diamonds, then Diamonds were 5-1 and Spades 6-1. So you cash the Diamonds and Hearts to complete this Type R double squeeze.

If a gullible or hasty South pushes out a Heart, T. 2, he kills the squeeze right there. He has no recourse except to finish the Hearts, with East discarding Clubs. Now, South must select Suit L at a time when both ambiguous suits are still doubly defended; and in such a spot, the squeeze can always be defeated very easily.

Unfortunately, we must also remember Anal. 111 (last paragraph). If Declarer cashes the Spades, making Spades Suit L, even a pair of dubs will defeat him (as the cards lie). But if he cashes the Diamonds, each defender will have to keep awake. However, no taint of double-dummy defense is involved, because the situation is clearly readable.

Let us replay the hand with ♡ 10, ♣ 2 traded. Now if Declarer takes another Heart, T. 2, then claims the rest, how many would realize that the hand had been misplayed? That Rule of § 35 is a good tool to keep handy.

Problem 32.*

NORTH	Bidding:
♠ 10 9 2	
♡ K 8 5	
◇ K 9 4	
♣ A K 7 4	

SOUTH	WEST	NORTH	EAST
1 ♠	P	2 ♣	P
2 ♠	P	2 NT	P
4 ♠	P	P	P

SOUTH	
♠ K Q J 6 4 3	West leads ♣ Q.
♡ A 9 3	
◇ A 7 3	
♣ 6	

* This hand was reported in NEA service.

T. 1: King wins. East plays ♣ 2.
T. 2: Spade. East plays ♠ 7; Ace wins.
T. 3: ♣ J led. East discards ◊ 8; Declarer ruffs.
T. 4: Spade. Both follow.

Solution 32.

WEST	EAST
♠ A 5	♠ 8 7
♡ 6	♡ Q J 10 7 4 2
◊ 10 5 2	◊ Q J 8 6
♣ Q J 10 9 8 5 3	♣ 2

A contract of four Spades was reached at twelve tables (though not in most cases, let us hope, on precisely this bidding sequence). One poor fish covered the second Club, making four; the others made five. Apparently no one so much as thought of a squeeze. Yet the presence of a squeeze, against any distribution or any defense, is mathematically proved after four tricks; and the same would be true even if West had room for stoppers in both red suits. However, this does not mean that Declarer can claim the rest (§ 71, last paragraph).

Of course you took care to win in Dummy, T. 4. On ♣ A East discards ♡ 7. Declarer's discard is immaterial—say a Heart. After two more Spades East's discards have made it abundantly clear that West cannot stop Hearts, which means Type B_1 (a) double squeeze with threats R, ♡ 8; L, ♣ 7; B, ◊ 7. "The last R must precede the last F," which says ♡ K A, Spade.

You should also play it with a Diamond discarded, T. 5.

One table played the hand in Notrump by North, making five: "there were eleven tricks for the asking." Change "eleven" to "twelve" and we will agree. With ♡ Q opened, ♠ A driven out and ♣ Q returned, an easier double squeeze would be hard to find.

Problem 33.

NORTH
♠ A K 6
♡ A 8 6 2
◊ A K Q J 4
♣ 7

SOUTH
♠ 7 5 4 2
♡ K 9
◊ 10 6 3
♣ A K Q 5

Bidding:

EAST	SOUTH	WEST	NORTH
P	1 ♣	P	2 ◊
P	2 NT	P	4 NT
P	5 ◊	P	5 NT
P	6 ♡	P	7 NT
P	P	P	

West leads ♠ Q.

T. 1: King wins. East plays ♠ 9.
T. 2-3: Diamonds. Both follow.
T. 4: Diamond. West discards ♡ 7.
T. 5: Diamond. East discards ♡ 4; West ♠ 10.

Solution 33.

WEST	EAST
♠ Q J 10	♠ 9 8 3
♡ Q J 7 3	♡ 10 5 4
◊ 8 7	◊ 9 5 2
♣ 10 6 4 3	♣ J 9 8 2

As the cards lie, all three suits are doubly stopped, which means of course that there is no genuine squeeze. But pseudo compound squeezes are often very difficult to defend.

After five tricks: unless some terrific fakery has been going on, East has ♠ 8 x remaining, which puts West out of Spades, while West has ♡ Q 10 x, which eliminates East's Hearts. Clubs are probably 4-4, but this is immaterial (§ 24). Due to the presence of a Spade threat in each hand, two techniques are available. (a) Type R double squeeze with threats R, ♡ 8; L, ♠ 7; B, ♣ 5. Or (b), Type B₂ double squeeze with threats R, ♠ 6; L, ♡ 8; B, ♣ 5. Of course this is not an "alternate threat squeeze" (§ 84), where both threats are essential; instead, it is of the same kind as Ex. 31.

We have spoken of "defensive errors" (Anal. 111). But in this hand, to ask that West abandon Hearts, East Clubs, is asking almost too much of human nature. Yet this is the only way to beat the hand.

Problem 34.*

NORTH	Bidding:			
♠ A 9 8 7 2				
♡ 3 2	SOUTH	WEST	NORTH	EAST
◊ 9 2	2 ◊	P	2 ♠	P
♣ A J 6 4	3 ◊	P	4 ♣	P
	4 ♡	P	4 ♠	P
SOUTH	4 NT	P	5 ♡	P
♠ K	7 NT	P	P	P
♡ A K 9 7				
◊ A K Q 10 8 7 6	West leads ♠ 5.			
♣ 10				

T. 1: East plays ♠ Q.

T. 2-3: Diamonds. Both follow.

T. 4: Diamond. West discards ♠ 4; East, ♠ 3.

Solution 34.

WEST	EAST
♠ J 10 6 5 4	♠ Q 3
♡ Q 10 5	♡ J 8 6 4
◊ J 4	◊ 5 3
♣ K 7 5	♣ Q 9 8 3 2

West does not have both Club pictures, for if so, he would have opened that suit. In case East has both Clubs, Type B$_2$ double with B threat ♡ 9. If the Clubs are divided, the compound squeeze is strictly counterfeit, but even in that event some manna might fall.

In the actual play, seeing that there is no chance unless his partner holds ♣ Q, West threw all his Clubs (as most players would do). And now, the black Aces smoothly completed the double squeeze.

If West is thoroughly familiar with the various types of double squeeze, he can come up infallibly with the correct defense. He can see very easily what will happen if he abandons Clubs. But

* This hand was played by Mr. J. C. Barefoot, Jr., of Greensboro, N. C.

the closed hand has no more Spades. Thus if West yields Hearts, the Type R squeeze will fail due to inability to cash the L (Spade) winner. This requires that East hold ♡ J 9 x, but it is the only chance.

Declarer pushes out the last Diamond, intending to discard a Heart (if he has already thrown a Heart, he is fresh out of luck). But when that ♡ 10 comes thundering down, it looks as if West has two Spades, two Clubs, and a Heart face. So, pitch the Spade threat and cash one Heart (compare Ex. 124); the rest is obvious.

Thus it turns out that the squeeze is genuine after all: when the compound blows up, the double guard comes to the rescue. Against correct defense, the key card is that insignificant-looking little ♡ 9!

CHAPTER VIII

THE TRUMP SQUEEZE

87. *Definition.* It is difficult to find in the books an explicit, clean-cut definition of the trump squeeze. The definition that will be used in this book is as follows:

The *trump squeeze* is a squeeze in which Declarer's ability to ruff plays an essential role *after the squeeze is established.*

This evidently excludes all such hands as (for instance) Ex. 11, where the squeeze is established by ruffing one opponent out of one threat-suit, after which the play is strictly of notrump character.

In a *simple trump squeeze*, one adversary is squeezed in two suits. It is easy to construct double, triple and compound trump squeezes, but such situations are rare in play and apt to be difficult to recognize: therefore, we shall not discuss these higher forms, beyond a typical example or two. Further, since this book has already grown beyond the bounds originally set for it, we shall present only the principal forms of two-suit trump squeeze.

88. *The simple trump squeeze.* A simple trump squeeze arises when, in one threat-suit, the victim has to retain *an extra guard* to his stopper in order to save that stopper from being ruffed out. In the typical case BLUE must be present with the exception of some one condition. Presence of an extra busy card in the defender's hand means that the squeeze will occur one trick earlier than in the notrump squeeze—that is, on the *next-to-last free winner* (usually but not necessarily a trump). This means that Declarer has a trump still in hand *after the squeeze has occurred,* and this may save the day.

Do not confuse this problem with that of § 10, where the victim's *partner* was ruffed out.

Exercise 127.

	NORTH
♠	A 6 4 2
♡	3
◇	10 4 3 2
♣	A K 8 5

	SOUTH
♠	K 3
♡	A
◇	A K Q J 8 6 5
♣	J 4 3

Bidding:

NORTH	EAST	SOUTH	WEST
1 ♣	P	2 ◇	3 ♡
4 ◇	P	4 ♡	P
4 ♠	P	4 NT	P
5 ♡	P	5 NT	P
6 ◇	P	7 ◇	P
P	P		

West leads ♡ K.

T. 1: East follows.

T. 2-3: Diamonds. East discards Hearts.

Analysis 127.

	WEST		EAST
♠	Q 9 8	♠	J 10 7 5
♡	K Q J 10 9 7 2	♡	8 6 5 4
◇	9 7	◇	—
♣	10	♣	Q 9 7 6 2

West is probably defunct. If East has five Spades and four Clubs, he is ripe: cash the Clubs (Vienna Coup), then run the trumps. But while this is not improbable, we can do better. If East has *four* Spades and four Clubs, West can be ruffed out of Spades—no! This puts us in the failing case of § 14—North's only entry in South's suit, South with no entry in either suit.

Look once more. If East has four Spades and four Clubs, he is dead. Cash one Club on general principles—might drop a blank Queen from West. Then run four more trumps, discarding Clubs. East's last six cards will be four Spades and two Clubs. If he discards a Club, the Ace will drop his Queen; if he yields a Spade the suit can be ruffed out, with ♣ A for entry.

An equally good sequence would be Spades, T. 4-5, followed by four trumps. If East gives a Spade, cross in Clubs, ruff a Spade, return in Clubs; if East unguards Clubs, cash the tops and return by a ruff.

Evidently this is merely a criss-cross squeeze, differing from that of § 13 only in that the element of trumps is necessary: North has an entry in South's suit, and South an entry in North's, either literally (first sequence above) or by means of a ruff in North's suit (second sequence). But do not fail to see clearly that the Spade ruff must be postponed until *after the squeeze has taken place*: if you ruff earlier, you will fail.

Exercise 128.*

NORTH
♠ A Q 4
♡ A K 7 6
◊ A 8 6 3
♣ 5 2

Bidding:

NORTH	EAST	SOUTH	WEST
1 ♡	P	1 ♠	P
3 ♠	P	4 ♠	P
P	P		

SOUTH
♠ K J 10 9 7 2
♡ 10 3
◊ Q J 2
♣ 8 6

West leads ♣ K.

T. 1: East plays ♣ 9.
T. 2: ♣ 4 led. Ace wins.
T. 3: ◊ 4 led. Queen wins; West plays ◊ 7.
T. 4: Spade. Both follow.
T. 5-6: Spades. East discards ◊ 5, ♣ 7.

Analysis 128.

WEST	EAST
♠ 8 6 5	♠ 3
♡ Q 8 5	♡ J 9 4 2
◊ 10 7	◊ K 9 5 4
♣ K Q 10 4 3	♣ A J 9 7

After six tricks it begins to look as if East has the Heart length. If so, the fifth Spade will pin him. (a) If he blanks ◊ K, the Ace will drop the King and the last trump will provide entry for ◊ J. (b) If East trims down to three Hearts, Dummy's thirteener can be ruffed out.

* This hand was played by Mr. Richard M. Carter, of Louisville, Ky.

Exercise 129.

	NORTH			
	♠ 5 3			
	♡ 1 0 9 8 7 4 3			
	◇ 8			
	♣ A K 7 3			

Bidding:

WEST	NORTH	EAST	SOUTH
P	P	1 ♠	2 ♡
P	4 ♡	P	P
P			

	SOUTH	
	♠ K 10 2	
	♡ A K Q 2	
	◇ A J 7 4	
	♣ 5 4	

West leads ♠ 9.

T. 1: East plays ♠ A.
T. 2: East returns ♣ Q, won by King.
T. 3: ♡ A. East discards ♠ 4.

Analysis 129.

	WEST		EAST	
	♠ 9 8 6		♠ A Q J 7 4	
	♡ J 5 2		♡ —	
	◇ 1 0 6 5 2		◇ K Q 9 3	
	♣ 1 0 6 2		♣ Q J 9 8	

With five-odd tricks assured, Declarer plays for six. The bad
Heart division prevents ruffing the second Club, but East is
unable to cause any ambiguity. We leave it to you.

PROBLEMS

Problem 35.

NORTH
- ♠ A 2
- ♡ A K J 9 3 2
- ◊ A K J
- ♣ 10 5

Bidding:

SOUTH	WEST	NORTH	EAST
4 ♣	4 ♠	7 ♣	P
P	P		

West leads ♠ K.

SOUTH
- ♠ 7 6
- ♡ 8
- ◊ 5 4 2
- ♣ A K Q J 8 6 4

T. 1:   East plays ♠ 3.
T. 2-5: Clubs. East discards ◊ 10, 6, ♠ 8, 9.
T. 6:   Heart. Both follow.
T. 7:   Heart. West discards ♠ 4.

Show that the contract is guaranteed on the one assumption that West had six Spades.

Solution 35.

WEST	EAST
♠ K Q J 10 5 4	♠ 9 8 3
♡ 4	♡ Q 10 7 6 5
◊ Q 3	◊ 10 9 8 7 6
♣ 9 7 3 2	♣ —

Of course you ruff a Heart, then lead a trump. If East discards a Heart, he is through. If not, he throws down to two Diamonds, whereupon the Queen will fall no matter where it may be, setting up the Five.

This is the first case we have had where the sufferer has to keep two extra guards to his stopper. Do not fail to note that if you have cashed one Diamond earlier, "on general principles," it will be just too bad.

Problem 36.*

NORTH   Contract:
♠ A 9
♡ 1 0 7 5 2   5 Spades by South.
♢ J 9 8 4
♣ K 9 2   West leads ♡ 6.

SOUTH
♠ K Q J 10 7 6 4 2
♡ —
♢ 5 2
♣ A 10 8

T. 1: East's Ace wins. Declarer discards a Diamond.
T. 2: ♡ 3 led. Declarer ruffs; West plays ♡ 4.
T. 3: Diamond. West's Queen wins; East plays ♢ 10.
T. 4: ♡ 8 led. East plays ♡ J; Declarer ruffs.
T. 5: ♠ A. West discards ♡ 9.
T. 6: Diamond ruff. East plays ♢ K.
T. 7: ♠ 9. West discards ♢ 3.
T. 8: Diamond ruff. East discards ♣ 3.

Solution 36.

WEST   EAST
♠ —   ♠ 8 5 3
♡ K 9 8 6 4   ♡ A Q J 3
♢ A Q 7 6 3   ♢ K 10
♣ Q 7 6   ♣ J 5 4 3

After four tricks: as long as each opponent stops both red suits, there is no squeeze, regardless of the Club situation. If both Club pictures are in one hand, the opposite hand can defend both red suits; if the Clubs are divided, either opponent can take up the red burden. And the situation is so exposed that the defense could hardly make a mistake. But it looks as if East can be ruffed out of Diamonds.

After eight tricks: if East has both Clubs, failure. If West has

* This hand was played by Mr. Ted Nellis, of Pontiac, Mich., and reported by Mr. Frank S. Eaton in the Detroit Free Press. The bidding is not available.

both, Diamond-Club simple squeeze. Clubs divided, double guard squeeze. West will discard two Clubs on the chance that East's last three Clubs are J 10 x.

Problem 37.

NORTH		Bidding:			
♠ K J 9 8 6 3 2					
♡ J 3		SOUTH	WEST	NORTH	EAST
◇ 10		1 ♣	P	1 ♠	P
♣ J 8 7		3 ♣	P	3 ♠	P
		4 ♣	P	4 ♠	Dbl.
SOUTH		5 ♣	P	P	Dbl.
♠ A		P	P	P	
♡ 9 4 2					
◇ K Q J		West leads ♠ 4.			
♣ A K Q 10 4 2					

T. 1: Dummy plays ♠ 8; East, ♠ 5.

Solution 37.

WEST	EAST
♠ 4	♠ Q 10 7 5
♡ Q 8 7 6 5	♡ A K 10
◇ 9 6 4 3 2	◇ A 8 7 5
♣ 9 5	♣ 6 3

The lead is surely a singleton; therefore, three entries to Dummy must be found. Two methods are available. (a) Lead ♣ 10 and overtake, succeeding if ♣ 9 is blank: a 1-in-8 chance. (b) Lead low and finesse ♣ 7, succeeding (unless West is super) if Clubs are 2-2 with West holding the Nine: a 1-in-5 chance. So, Club finesse, T. 2; Spade ruff, T. 3; ♣ 10 overtaken, T. 4: concede one and claim the rest.

West is the goat, but excusably so—at least as bridge is played out here in the sticks. If he stops to look, he can see that insertion of the Nine will block the suit provided East has two small Clubs.

Problem 38.*

	NORTH
♠	A K 5
♡	Q
◇	Q 10 7 3
♣	A Q J 10 4

Bidding:

EAST	SOUTH	WEST	NORTH
P	P	P	1 ♣
1 ♡	1 ♠	Dbl.	P
2 ♡	3 ♣	3 ♡	3 ♠
4 ♡	4 ♠	Dbl.	P
P	P		

	SOUTH
♠	9 8 7 6 2
♡	8
◇	A J 9
♣	K 8 5 2

West leads ♡ A.

T. 1: East plays ♡ 7.
T. 2: ♡ 4 led.

Solution 38.

	WEST		EAST
♠	Q J 10 4 3	♠	—
♡	A 9 6 4 2	♡	K J 10 7 5 3
◇	6 4	◇	K 8 5 2
♣	3	♣	9 7 6

West's first double, horrific at best, can only be explained on the ground that he has five Spades. So Declarer ruffs with the Six and leads the Deuce; West, momentarily napping, shoves out his Trey and the Five wins!

With one high hurdle safely cleared, another lies ahead. Declarer plans to force West twice, with West forcing the closed hand twice, in return, after which West's trumps can be picked up. So, T. 4, ♣ Q: both follow. T. 5, ♣ J: West discards a Diamond. Were West to make the mistake of ruffing the second and presently the third Club, the Diamond finesse could be avoided. But now, if Declarer leads a third Club, he will ultimately have to yield a trick to ◇ K (check it). So, T. 6: ◇ Q, which holds. T. 7: Diamond finesse. And now West is helpless.

* This hand was played by Mr. Richard M. Carter.

Problem 39.

	NORTH		Bidding:			
♠	—					
♡	A 10 8 6 2		EAST	SOUTH	WEST	NORTH
◊	A 3		P	1 ♣	P	1 ♡
♣	Q J 7 6 5 2		P	2 ♠	P	3 ♣
			P	3 ♡	P	6 ♣
	SOUTH		P	7 ♣	P	P
♠	A K J 2					
♡	K Q 3		West leads	◊ 4.		
◊	Q 10 5					
♣	A K 8					

T. 1: Ace wins. East plays ◊ 9.
T. 2: ♣ A. East plays ◊ 2.

Solution 39.

	WEST			EAST	
♠	8 7 6 4		♠	Q 10 9 5 3	
♡	4		♡	J 9 7 5	
◊	J 8 7 4		◊	K 9 6 2	
♣	10 9 4 3		♣	—	

This being a three-suit-squeeze, East is in trouble almost from the start. The squeeze takes place on the second-from-last free winner. With East having been squeezed twice, there will be no ambiguity.

MISCELLANEOUS PROBLEMS

Problem 40.*

NORTH
♠ 7 5
♡ A K 9 5
◇ J 10 7 4 2
♣ 6 5

SOUTH
♠ A K Q 9 8 6 4
♡ 4 2
◇ —
♣ A 10 3 2

Bidding:

WEST	NORTH	EAST	SOUTH
P	P	1 ♣	2 ♠
3 ♣	3 ♡	P	4 ♣
P	4 ♠	P	6 ♠
P	P	P	

West leads ◇ K.

T. 1: Declarer ruffs.

Solution 40.

WEST
♠ J 3
♡ Q 10 3
◇ K Q 9 5 3
♣ J 7 4

EAST
♠ 10 2
♡ J 8 7 6
◇ A 8 6
♣ K Q 9 8

With proper divisions in the black suits, there are squeeze possibilities. Declarer lost a Club, captured the Spade return, cashed ♣ A and ruffed a Club, ruffed a Diamond and played the trumps.

* This hand was played by Mr. Clyde Morrison, of Detroit, and reported by Mr. William S. Mouser in the Detroit News.

Problem 41.

	NORTH
♠	A Q 7 5
♡	Q 7
♢	8 7 4 2
♣	A K Q

Bidding:

NORTH	EAST	SOUTH	WEST
1 ♣	1 ♢	1 ♡	P
1 ♠	P	1 NT	P
2 NT	P	3 NT	P
P	P		

	SOUTH
♠	K 6
♡	A 9 8 6 5
♢	A 10
♣	9 6 4 2

West leads ♢ 6.

T. 1: ♢ J wins.
T. 2: ♢ K led. ♢ A wins.
T. 3-4: Clubs.
T. 5: Club. East discards ♡ 3.

Solution 41.

WEST	EAST
♠ J 10 8 3	♠ 9 4 2
♡ J 4 2	♡ K 10 3
♢ 6 5	♢ K Q J 9 3
♣ J 8 7 5	♣ 10 3

It is perhaps a close question whether East or West has ♡ K, but Declarer decides on East on the strength of the bidding. He throws East in with a Diamond, T. 9, and waits with bated breath for the twelfth trick.

Problem 42.*

```
           NORTH                Bidding:
        ♠ K 10 7 4
        ♡ K 7 6 2         SOUTH   WEST   NORTH   EAST
        ◊ 7               1 ♡     2 ♣    2 ♡     P
        ♣ J 10 6 5        2 ♠     P      3 ♠     P
                          3 NT    P      P       P
           SOUTH
        ♠ 3                   West leads ♣ 7.
        ♡ Q 9 5
        ◊ A K J 10 4 3
        ♣ A K 3
```

T. 1: Ten wins. East discards ♠ 9.

T. 2: Diamond finesse wins.

T. 3: ◊ A. West plays ♣ 2.

T. 4: ♡ Q won by West's Ace.

T. 5: ♠ 2 led. North plays Ten, East Jack.

T. 6: ♠ 6 led. West's Ace wins.

T. 7: ♠ 5 led.

Solution 42.

```
           WEST                     EAST
        ♠ A 5 2                  ♠ Q J 9 8 6
        ♡ A 8 4                  ♡ J 10 3
        ◊ 8                      ◊ Q 9 6 5 2
        ♣ Q 9 8 7 4 2            ♣ —
```

South wins with Dummy's ♠ K, cashes South's ♣ A K, returns to ♡ K and throws East in with ♠ 7.

---

* This hand was played by Mr. Martin J. Cohn, of Detroit, and reported by Mr. William S. Mouser in the Detroit News.

Problem 43.*

NORTH
♠ A K J 9
♡ A Q J 9 3
◊ J 10 8
♣ A

SOUTH
♠ Q 7 6 4 3
♡ K 6
◊ K Q 9
♣ 8 7 5

Contract:

Six Spades by South.

West leads ♣ K.

T. 1:   Ace wins.

T. 2-4:   Trumps drawn. West discards Clubs.

Solution 43.

WEST
♠ 2
♡ 10 7 4
◊ 6 3 2
♣ K Q J 10 9 2

EAST
♠ 10 8 5
♡ 8 5 2
◊ A 7 5 4
♣ 6 4 3

Declarer ran the Hearts, discarding Diamonds. East passed
◊ J, South discarding a Club, after which the cross-ruff completed the score for seven. Had East gone in on the first Diamond, the result would have been the same.

* This hand was played by Mr. Ted Nellis, of Pontiac, Mich., and reported by Mr. Frank S. Eaton in the Detroit Free Press.

Problem 44.

NORTH
- ♠ K 4
- ♡ A 10 5
- ◇ 7 3
- ♣ K J 9 7 4 2

SOUTH
- ♠ A J 8 7 3
- ♡ Q 8 7
- ◇ A J 9 6 4
- ♣ —

Bidding:

EAST	SOUTH	WEST	NORTH
1 NT	2 ♠	P	3 ♣
P	3 ◇	P	3 ♠
Dbl.	P	P	P

West leads ♣ 5.

T. 1: ♣ 9 to ♣ A. Declarer ruffs.
T. 2: ♠ K. Both follow.
T. 3: ♠ J finessed. Both follow.
T. 4: ♠ A. West discards ♡ 2.

Solution 44.

WEST
- ♠ 9 2
- ♡ 9 4 3 2
- ◇ 8 5 2
- ♣ Q 10 8 5

EAST
- ♠ Q 10 6 5
- ♡ K J 6
- ◇ K Q 10
- ♣ A 6 3

After four tricks, East was a sitting pigeon for a throw-in.

Problem 45.

NORTH
- ♠ K Q J
- ♡ 4
- ◇ A 10 5 4 2
- ♣ A 9 6 5

SOUTH
- ♠ 7 4 3
- ♡ A Q 10 9 6 3
- ◇ 8 7 3
- ♣ 8

Bidding:

WEST	NORTH	EAST	SOUTH
P	1 ◇	Dbl.	4 ♡
P	P	P	

West leads ♠ 2.

T. 1: East plays ♠ A.
T. 2: ♣ K led; Ace wins.
T. 3: Heart. Ten wins; West plays ♡ 7.

Solution 45.

	WEST		EAST
♠	10 6 5 2	♠	A 9 8
♡	7	♡	K J 8 5 2
◊	Q 6	◊	K J 9
♣	J 10 7 4 3 2	♣	K Q

If West's lead is honest, East has two Spades remaining. Therefore, Declarer can make the hand. T. 4: Spade. T. 5: Club ruff. T. 6: Spade. T. 7: Club ruff. T. 8: ◊ A. T. 9: Club ruff. And now the exit in Diamonds assures Declarer of making ♡ A Q.

Problem 46.

	NORTH			Bidding:			
♠	A K Q 10			NORTH	EAST	SOUTH	WEST
♡	A Q 8			1 ♣	P	1 ♡	P
◊	6 5			1 ♠	P	3 ♡	P
♣	A K 4 2			4 NT	P	5 ◊	P
	SOUTH			6 ♡	P	P	P
♠	—			West leads ◊ K.			
♡	K J 10 9 6 2						
◊	A 10 3						
♣	7 6 5 3						

T. 1:   ◊ A.
T. 2-3:   ♡ A Q. Both follow.

Solution 46.

	WEST		EAST
♠	8 5 3 2	♠	J 9 7 6 4
♡	7 5	♡	4 3
◊	K Q J 9	◊	8 7 4 2
♣	Q 9 8	♣	J 10

With so many squeeze possibilities, Declarer plays for the overtrick. If West shows up with ◊ Q J and either ♠ J or three Clubs, he is elected. We leave it to you.

It is equally reasonable to play for the Clubs to split 3-2 after the trumps break favorably. Cash the Spades, discarding a Diamond and two Clubs. Take the top Clubs and ruff a Club. Return to Dummy with ♡ 8 to discard another Diamond on the last Club.

Problem 47.

	NORTH
♠	Q 9 5
♡	A Q 4 3
◇	Q J 9 7
♣	K 6

Bidding:

NORTH	EAST	SOUTH	WEST
1 ♡	2 ♣	3 ◇	P
3 NT	P	4 ♣	P
5 ◇	P	7 ◇	P
P	P		

	SOUTH
♠	A 10 8
♡	K 5 2
◇	A K 8 5 4 3 2
♣	—

West leads ♣ J.

Plan Declarer's play.

Solution 47.

WEST	
♠	7 6 4 3
♡	9 6
◇	10 6
♣	J 10 9 4 3

EAST	
♠	K J 2
♡	J 10 8 7
◇	—
♣	A Q 8 7 5 2

Declarer ducks and ruffs, T. 1. Even if Hearts break, the only hope is a squeeze, which requires that East hold ♠ K J. But if Hearts do not break, there is still a chance: East may have the length. If so, to discard the Club or Heart stopper will leave him under the gun for a second squeeze; to discard down to ♠ K will establish the double threat—♠ 10 8.

Problem 48.

	NORTH
♠	A 8
♡	A K Q
◇	J 7 4
♣	Q 8 7 6 4

Bidding:

EAST	SOUTH	WEST	NORTH
1 ♣	3 ◇	P	6 ◇
P	P	P	

	SOUTH
♠	Q 4
♡	8 7 6 3
◇	A K Q 10 6 5 3
♣	—

West leads ♣ 9.

T. 1: Duck and ruff.
T. 2: ◇ A. West discards a Spade.

Solution 48.

	WEST		EAST
♠	J 10 7 6 3 2	♠	K 9 5
♡	J 10 9 4	♡	5 2
◇	—	◇	9 8 2
♣	9 3 2	♣	A K J 10 5

The obvious plan—ruff the fourth heart if necessary—is spoiled by the 3-0 trump division. Still, everything is under control unless East shows up with four Hearts, because his bid places ♠ K in his hand.

East cannot escape the throw-in. South runs the Trumps and Hearts, after which a Club puts East in for a Spade return. East should make things tough by discarding two Spades very early and then falsecarding in Clubs to give the appearance of four in each black suit, but the nature of West's opening lead should prevent South from being deceived.

Problem 49.*

	NORTH
♠	K 9 8 2
♡	10 8 7 4 2
◇	8
♣	K 8 4

	SOUTH
♠	7 5 4 3
♡	A K J 6
◇	A J
♣	A 3 2

Bidding:

NORTH	EAST	SOUTH	WEST
P	P	1 ♡	2 ◇
2 ♡	P	4 ♡	P
P	P		

West leads ♠ A.

T. 1: Ace wins.
T. 2: ♣ Q led.

Solution 49.

	WEST		EAST
♠	A	♠	Q J 10 6
♡	Q 5	♡	9 3
◇	K Q 9 7 3 2	◇	10 6 5 4
♣	Q J 9 7	♣	10 6 5

* This hand was played by Mrs. Dean Carron of Ann Arbor, Mich., and reported by Mr. William S. Mouser in the Detroit News.

The Ace followed by a shift caused Declarer to think that the lead was a singleton. Therefore, Declarer played to toss West in at a time when his only return would hand Declarer a trick.

The best chance is to let West hold the ♣ Q. South wins any continuation, draws two Trumps, cashes top Clubs, ♠ K and ◊ A. West is then put in with a Diamond.

Problem 50.

	NORTH
♠	A 7 5
♡	A K 4 2
◊	A K 3
♣	6 3 2

Bidding:

SOUTH	WEST	NORTH	EAST
3 ♣	P	6 ♣	P
P	P		

West leads ♡ Q.

	SOUTH
♠	2
♡	7 3
◊	Q 9 7 4
♣	A K Q J 9 4

T. 1: King wins.
T. 2-5: Clubs. North discards ♠ 5. East discards ♠ 8 3 4, ♡ 8.
T. 6-7: ◊ A K. All follow.
T. 8: ◊ Q. West discards ♠ 6.

Solution 50.

	WEST		EAST
♠	Q 9 6	♠	K J 10 8 4 3
♡	Q J 10 5	♡	9 8 6
◊	8 6	◊	J 10 5 2
♣	10 8 7 5	♣	—

With the contract assured, Declarer plays for the overtrick. He hopes for a 3-3 split in Diamonds. When this does not develop, perhaps a double squeeze will do as well.

Problem 51.*

	NORTH
♠	10 8
♡	K J 9 5
◇	A 7 5
♣	Q 9 6 5

	SOUTH
♠	K J 4
♡	A 10 8 2
◇	K Q
♣	A 10 7 2

Bidding:

SOUTH	WEST	NORTH	EAST
1 NT	P	2 ♣	2 ◇
2 ♡	P	4 ♡	P
P	Dbl.	P	P
P			

West leads ◇ 8.

T. 1: King wins.
T. 2: ♡ A led. East discards a Diamond.
T. 3: ♡ 2 to ♡ 9.
T. 4: ♣ Q to ♣ K.
T. 5: Low Heart to ♡ J.
T. 6: Low Club finessed.

Solution 51.

	WEST
♠	A Q 9 6 5
♡	Q 7 6 4 3
◇	8
♣	K 4

	EAST
♠	7 3 2
♡	—
◇	J 10 9 6 4 3 2
♣	J 8 3

West can see the throw-in developing, but he is helpless. We leave it to you.

---

* This hand was played by Mr. Holton Sexton, of Greensfork, Ind., and reported by Mr. William S. Mouser in the Detroit News.

Problem 52.

NORTH
♠ K 4 3 2
♡ A K 6 5
◇ —
♣ A Q 7 5 2

SOUTH
♠ Q 10 9 7 5
♡ Q 7 2
◇ 9 7 4 2
♣ J

Bidding:

EAST	SOUTH	WEST	NORTH
1 ◇	P	P	Dbl.
1 NT	P	P	Dbl.
P	2 ♠	P	3 ♠
P	4 ♠	P	P
P			

West leads ◇ 8.

T. 1: Ruff.
T. 2-4: ♡ A Q K.

Solution 52.

WEST
♠ J 8 6
♡ 9 8 4
◇ 8 6 3
♣ 9 8 6 4

EAST
♠ A
♡ J 10 3
◇ A K Q J 10 5
♣ K 10 3

Declarer tries the Hearts at once. Then, T. 5: ♣ A. T. 6: Club ruff. T. 7: Diamond ruff. T. 8: Club ruff. T. 9: Diamond ruff. Now, ♣ Q is ruffed by ♠ A, and West's Jack is smothered by the Diamond return.

If East had refused to ruff, Declarer would, of course, have ruffed with ♠ 9, then made his Queen good by a lead from the board.

* This hand was played by Mr. William B. Woodson.

Problem 53.*

NORTH
♠ J 9
♡ K 4
◇ Q J 6 4 3
♣ A K 9 3

SOUTH
♠ K Q 10 5
♡ A Q 10 8 3 2
◇ —
♣ J 8 4

Bidding:

EAST	SOUTH	WEST	NORTH
1 ◇	1 ♡	P	2 ♣
P	3 ♠	P	6 ♡
P	P	P	

West leads ◇ 8.

T. 1: North plays ◇ J, East plays ◇ K. Declarer ruffs.
T. 2-4: Trumps exhausted. East discards ◇ 2.

Solution 53.

WEST
♠ 7 6 4 2
♡ J 9 5
◇ 8 7 5
♣ 10 7 5

EAST
♠ A 8 3
♡ 7 6
◇ A K 10 9 2
♣ Q 6 2

Declarer led to ♠ J; East won with Ace and returned the suit. Now Declarer led Spades and Hearts to produce the trump squeeze.

At the end, Dummy saves two top Clubs and two Diamonds. South has a Trump and three Clubs. East must unguard the Queen of Clubs or allow South to ruff out the ◇ A.

* This hand was played by Mr. H. Sanborn Brown, of Detroit, and reported by Mr. Frank S. Eaton in the Detroit Free Press.

Problem 54.

```
        NORTH              Bidding:
     ♠ A 7 3 2
     ♡ A 7 2          EAST    SOUTH   WEST   NORTH
     ◊ J 9 5           P       5 ◊     P      6 ◊
     ♣ A K 10          P       P       P
        SOUTH
     ♠ 10              West leads ♣ 5.
     ♡ 10
     ◊ A K Q 10 8 6 4 3
     ♣ 8 7 4
```

T. 1: King wins. East plays ♣ 6.

Solution 54.

```
        WEST                      EAST
     ♠ K J 9 6 4              ♠ Q 8 5
     ♡ K J 8 6 5             ♡ Q 9 4 3
     ◊ 7 2                    ◊ —
     ♣ 5                      ♣ Q J 9 6 3 2
```

Well, fellows, can you guess correctly, against average defense, so as to make seven out of this six hand?

Two Trumps, Club Ace, and three more Trumps compel East to bear down to a doubleton in one of the majors. South leads that major suit to Dummy's Ace, ruffs the return, and runs trumps for Type R double squeeze. (Deceptive discarding by East may mislead South.)

Problem 55.*

```
        NORTH              Bidding:
     ♠ A 4 3
     ♡ A 7 2          NORTH   EAST   SOUTH   WEST
     ◊ A K Q 8 6       2 ◊     P      3 NT    P
     ♣ A 8             6 NT    P      P       P
        SOUTH
     ♠ K J 10          West leads ♡ J.
     ♡ K 9 5 3
     ◊ 10 5
     ♣ K 9 3 2
```

* This hand was played by Mr. John W. Norwood, Jr.

T. 1:   ♡ A.
T. 2-4: ◊ A K Q. Both follow.

Solution 55.

	WEST		EAST
♠	Q 8 2	♠	9 7 6 5
♡	J 10 8 6	♡	Q 4
◊	J 7 4	◊	9 3 2
♣	10 6 4	♣	Q J 7 5

The question is, should Declarer go for seven by trying to place ♠ Q by guess or for six by ducking a Club. Declarer quite properly chose the latter.

Problem 56.*

	NORTH	
♠	K Q 5 3	Contract:
♡	A 10 9 6	4 ♡ by South.
◊	K 10 8	
♣	A 6	West leads ♠ A.

	SOUTH
♠	8
♡	K Q 7 5 3 2
◊	A 6 3
♣	J 8 3

T. 1: Ace wins.
T. 2: ♠ J to K.

Solution 56.

	WEST		EAST
♠	A J 10 7 6	♠	9 4 2
♡	J 4	♡	8
◊	Q 9 7	◊	J 5 4 2
♣	K 4 2	♣	Q 10 9 7 5

Until West discards to the fifth Heart, one cannot tell whether the doubly-stopped threats are ◊ 10, ♣ J, or ◊ 6, ♣ 6.

---

* This hand was played by Mr. Robert White of Ann Arbor, Michigan. The bidding is not available.

Problem 57.*

NORTH
♠ K 9 3
♡ 9
◇ 10 8 6 2
♣ A J 7 6 5

Bidding:

SOUTH	WEST	NORTH	EAST
1 ♡	P	2 ♣	3 ◇
4 NT	P	5 ◇	P
6 ♡	P	P	P

SOUTH
♠ A Q 4
♡ A Q J 10 6 5 3
◇ A
♣ Q 4

West leads ◇ 9.

T. 1: Ace wins.
T. 2: ♡ A wins.
T. 3: ♡ Q to K. East discards ♣ 9.
T. 4: ◇ 3 led.

Solution 57.

WEST
♠ 10 8 5 2
♡ K 8 4 2
◇ 9 3
♣ 10 3 2

EAST
♠ J 7 6
♡ 7
◇ K Q J 7 5 4
♣ K 9 8

At trick nine this was the situation: North ♠ K, ◇ 10 8, ♣ A; East ◇ K Q, ♣ K 8; South ♠ 4, ♡ 5, ♣ Q 4. When ♠ K was cashed, East glared at partner.

Problem 58.

NORTH
♠ K 5
♡ K 6 3
◇ 8 5 4
♣ K 9 5 3 2

Bidding:

SOUTH	WEST	NORTH	EAST
2 ♠	P	3 ♣	P
3 ♠	P	4 ♠	P
4 NT	P	5 ♣	P
5 NT	P	7 ♠	P
P	P		

SOUTH
♠ A Q J 10 7 3 2
♡ A 5 2
◇ A 3
♣ A

West leads ♣ Q.

* This hand was played by Miss Frances Taylor of Detroit, Michigan, and reported by Mr. Frank S. Eaton in the Detroit Free Press.

Solution 58.

WEST	EAST
♠ 9 8	♠ 6 4
♡ J 10 8 4	♡ Q 9 7
◇ K J 9	◇ Q 10 7 6 2
♣ Q J 10 4	♣ 8 7 6

North, as soon as he was sure of his side holding all the Aces, went for a top. You take it from there.

*Problem 59.**

NORTH
♠ A Q 6
♡ 6 5 3
◇ A 10 2
♣ A 8 6 4

SOUTH
♠ K 7 4
♡ 9
◇ Q J 9 8 7 5
♣ K 10 5

Bidding:

NORTH	EAST	SOUTH	WEST
1 ♣	1 ♡	2 ◇	P
3 ◇	P	5 ◇	P
P	P		

West leads ♡ K.

T. 1: King wins.
T. 2: ♡ Q, ruffed.
T. 3: ◇ J. East discards a Heart.

Solution 59.

WEST	EAST
♠ J 8 5	♠ 10 9 3 2
♡ K Q 2	♡ A J 10 8 7 4
◇ K 6 4 3	◇ —
♣ 9 3 2	♣ Q J 7

Declarer sees but one way to make it. He finesses ◇ 10, trumps Dummy's last Heart, cashes ♠ K Q A and ♣ A K. When ♣ 10 throws East in, East has to lead a Heart and ◇ K is trapped.

* This hand was played by Mr. Grant Shaffer, of Detroit, and reported by Mr. William S. Mouser in the Detroit News.

INDEX

A CATALOGUE OF SELECTED DOVER BOOKS
IN ALL FIELDS OF INTEREST

A CATALOGUE OF SELECTED DOVER BOOKS
IN ALL FIELDS OF INTEREST

WHAT IS SCIENCE?, *N. Campbell*
The role of experiment and measurement, the function of mathematics, the nature of scientific laws, the difference between laws and theories, the limitations of science, and many similarly provocative topics are treated clearly and without technicalities by an eminent scientist. "Still an excellent introduction to scientific philosophy," H. Margenau in *Physics Today*. "A first-rate primer . . . deserves a wide audience," *Scientific American*. 192pp. 5⅜ x 8.
Paperbound $1.25

THE NATURE OF LIGHT AND COLOUR IN THE OPEN AIR, *M. Minnaert*
Why are shadows sometimes blue, sometimes green, or other colors depending on the light and surroundings? What causes mirages? Why do multiple suns and moons appear in the sky? Professor Minnaert explains these unusual phenomena and hundreds of others in simple, easy-to-understand terms based on optical laws and the properties of light and color. No mathematics is required but artists, scientists, students, and everyone fascinated by these "tricks" of nature will find thousands of useful and amazing pieces of information. Hundreds of observational experiments are suggested which require no special equipment. 200 illustrations; 42 photos. xvi + 362pp. 5⅜ x 8.
Paperbound $2.00

THE STRANGE STORY OF THE QUANTUM, AN ACCOUNT FOR THE GENERAL READER OF THE GROWTH OF IDEAS UNDERLYING OUR PRESENT ATOMIC KNOWLEDGE, *B. Hoffmann*
Presents lucidly and expertly, with barest amount of mathematics, the problems and theories which led to modern quantum physics. Dr. Hoffmann begins with the closing years of the 19th century, when certain trifling discrepancies were noticed, and with illuminating analogies and examples takes you through the brilliant concepts of Planck, Einstein, Pauli, Broglie, Bohr, Schroedinger, Heisenberg, Dirac, Sommerfeld, Feynman, etc. This edition includes a new, long postscript carrying the story through 1958. "Of the books attempting an account of the history and contents of our modern atomic physics which have come to my attention, this is the best," H. Margenau, Yale University, in *American Journal of Physics*. 32 tables and line illustrations. Index. 275pp. 5⅜ x 8.
Paperbound $1.75

GREAT IDEAS OF MODERN MATHEMATICS: THEIR NATURE AND USE, *Jagjit Singh*
Reader with only high school math will understand main mathematical ideas of modern physics, astronomy, genetics, psychology, evolution, etc. better than many who use them as tools, but comprehend little of their basic structure. Author uses his wide knowledge of non-mathematical fields in brilliant exposition of differential equations, matrices, group theory, logic, statistics, problems of mathematical foundations, imaginary numbers, vectors, etc. Original publication. 2 appendixes. 2 indexes. 65 ills. 322pp. 5⅜ x 8.
Paperbound $2.00

THE MUSIC OF THE SPHERES: THE MATERIAL UNIVERSE — FROM ATOM TO QUASAR, SIMPLY EXPLAINED, *Guy Murchie*
Vast compendium of fact, modern concept and theory, observed and calculated data, historical background guides intelligent layman through the material universe. Brilliant exposition of earth's construction, explanations for moon's craters, atmospheric components of Venus and Mars (with data from recent fly-by's), sun spots, sequences of star birth and death, neighboring galaxies, contributions of Galileo, Tycho Brahe, Kepler, etc.; and (Vol. 2) construction of the atom (describing newly discovered sigma and xi subatomic particles), theories of sound, color and light, space and time, including relativity theory, quantum theory, wave theory, probability theory, work of Newton, Maxwell, Faraday, Einstein, de Broglie, etc. "Best presentation yet offered to the intelligent general reader," *Saturday Review*. Revised (1967). Index. 319 illustrations by the author. Total of xx + 644pp. 5⅜ x 8½.
Vol. 1 Paperbound $2.00, Vol. 2 Paperbound $2.00,
The set $4.00

FOUR LECTURES ON RELATIVITY AND SPACE, *Charles Proteus Steinmetz*
Lecture series, given by great mathematician and electrical engineer, generally considered one of the best popular-level expositions of special and general relativity theories and related questions. Steinmetz translates complex mathematical reasoning into language accessible to laymen through analogy, example and comparison. Among topics covered are relativity of motion, location, time; of mass; acceleration; 4-dimensional time-space; geometry of the gravitational field; curvature and bending of space; non-Euclidean geometry. Index. 40 illustrations. x + 142pp. 5⅜ x 8½.　　　　　　　　Paperbound $1.35

HOW TO KNOW THE WILD FLOWERS, *Mrs. William Starr Dana*
Classic nature book that has introduced thousands to wonders of American wild flowers. Color-season principle of organization is easy to use, even by those with no botanical training, and the genial, refreshing discussions of history, folklore, uses of over 1,000 native and escape flowers, foliage plants are informative as well as fun to read. Over 170 full-page plates, collected from several editions, may be colored in to make permanent records of finds. Revised to conform with 1950 edition of Gray's Manual of Botany. xlii + 438pp. 5⅜ x 8½.　　　　　　　　　　　　　　　　　　　　Paperbound $2.00

MANUAL OF THE TREES OF NORTH AMERICA, *Charles Sprague Sargent*
Still unsurpassed as most comprehensive, reliable study of North American tree characteristics, precise locations and distribution. By dean of American dendrologists. Every tree native to U.S., Canada, Alaska; 185 genera, 717 species, described in detail—leaves, flowers, fruit, winterbuds, bark, wood, growth habits, etc. plus discussion of varieties and local variants, immaturity variations. Over 100 keys, including unusual 11-page analytical key to genera, aid in identification. 783 clear illustrations of flowers, fruit, leaves. An unmatched permanent reference work for all nature lovers. Second enlarged (1926) edition. Synopsis of families. Analytical key to genera. Glossary of technical terms. Index. 783 illustrations, 1 map. Total of 982pp. 5⅜ x 8.
Vol. 1 Paperbound $2.25, Vol. 2 Paperbound $2.25,
The set $4.50

IT's FUN TO MAKE THINGS FROM SCRAP MATERIALS,
Evelyn Glantz Hershoff
What use are empty spools, tin cans, bottle tops? What can be made from
rubber bands, clothes pins, paper clips, and buttons? This book provides
simply worded instructions and large diagrams showing you how to make
cookie cutters, toy trucks, paper turkeys, Halloween masks, telephone sets,
aprons, linoleum block- and spatter prints — in all 399 projects! Many are easy
enough for young children to figure out for themselves; some challenging
enough to entertain adults; all are remarkably ingenious ways to make things
from materials that cost pennies or less! Formerly "Scrap Fun for Everyone."
Index. 214 illustrations. 373pp. 5⅜ x 8½.   Paperbound $1.50

SYMBOLIC LOGIC and THE GAME OF LOGIC, *Lewis Carroll*
"Symbolic Logic" is not concerned with modern symbolic logic, but is instead
a collection of over 380 problems posed with charm and imagination, using
the syllogism and a fascinating diagrammatic method of drawing conclusions.
In "The Game of Logic" Carroll's whimsical imagination devises a logical game
played with 2 diagrams and counters (included) to manipulate hundreds of
tricky syllogisms. The final section, "Hit or Miss" is a lagniappe of 101 additional puzzles in the delightful Carroll manner. Until this reprint edition,
both of these books were rarities costing up to $15 each. Symbolic Logic:
Index. xxxi + 199pp. The Game of Logic: 96pp. 2 vols. bound as one. 5⅜ x 8.
                                                            Paperbound $2.00

MATHEMATICAL PUZZLES OF SAM LOYD, PART I
selected and edited by M. Gardner
Choice puzzles by the greatest American puzzle creator and innovator. Selected
from his famous collection, "Cyclopedia of Puzzles," they retain the unique
style and historical flavor of the originals. There are posers based on arithmetic,
algebra, probability, game theory, route tracing, topology, counter and sliding
block, operations research, geometrical dissection. Includes the famous "14-15"
puzzle which was a national craze, and his "Horse of a Different Color" which
sold millions of copies. 117 of his most ingenious puzzles in all. 120 line
drawings and diagrams. Solutions. Selected references. xx + 167pp. 5⅜ x 8.
                                                            Paperbound $1.00

STRING FIGURES AND HOW TO MAKE THEM, *Caroline Furness Jayne*
107 string figures plus variations selected from the best primitive and modern
examples developed by Navajo, Apache, pygmies of Africa, Eskimo, in Europe,
Australia, China, etc. The most readily understandable, easy-to-follow book in
English on perennially popular recreation. Crystal-clear exposition; step-by-
step diagrams. Everyone from kindergarten children to adults looking for
unusual diversion will be endlessly amused. Index. Bibliography. Introduction
by A. C. Haddon. 17 full-page plates, 960 illustrations. xxiii + 401pp. 5⅜ x 8½.
                                                            Paperbound $2.00

PAPER FOLDING FOR BEGINNERS, *W. D. Murray and F. J. Rigney*
A delightful introduction to the varied and entertaining Japanese art of
origami (paper folding), with a full, crystal-clear text that anticipates every
difficulty; over 275 clearly labeled diagrams of all important stages in creation.
You get results at each stage, since complex figures are logically developed
from simpler ones. 43 different pieces are explained: sailboats, frogs, roosters,
etc. 6 photographic plates. 279 diagrams. 95pp. 5⅝ x 8⅜. Paperbound $1.00

PRINCIPLES OF ART HISTORY,
H. Wölfflin
Analyzing such terms as "baroque," "classic," "neoclassic," "primitive," "picturesque," and 164 different works by artists like Botticelli, van Cleve, Dürer, Hobbema, Holbein, Hals, Rembrandt, Titian, Brueghel, Vermeer, and many others, the author establishes the classifications of art history and style on a firm, concrete basis. This classic of art criticism shows what really occurred between the 14th-century primitives and the sophistication of the 18th century in terms of basic attitudes and philosophies. "A remarkable lesson in the art of seeing," *Sat. Rev. of Literature*. Translated from the 7th German edition. 150 illustrations. 254pp. 6⅛ x 9¼.   Paperbound $2.00

PRIMITIVE ART,
Franz Boas
This authoritative and exhaustive work by a great American anthropologist covers the entire gamut of primitive art. Pottery, leatherwork, metal work, stone work, wood, basketry, are treated in detail. Theories of primitive art, historical depth in art history, technical virtuosity, unconscious levels of patterning, symbolism, styles, literature, music, dance, etc. A must book for the interested layman, the anthropologist, artist, handicrafter (hundreds of unusual motifs), and the historian. Over 900 illustrations (50 ceramic vessels, 12 totem poles, etc.). 376pp. 5⅜ x 8.   Paperbound $2.25

THE GENTLEMAN AND CABINET MAKER'S DIRECTOR,
Thomas Chippendale
A reprint of the 1762 catalogue of furniture designs that went on to influence generations of English and Colonial and Early Republic American furniture makers. The 200 plates, most of them full-page sized, show Chippendale's designs for French (Louis XV), Gothic, and Chinese-manner chairs, sofas, canopy and dome beds, cornices, chamber organs, cabinets, shaving tables, commodes, picture frames, frets, candle stands, chimney pieces, decorations, etc. The drawings are all elegant and highly detailed; many include construction diagrams and elevations. A supplement of 24 photographs shows surviving pieces of original and Chippendale-style pieces of furniture. Brief biography of Chippendale by N. I. Bienenstock, editor of *Furniture World*. Reproduced from the 1762 edition. 200 plates, plus 19 photographic plates. vi + 249pp. 9⅛ x 12¼.   Paperbound $3.50

AMERICAN ANTIQUE FURNITURE: A BOOK FOR AMATEURS,
Edgar G. Miller, Jr.
Standard introduction and practical guide to identification of valuable American antique furniture. 2115 illustrations, mostly photographs taken by the author in 148 private homes, are arranged in chronological order in extensive chapters on chairs, sofas, chests, desks, bedsteads, mirrors, tables, clocks, and other articles. Focus is on furniture accessible to the collector, including simpler pieces and a larger than usual coverage of Empire style. Introductory chapters identify structural elements, characteristics of various styles, how to avoid fakes, etc. "We are frequently asked to name some book on American furniture that will meet the requirements of the novice collector, the beginning dealer, and . . . the general public. . . . We believe Mr. Miller's two volumes more completely satisfy this specification than any other work," *Antiques*. Appendix. Index. Total of vi + 1106pp. 7⅞ x 10¾.
Two volume set, paperbound $7.50

THE BAD CHILD'S BOOK OF BEASTS, MORE BEASTS FOR WORSE CHILDREN, and A MORAL ALPHABET, *H. Belloc*
Hardly and anthology of humorous verse has appeared in the last 50 years without at least a couple of these famous nonsense verses. But one must see the entire volumes — with all the delightful original illustrations by Sir Basil Blackwood — to appreciate fully Belloc's charming and witty verses that play so subacidly on the platitudes of life and morals that beset his day — and ours. A great humor classic. Three books in one. Total of 157pp. 5⅜ x 8.
Paperbound $1.00

THE DEVIL'S DICTIONARY, *Ambrose Bierce*
Sardonic and irreverent barbs puncturing the pomposities and absurdities of American politics, business, religion, literature, and arts, by the country's greatest satirist in the classic tradition. Epigrammatic as Shaw, piercing as Swift, American as Mark Twain, Will Rogers, and Fred Allen, Bierce will always remain the favorite of a small coterie of enthusiasts, and of writers and speakers whom he supplies with "some of the most gorgeous witticisms of the English language" (H. L. Mencken). Over 1000 entries in alphabetical order. 144pp. 5⅜ x 8.
Paperbound $1.00

THE COMPLETE NONSENSE OF EDWARD LEAR.
This is the only complete edition of this master of gentle madness available at a popular price. *A Book of Nonsense, Nonsense Songs, More Nonsense Songs and Stories* in their entirety with all the old favorites that have delighted children and adults for years. The Dong With A Luminous Nose, The Jumblies, The Owl and the Pussycat, and hundreds of other bits of wonderful nonsense. 214 limericks, 3 sets of Nonsense Botany, 5 Nonsense Alphabets, 546 drawings by Lear himself, and much more. 320pp. 5⅜ x 8.
Paperbound $1.00

THE WIT AND HUMOR OF OSCAR WILDE, *ed. by Alvin Redman*
Wilde at his most brilliant, in 1000 epigrams exposing weaknesses and hypocrisies of "civilized" society. Divided into 49 categories—sin, wealth, women, America, etc.—to aid writers, speakers. Includes excerpts from his trials, books, plays, criticism. Formerly "The Epigrams of Oscar Wilde." Introduction by Vyvyan Holland, Wilde's only living son. Introductory essay by editor. 260pp. 5⅜ x 8.
Paperbound $1.00

A CHILD'S PRIMER OF NATURAL HISTORY, *Oliver Herford*
Scarcely an anthology of whimsy and humor has appeared in the last 50 years without a contribution from Oliver Herford. Yet the works from which these examples are drawn have been almost impossible to obtain! Here at last are Herford's improbable definitions of a menagerie of familiar and weird animals, each verse illustrated by the author's own drawings. 24 drawings in 2 colors; 24 additional drawings. vii + 95pp. 6½ x 6.
Paperbound $1.00

THE BROWNIES: THEIR BOOK, *Palmer Cox*
The book that made the Brownies a household word. Generations of readers have enjoyed the antics, predicaments and adventures of these jovial sprites, who emerge from the forest at night to play or to come to the aid of a deserving human. Delightful illustrations by the author decorate nearly every page. 24 short verse tales with 266 illustrations. 155pp. 6⅝ x 9¼.
Paperbound $1.50

THE PRINCIPLES OF PSYCHOLOGY,
William James

The full long-course, unabridged, of one of the great classics of Western literature and science. Wonderfully lucid descriptions of human mental activity, the stream of thought, consciousness, time perception, memory, imagination, emotions, reason, abnormal phenomena, and similar topics. Original contributions are integrated with the work of such men as Berkeley, Binet, Mills, Darwin, Hume, Kant, Royce, Schopenhauer, Spinoza, Locke, Descartes, Galton, Wundt, Lotze, Herbart, Fechner, and scores of others. All contrasting interpretations of mental phenomena are examined in detail—introspective analysis, philosophical interpretation, and experimental research. "A classic," *Journal of Consulting Psychology*. "The main lines are as valid as ever," *Psychoanalytical Quarterly*. "Standard reading ... a classic of interpretation," *Psychiatric Quarterly*. 94 illustrations. 1408pp. 5⅜ x 8.

Vol. 1 Paperbound $2.50, Vol. 2 Paperbound $2.50,
The set $5.00

VISUAL ILLUSIONS: THEIR CAUSES, CHARACTERISTICS AND APPLICATIONS,
M. Luckiesh

"Seeing is deceiving," asserts the author of this introduction to virtually every type of optical illusion known. The text both describes and explains the principles involved in color illusions, figure-ground, distance illusions, etc. 100 photographs, drawings and diagrams prove how easy it is to fool the sense: circles that aren't round, parallel lines that seem to bend, stationary figures that seem to move as you stare at them — illustration after illustration strains our credulity at what we see. Fascinating book from many points of view, from applications for artists, in camouflage, etc. to the psychology of vision. New introduction by William Ittleson, Dept. of Psychology, Queens College. Index. Bibliography. xxi + 252pp. 5⅜ x 8½. Paperbound $1.50

FADS AND FALLACIES IN THE NAME OF SCIENCE,
Martin Gardner

This is the standard account of various cults, quack systems, and delusions which have masqueraded as science: hollow earth fanatics. Reich and orgone sex energy, dianetics, Atlantis, multiple moons, Forteanism, flying saucers, medical fallacies like iridiagnosis, zone therapy, etc. A new chapter has been added on Bridey Murphy, psionics, and other recent manifestations in this field. This is a fair, reasoned appraisal of eccentric theory which provides excellent inoculation against cleverly masked nonsense. "Should be read by everyone, scientist and non-scientist alike," R. T. Birge, Prof. Emeritus of Physics, Univ. of California; Former President, American Physical Society. Index. x + 365pp. 5⅜ x 8. Paperbound $1.85

ILLUSIONS AND DELUSIONS OF THE SUPERNATURAL AND THE OCCULT,
D. H. Rawcliffe

Holds up to rational examination hundreds of persistent delusions including crystal gazing, automatic writing, table turning, mediumistic trances, mental healing, stigmata, lycanthropy, live burial, the Indian Rope Trick, spiritualism, dowsing, telepathy, clairvoyance, ghosts, ESP, etc. The author explains and exposes the mental and physical deceptions involved, making this not only an exposé of supernatural phenomena, but a valuable exposition of characteristic types of abnormal psychology. Originally titled "The Psychology of the Occult." 14 illustrations. Index. 551pp. 5⅜ x 8. Paperbound $2.25

FAIRY TALE COLLECTIONS, *edited by Andrew Lang*
Andrew Lang's fairy tale collections make up the richest shelf-full of traditional children's stories anywhere available. Lang supervised the translation of stories from all over the world—familiar European tales collected by Grimm, animal stories from Negro Africa, myths of primitive Australia, stories from Russia, Hungary, Iceland, Japan, and many other countries. Lang's selection of translations are unusually high; many authorities consider that the most familiar tales find their best versions in these volumes. All collections are richly decorated and illustrated by H. J. Ford and other artists.

THE BLUE FAIRY BOOK. 37 stories. 138 illustrations. ix + 390pp. 5⅜ x 8½.
Paperbound $1.50

THE GREEN FAIRY BOOK. 42 stories. 100 illustrations. xiii + 366pp. 5⅜ x 8½.
Paperbound $1.50

THE BROWN FAIRY BOOK. 32 stories. 50 illustrations, 8 in color. xii + 350pp. 5⅜ x 8½.
Paperbound $1.50

THE BEST TALES OF HOFFMANN, *edited by E. F. Bleiler*
10 stories by E. T. A. Hoffmann, one of the greatest of all writers of fantasy. The tales include "The Golden Flower Pot," "Automata," "A New Year's Eve Adventure," "Nutcracker and the King of Mice," "Sand-Man," and others. Vigorous characterizations of highly eccentric personalities, remarkably imaginative situations, and intensely fast pacing has made these tales popular all over the world for 150 years. Editor's introduction. 7 drawings by Hoffmann. xxxiii + 419pp. 5⅜ x 8½.
Paperbound $2.00

GHOST AND HORROR STORIES OF AMBROSE BIERCE,
edited by E. F. Bleiler
Morbid, eerie, horrifying tales of possessed poets, shabby aristocrats, revived corpses, and haunted malefactors. Widely acknowledged as the best of their kind between Poe and the moderns, reflecting their author's inner torment and bitter view of life. Includes "Damned Thing," "The Middle Toe of the Right Foot," "The Eyes of the Panther," "Visions of the Night," "Moxon's Master," and over a dozen others. Editor's introduction. xxii + 199pp. 5⅜ x 8½.
Paperbound $1.25

THREE GOTHIC NOVELS, *edited by E. F. Bleiler*
Originators of the still popular Gothic novel form, influential in ushering in early 19th-century Romanticism. Horace Walpole's *Castle of Otranto*, William Beckford's *Vathek*, John Polidori's *The Vampyre*, and a *Fragment* by Lord Byron are enjoyable as exciting reading or as documents in the history of English literature. Editor's introduction. xi + 291pp. 5⅜ x 8½.
Paperbound $2.00

BEST GHOST STORIES OF LEFANU, *edited by E. F. Bleiler*
Though admired by such critics as V. S. Pritchett, Charles Dickens and Henry James, ghost stories by the Irish novelist Joseph Sheridan LeFanu have never become as widely known as his detective fiction. About half of the 16 stories in this collection have never before been available in America. Collection includes "Carmilla" (perhaps the best vampire story ever written), "The Haunted Baronet," "The Fortunes of Sir Robert Ardagh," and the classic "Green Tea." Editor's introduction. 7 contemporary illustrations. Portrait of LeFanu. xii + 467pp. 5⅜ x 8.
Paperbound $2.00

EASY-TO-DO ENTERTAINMENTS AND DIVERSIONS WITH COINS, CARDS, STRING, PAPER AND MATCHES, *R. M. Abraham*
Over 300 tricks, games and puzzles will provide young readers with absorbing fun. Sections on card games; paper-folding; tricks with coins, matches and pieces of string; games for the agile; toy-making from common household objects; mathematical recreations; and 50 miscellaneous pastimes. Anyone in charge of groups of youngsters, including hard-pressed parents, and in need of suggestions on how to keep children sensibly amused and quietly content will find this book indispensable. Clear, simple text, copious number of delightful line drawings and illustrative diagrams. Originally titled "Winter Nights' Entertainments." Introduction by Lord Baden Powell. 329 illustrations. v + 186pp. 5⅜ x 8½.   Paperbound $1.00

AN INTRODUCTION TO CHESS MOVES AND TACTICS SIMPLY EXPLAINED, *Leonard Barden*
Beginner's introduction to the royal game. Names, possible moves of the pieces, definitions of essential terms, how games are won, etc. explained in 30-odd pages. With this background you'll be able to sit right down and play. Balance of book teaches strategy — openings, middle game, typical endgame play, and suggestions for improving your game. A sample game is fully analyzed. True middle-level introduction, teaching you all the essentials without oversimplifying or losing you in a maze of detail. 58 figures. 102pp. 5⅜ x 8½.   Paperbound $1.00

LASKER'S MANUAL OF CHESS, *Dr. Emanuel Lasker*
Probably the greatest chess player of modern times, Dr. Emanuel Lasker held the world championship 28 years, independent of passing schools or fashions. This unmatched study of the game, chiefly for intermediate to skilled players, analyzes basic methods, combinations, position play, the aesthetics of chess, dozens of different openings, etc., with constant reference to great modern games. Contains a brilliant exposition of Steinitz's important theories. Introduction by Fred Reinfeld. Tables of Lasker's tournament record. 3 indices. 308 diagrams. 1 photograph. xxx + 349pp. 5⅜ x 8.   Paperbound $2.25

COMBINATIONS: THE HEART OF CHESS, *Irving Chernev*
Step-by-step from simple combinations to complex, this book, by a well-known chess writer, shows you the intricacies of pins, counter-pins, knight forks, and smothered mates. Other chapters show alternate lines of play to those taken in actual championship games; boomerang combinations; classic examples of brilliant combination play by Nimzovich, Rubinstein, Tarrasch, Botvinnik, Alekhine and Capablanca. Index. 356 diagrams. ix + 245pp. 5⅜ x 8½.   Paperbound $1.85

HOW TO SOLVE CHESS PROBLEMS, *K. S. Howard*
Full of practical suggestions for the fan or the beginner — who knows only the moves of the chessmen. Contains preliminary section and 58 two-move, 46 three-move, and 8 four-move problems composed by 27 outstanding American problem creators in the last 30 years. Explanation of all terms and exhaustive index. "Just what is wanted for the student," Brian Harley. 112 problems, solutions. vi + 171pp. 5⅜ x 8.   Paperbound $1.35

SOCIAL THOUGHT FROM LORE TO SCIENCE,
H. E. Barnes and H. Becker
An immense survey of sociological thought and ways of viewing, studying, planning, and reforming society from earliest times to the present. Includes thought on society of preliterate peoples, ancient non-Western cultures, and every great movement in Europe, America, and modern Japan. Analyzes hundreds of great thinkers: Plato, Augustine, Bodin, Vico, Montesquieu, Herder, Comte, Marx, etc. Weighs the contributions of utopians, sophists, fascists and communists; economists, jurists, philosophers, ecclesiastics, and every 19th and 20th century school of scientific sociology, anthropology, and social psychology throughout the world. Combines topical, chronological, and regional approaches, treating the evolution of social thought as a process rather than as a series of mere topics. "Impressive accuracy, competence, and discrimination . . . easily the best single survey," *Nation*. Thoroughly revised, with new material up to 1960. 2 indexes. Over 2200 bibliographical notes. Three volume set. Total of 1586pp. 5⅜ x 8.
Vol. 1 Paperbound $2.75, Vol. 2 Paperbound $2.75, Vol. 3 Paperbound $2.50
The set $8.00

A HISTORY OF HISTORICAL WRITING, *Harry Elmer Barnes*
Virtually the only adequate survey of the whole course of historical writing in a single volume. Surveys developments from the beginnings of historiography in the ancient Near East and the Classical World, up through the Cold War. Covers major historians in detail, shows interrelationship with cultural background, makes clear individual contributions, evaluates and estimates importance; also enormously rich upon minor authors and thinkers who are usually passed over. Packed with scholarship and learning, clear, easily written. Indispensable to every student of history. Revised and enlarged up to 1961. Index and bibliography. xv + 442pp. 5⅜ x 8½.   Paperbound $2.50

JOHANN SEBASTIAN BACH, *Philipp Spitta*
The complete and unabridged text of the definitive study of Bach. Written some 70 years ago, it is still unsurpassed for its coverage of nearly all aspects of Bach's life and work. There could hardly be a finer non-technical introduction to Bach's music than the detailed, lucid analyses which Spitta provides for hundreds of individual pieces. 26 solid pages are devoted to the B minor mass, for example, and 30 pages to the glorious St. Matthew Passion. This monumental set also includes a major analysis of the music of the 18th century: Buxtehude, Pachelbel, etc. "Unchallenged as the last word on one of the supreme geniuses of music," John Barkham, *Saturday Review Syndicate*. Total of 1819pp. Heavy cloth binding. 5⅜ x 8.
Two volume set, clothbound $13.50

BEETHOVEN AND HIS NINE SYMPHONIES, *George Grove*
In this modern middle-level classic of musicology Grove not only analyzes all nine of Beethoven's symphonies very thoroughly in terms of their musical structure, but also discusses the circumstances under which they were written, Beethoven's stylistic development, and much other background material. This is an extremely rich book, yet very easily followed; it is highly recommended to anyone seriously interested in music. Over 250 musical passages. Index. viii + 407pp. 5⅜ x 8.   Paperbound $2.00

THREE SCIENCE FICTION NOVELS,
John Taine
Acknowledged by many as the best SF writer of the 1920's, Taine (under the name Eric Temple Bell) was also a Professor of Mathematics of considerable renown. Reprinted here are *The Time Stream*, generally considered Taine's best, *The Greatest Game*, a biological-fiction novel, and *The Purple Sapphire*, involving a supercivilization of the past. Taine's stories tie fantastic narratives to frameworks of original and logical scientific concepts. Speculation is often profound on such questions as the nature of time, concept of entropy, cyclical universes, etc. 4 contemporary illustrations. v + 532pp. 5⅜ x 8⅜.
Paperbound $2.00

SEVEN SCIENCE FICTION NOVELS,
H. G. Wells
Full unabridged texts of 7 science-fiction novels of the master. Ranging from biology, physics, chemistry, astronomy, to sociology and other studies, Mr. Wells extrapolates whole worlds of strange and intriguing character. "One will have to go far to match this for entertainment, excitement, and sheer pleasure . . ."*New York Times*. Contents: The Time Machine, The Island of Dr. Moreau, The First Men in the Moon, The Invisible Man, The War of the Worlds, The Food of the Gods, In The Days of the Comet. 1015pp. 5⅜ x 8.
Clothbound $5.00

28 SCIENCE FICTION STORIES OF H. G. WELLS.
Two full, unabridged novels, *Men Like Gods* and *Star Begotten,* plus 26 short stories by the master science-fiction writer of all time! Stories of space, time, invention, exploration, futuristic adventure. Partial contents: *The Country of the Blind, In the Abyss, The Crystal Egg, The Man Who Could Work Miracles, A Story of Days to Come, The Empire of the Ants, The Magic Shop, The Valley of the Spiders, A Story of the Stone Age, Under the Knife, Sea Raiders,* etc. An indispensable collection for the library of anyone interested in science fiction adventure. 928pp. 5⅜ x 8.　　Clothbound $4.50

THREE MARTIAN NOVELS,
Edgar Rice Burroughs
Complete, unabridged reprinting, in one volume, of Thuvia, Maid of Mars; Chessmen of Mars; The Master Mind of Mars. Hours of science-fiction adventure by a modern master storyteller. Reset in large clear type for easy reading. 16 illustrations by J. Allen St. John. vi + 490pp. 5⅜ x 8½.
Paperbound $1.85

AN INTELLECTUAL AND CULTURAL HISTORY OF THE WESTERN WORLD,
Harry Elmer Barnes
Monumental 3-volume survey of intellectual development of Europe from primitive cultures to the present day. Every significant product of human intellect traced through history: art, literature, mathematics, physical sciences, medicine, music, technology, social sciences, religions, jurisprudence, education, etc. Presentation is lucid and specific, analyzing in detail specific discoveries, theories, literary works, and so on. Revised (1965) by recognized scholars in specialized fields under the direction of Prof. Barnes. Revised bibliography. Indexes. 24 illustrations. Total of xxix + 1318pp.
Vol. 1 Paperbound $2.00, Vol. 2 Paperbound $2.00, Vol. 3 Paperbound $2.00,
The set $6.00

HEAR ME TALKIN' TO YA, *edited by Nat Shapiro and Nat Hentoff*
In their own words, Louis Armstrong, King Oliver, Fletcher Henderson, Bunk Johnson, Bix Beiderbecke, Billy Holiday, Fats Waller, Jelly Roll Morton, Duke Ellington, and many others comment on the origins of jazz in New Orleans and its growth in Chicago's South Side, Kansas City's jam sessions, Depression Harlem, and the modernism of the West Coast schools. Taken from taped conversations, letters, magazine articles, other first-hand sources. Editors' introduction. xvi + 429pp. 5⅜ x 8½.　　Paperbound $2.00

THE JOURNAL OF HENRY D. THOREAU
A 25-year record by the great American observer and critic, as complete a record of a great man's inner life as is anywhere available. Thoreau's Journals served him as raw material for his formal pieces, as a place where he could develop his ideas, as an outlet for his interests in wild life and plants, in writing as an art, in classics of literature, Walt Whitman and other contemporaries, in politics, slavery, individual's relation to the State, etc. The Journals present a portrait of a remarkable man, and are an observant social history. Unabridged republication of 1906 edition, Bradford Torrey and Francis H. Allen, editors. Illustrations. Total of 1888pp. 8⅜ x 12¼.
　　Two volume set, clothbound $25.00

A SHAKESPEARIAN GRAMMAR, *E. A. Abbott*
Basic reference to Shakespeare and his contemporaries, explaining through thousands of quotations from Shakespeare, Jonson, Beaumont and Fletcher, North's *Plutarch* and other sources the grammatical usage differing from the modern. First published in 1870 and written by a scholar who spent much of his life isolating principles of Elizabethan language, the book is unlikely ever to be superseded. Indexes. xxiv + 511pp. 5⅜ x 8½.　　Paperbound $2.75

FOLK-LORE OF SHAKESPEARE, *T. F. Thistelton Dyer*
Classic study, drawing from Shakespeare a large body of references to supernatural beliefs, terminology of falconry and hunting, games and sports, good luck charms, marriage customs, folk medicines, superstitions about plants, animals, birds, argot of the underworld, sexual slang of London, proverbs, drinking customs, weather lore, and much else. From full compilation comes a mirror of the 17th-century popular mind. Index. ix + 526pp. 5⅜ x 8½.
　　Paperbound $2.50

THE NEW VARIORUM SHAKESPEARE, *edited by H. H. Furness*
By far the richest editions of the plays ever produced in any country or language. Each volume contains complete text (usually First Folio) of the play, all variants in Quarto and other Folio texts, editorial changes by every major editor to Furness's own time (1900), footnotes to obscure references or language, extensive quotes from literature of Shakespearian criticism, essays on plot sources (often reprinting sources in full), and much more.

HAMLET, *edited by H. H. Furness*
Total of xxvi + 905pp. 5⅜ x 8½.　　Two volume set, paperbound $4.75

TWELFTH NIGHT, *edited by H. H. Furness*
Index. xxii + 434pp. 5⅜ x 8½.　　Paperbound $2.25

LA BOHEME BY GIACOMO PUCCINI,
translated and introduced by Ellen H. Bleiler
Complete handbook for the operagoer, with everything needed for full enjoyment except the musical score itself. Complete Italian libretto, with new, modern English line-by-line translation—the only libretto printing all repeats; biography of Puccini; the librettists; background to the opera, Murger's La Boheme, etc.; circumstances of composition and performances; plot summary; and pictorial section of 73 illustrations showing Puccini, famous singers and performances, etc. Large clear type for easy reading. 124pp. 5⅜ x 8½.
Paperbound $1.00

ANTONIO STRADIVARI: HIS LIFE AND WORK (1644-1737),
W. Henry Hill, Arthur F. Hill, and Alfred E. Hill
Still the only book that really delves into life and art of the incomparable Italian craftsman, maker of the finest musical instruments in the world today. The authors, expert violin-makers themselves, discuss Stradivari's ancestry, his construction and finishing techniques, distinguished characteristics of many of his instruments and their locations. Included, too, is story of introduction of his instruments into France, England, first revelation of their supreme merit, and information on his labels, number of instruments made, prices, mystery of ingredients of his varnish, tone of pre-1684 Stradivari violin and changes between 1684 and 1690. An extremely interesting, informative account for all music lovers, from craftsman to concert-goer. Republication of original (1902) edition. New introduction by Sydney Beck, Head of Rare Book and Manuscript Collections, Music Division, New York Public Library. Analytical index by Rembert Wurlitzer. Appendixes. 68 illustrations. 30 full-page plates. 4 in color. xxvi + 315pp. 5⅜ x 8½.
Paperbound $2.25

MUSICAL AUTOGRAPHS FROM MONTEVERDI TO HINDEMITH,
Emanuel Winternitz
For beauty, for intrinsic interest, for perspective on the composer's personality, for subtleties of phrasing, shading, emphasis indicated in the autograph but suppressed in the printed score, the mss. of musical composition are fascinating documents which repay close study in many different ways. This 2-volume work reprints facsimiles of mss. by virtually every major composer, and many minor figures—196 examples in all. A full text points out what can be learned from mss., analyzes each sample. Index. Bibliography. 18 figures. 196 plates. Total of 170pp. of text. 7⅞ x 10¾.
Vol. 1 Paperbound $2.00, Vol. 2 Paperbound $2.00,
The set $4.00

J. S. BACH,
Albert Schweitzer
One of the few great full-length studies of Bach's life and work, and the study upon which Schweitzer's renown as a musicologist rests. On first appearance (1911), revolutionized Bach performance. The only writer on Bach to be musicologist, performing musician, and student of history, theology and philosophy, Schweitzer contributes particularly full sections on history of German Protestant church music, theories on motivic pictorial representations in vocal music, and practical suggestions for performance. Translated by Ernest Newman. Indexes. 5 illustrations. 650 musical examples. Total of xix + 928pp. 5⅜ x 8½.
Vol. 1 Paperbound $2.00, Vol. 2 Paperbound $2.00,
The set $4.00

THE METHODS OF ETHICS, *Henry Sidgwick*
Propounding no organized system of its own, study subjects every major methodological approach to ethics to rigorous, objective analysis. Study discusses and relates ethical thought of Plato, Aristotle, Bentham, Clarke, Butler, Hobbes, Hume, Mill, Spencer, Kant, and dozens of others. Sidgwick retains conclusions from each system which follow from ethical premises, rejecting the faulty. Considered by many in the field to be among the most important treatises on ethical philosophy. Appendix. Index. xlvii + 528pp. 5⅜ x 8½.
Paperbound $2.50

TEUTONIC MYTHOLOGY, *Jakob Grimm*
A milestone in Western culture; the work which established on a modern basis the study of history of religions and comparative religions. 4-volume work assembles and interprets everything available on religious and folkloristic beliefs of Germanic people (including Scandinavians, Anglo-Saxons, etc.). Assembling material from such sources as Tacitus, surviving Old Norse and Icelandic texts, archeological remains, folktales, surviving superstitions, comparative traditions, linguistic analysis, etc. Grimm explores pagan deities, heroes, folklore of nature, religious practices, and every other area of pagan German belief. To this day, the unrivaled, definitive, exhaustive study. Translated by J. S. Stallybrass from 4th (1883) German edition. Indexes. Total of lxxvii + 1887pp. 5⅜ x 8½. Four volume set, paperbound $10.00

THE I CHING, *translated by James Legge*
Called "The Book of Changes" in English, this is one of the Five Classics edited by Confucius, basic and central to Chinese thought. Explains perhaps the most complex system of divination known, founded on the theory that all things happening at any one time have characteristic features which can be isolated and related. Significant in Oriental studies, in history of religions and philosophy, and also to Jungian psychoanalysis and other areas of modern European thought. Index. Appendixes. 6 plates. xxi + 448pp. 5⅜ x 8½.
Paperbound $2.75

HISTORY OF ANCIENT PHILOSOPHY, *W. Windelband*
One of the clearest, most accurate comprehensive surveys of Greek and Roman philosophy. Discusses ancient philosophy in general, intellectual life in Greece in the 7th and 6th centuries B.C., Thales, Anaximander, Anaximenes, Heraclitus, the Eleatics, Empedocles, Anaxagoras, Leucippus, the Pythagoreans, the Sophists, Socrates, Democritus (20 pages), Plato (50 pages), Aristotle (70 pages), the Peripatetics, Stoics, Epicureans, Sceptics, Neo-platonists, Christian Apologists, etc. 2nd German edition translated by H. E. Cushman. xv + 393pp. 5⅜ x 8. Paperbound $2.25

THE PALACE OF PLEASURE, *William Painter*
Elizabethan versions of Italian and French novels from *The Decameron*, Cinthio, Straparola, Queen Margaret of Navarre, and other continental sources — the very work that provided Shakespeare and dozens of his contemporaries with many of their plots and sub-plots and, therefore, justly considered one of the most influential books in all English literature. It is also a book that any reader will still enjoy. Total of cviii + 1,224pp.
Three volume set, Paperbound $6.75

THE WONDERFUL WIZARD OF OZ, *L. F. Baum*

All the original W. W. Denslow illustrations in full color—as much a part of "The Wizard" as Tenniel's drawings are of "Alice in Wonderland." "The Wizard" is still America's best-loved fairy tale, in which, as the author expresses it, "The wonderment and joy are retained and the heartaches and nightmares left out." Now today's young readers can enjoy every word and wonderful picture of the original book. New introduction by Martin Gardner. A Baum bibliography. 23 full-page color plates. viii + 268pp. 5⅜ x 8.

Paperbound $1.50

THE MARVELOUS LAND OF OZ, *L. F. Baum*

This is the equally enchanting sequel to the "Wizard," continuing the adventures of the Scarecrow and the Tin Woodman. The hero this time is a little boy named Tip, and all the delightful Oz magic is still present. This is the Oz book with the Animated Saw-Horse, the Woggle-Bug, and Jack Pumpkinhead. All the original John R. Neill illustrations, 10 in full color. 287pp. 5⅜ x 8.

Paperbound $1.50

ALICE'S ADVENTURES UNDER GROUND, *Lewis Carroll*

The original *Alice in Wonderland*, hand-lettered and illustrated by Carroll himself, and originally presented as a Christmas gift to a child-friend. Adults as well as children will enjoy this charming volume, reproduced faithfully in this Dover edition. While the story is essentially the same, there are slight changes, and Carroll's spritely drawings present an intriguing alternative to the famous Tenniel illustrations. One of the most popular books in Dover's catalogue. Introduction by Martin Gardner. 38 illustrations. 128pp. 5⅜ x 8½.

Paperbound $1.00

THE NURSERY "ALICE," *Lewis Carroll*

While most of us consider *Alice in Wonderland* a story for children of all ages, Carroll himself felt it was beyond younger children. He therefore provided this simplified version, illustrated with the famous Tenniel drawings enlarged and colored in delicate tints, for children aged "from Nought to Five." Dover's edition of this now rare classic is a faithful copy of the 1889 printing, including 20 illustrations by Tenniel, and front and back covers reproduced in full color. Introduction by Martin Gardner. xxiii + 67pp. 6⅛ x 9¼.

Paperbound $1.50

THE STORY OF KING ARTHUR AND HIS KNIGHTS, *Howard Pyle*

A fast-paced, exciting retelling of the best known Arthurian legends for young readers by one of America's best story tellers and illustrators. The sword Excalibur, wooing of Guinevere, Merlin and his downfall, adventures of Sir Pellias and Gawaine, and others. The pen and ink illustrations are vividly imagined and wonderfully drawn. 41 illustrations. xviii + 313pp. 6⅛ x 9¼.

Paperbound $1.50

Prices subject to change without notice.

Available at your book dealer or write for free catalogue to Dept. Adsci, Dover Publications, Inc., 180 Varick St., N.Y., N.Y. 10014. Dover publishes more than 150 books each year on science, elementary and advanced mathematics, biology, music, art, literary history, social sciences and other areas.